# "THE WORLD'S EASIEST GUIDE" FOR New Believers

# "THE WORLD'S EASIEST GUIDE"™ FOR New Believers

RANDY SOUTHERN

NORTHFIELD PUBLISHING
Chicago

Southern, Randy.
The world's easiest guide for new believers / Randy Southern
p. cm.
Includes index.
ISBN 1-881273-64-4
1. Christianity. 2. Title.

BR121.3 .S68 2002
230--dc21

2002025051

*If you are interested in information about other books written from a biblical perspective, please write to the following address:*
Northfield Publishing
215 West Locust Street
Chicago, IL 60610

ISBN: 1-881273-64-4
1 3 5 7 9 10 8 6 4 2
Printed in the United States of America

# Table of Contents

CHAPTER 1

# Christianity in 8,000 Words or Less

## SNAPSHOT

Tory closed the front door and turned off the porch light. "That went well," he said with a nervous chuckle. But Carol gave him an icy stare as she collected the punch glasses and cake plates from the coffee table.

Tory threw up his hands in mock surrender. "All right, I shouldn't have invited him," he said. "It was a mistake—I admit it. I'm sorry."

"You *promised* he wouldn't hit on Marcy if he came," Carol said.

"I didn't think he would!" Tory replied. "I told him she only goes out with Christian guys, and I figured that was the end of it. I didn't know he was gonna try to use it to pick her up."

"What kind of person pretends to be a Christian just to impress a girl?" Carol asked. "And why didn't you *do* something about it? He's your friend."

"What was I supposed to do?" Tory asked. "Make a

**SNEAK PREVIEW**

1. Salvation is necessary because sin creates a chasm between humans and God that only Jesus can bridge.
2. Repentance and belief are the two elements necessary for salvation.
3. Receiving God's gift of salvation results in a new set of privileges, responsibilities, and challenges for a believer.

citizen's arrest for impersonating a believer?"

"You should have done *something,*" Carol said.

"Yeah . . . well . . . maybe we should be giving him the benefit of the doubt," Tory replied. "Did you ever think about *that?* Maybe we've got him all wrong. Maybe he has a spiritual side that we've never seen before. Maybe he really *is* a committed Christian."

"And maybe Alan's story about his kidney stones was *really* interesting," Carol shot back. "Come on! I heard Marcy say she's been reading Paul's letters in her daily devotions. And do you know what Mr. Committed Christian asked her? 'Paul who?' He must have thought she was talking about an old boyfriend or something."

Tory shrugged. "Okay, so maybe he just misunder—"

Carol held up her hand to interrupt him, then continued. "Later, when Marcy asked him how long he'd been a Christian, he said, 'Since the day I was born.'"

"Okay, maybe his grasp of Christianity is a little shaky," Tory admitted. "But I don't see what the big deal is. Marcy seemed to have a sense of humor about the whole thing, so what's the problem?"

"The *problem,*" Carol replied, "is someone thinking he can call himself a Christian whenever it's convenient for him."

"You're right," Tory said, punching his fist into his open hand. "I'll send some goons from my Bible study group over to his house to rough him up and teach him a lesson."

Carol ignored him. "It's not just *him* that I'm worried about," she said. "I'm also thinking about the people from my office who were at the party. They know I'm a Christian, but I don't think they have any idea what that really means. So when they saw your friend doing his little song and dance for Marcy, I'm sure some of them wondered, *Is* that *what a Christian is?*"

"I see your point," Tory said.

Carol kissed him on the cheek and started up the stairs. "I'm going to bed," she said. "Maybe you can talk to him about it tomorrow."

"Or I could just go spray-paint the word *heathen* all over his car," Tory called after her. "Whatever you think would work better."

* * * * * * * * * * * * * * * * *

At what point in your life did you become a Christian?

From a biographical point of view, that's a pretty easy question to answer. (If you're a new believer, it's even easier, since the details are likely still fresh in your mind.)

But what if we weren't looking for *biographical information?* What if you had to answer the question without referring to a specific time, place, or situation in your life? What if you had to come up with a response that didn't focus on a . . .

- date ("I became a Christian on the day before Easter this year.") or
- location ("I accepted Jesus at Awana camp when I was twelve.") or
- specific circumstance ("I gave my life to Christ after I survived a car wreck that killed my best friend.")?

Could you do it?

If you're not one to let a challenge go unmet, pull out your blue notebook and #2 pencil and write your response. (When you're finished, raise your hand and someone will come around to collect your paper.)

If you're not even sure what we're asking, take a look at the front cover of this book. The title is *The World's Easiest Guide for New Believers,* a name that implies some kind of transition. You can't be a "new" something unless you're a "former" something else. New homeowners are former renters. New parolees are former prisoners. *New*lyweds are former singles. *New*borns are former zygotes. New believers are former unbelievers.

The question on the table is, *when* is that line crossed? Homeowners can point to the moment they signed their mortgage papers. Parolees can point to the moment they walked out of the prison doors. Newlyweds can point to the moment the pastor said, "I now pronounce you husband and wife." Newborns can point to their time of birth.

But at what moment does a person go from being an unbeliever to being a believer, from being a non-Christian to being a Christian, from being unsaved to being saved?

To put it another way: What makes a Christian a Christian?

If these questions trigger unpleasant flashbacks of middle-school vocabulary tests, we apologize. But it's important for believers to be able to define the word *Christian* as completely and specifically as possible.

**ON A PERSONAL NOTE**

Write (in a journal or your Bible) everything you can remember about your decision to follow Christ. Include the circumstances that caused you to start thinking about a relationship with Christ, the people you talked to about your decision, the Bible verses you read, the place where you made your decision, the prayer you said, and anything else that you can recall. Many Christians struggle with doubts about their salvation from time to time. A detailed autobiographical record of your salvation can be a helpful resource for preventing or combatting such doubt.

## Says Who?

If you don't define your beliefs yourself—if you don't know specifically what it means to be a Christian—you may be tempted to rely on other people's definitions. And that's where real trouble begins.

There's certainly no shortage of opinions about what it means to be a Christian. But if you asked one hundred people on the street what a Christian is, you'd probably have a hard time getting any kind of consensus.

- "A Christian is someone who believes in God."
- "A Christian is someone who's going to heaven when he dies."
- "A Christian is someone who needs a crutch to get through life because he can't face the big, bad world on his own."
- "A Christian is someone who goes to church."

- "A Christian is someone who doesn't believe in premarital sex."
- "A Christian is anyone who's not a Muslim, Hindu, or Buddhist."
- "A Christian is someone who loves Jesus."
- "A Christian is someone who acts nice to people even when she really hates them."
- "A Christian is someone who obeys the Ten Commandments."
- "A Christian is an uptight, self-righteous do-gooder whose main goal in life is to spoil everybody else's fun by—"

Well, you get the idea.

While many of those statements contain kernels of truth, none of them *defines* what a Christian is. Without more to go on, we're left with a Christian identity crisis, an uncertainty about what exactly makes us who we are.

In the next dozen or so pages, we're going to explore the specifics of what it means to be a Christian. Instead of focusing on the traditional questions of who, when, and where—

- *Who* led you to Christ?
- *When* did you become a believer?
- *Where* did you make your decision for Jesus?

—we're going to talk about why, how, and what:

- *Why* is it even necessary to become a Christian?
- *How* exactly does a person become a Christian?
- *What* happens when you become a Christian?

## A Word to the Whys

First Peter 3:15 offers an important instruction for all believers: "Always be prepared to give an answer to everyone who asks you to give the reason for the

**NOTABLE QUOTABLE**

Going to church doesn't make you a Christian any more than going to a garage makes you an automobile.

—BILLY SUNDAY

hope that you have." If you were to tell an unbelieving friend or family member that you've become a Christian, one of the first questions you'd probably get is . . . *Why?*

It's a legitimate question, but answering it is like peeling an onion. You've got to be prepared to make your way through several different layers. You could say, "I became a Christian because I realized that I was a sinner." But that raises more questions than it answers. For example . . .

- What does it mean to be a sinner?
- Why is it a problem to be a sinner?
- How does being a Christian change your "sinner-ness"?

To answer those questions, you've got to peel your way down to the next layer of information. And, of course, those answers would lead to more questions, and so on, and so on.

Getting a handle on the "big picture" of salvation can be difficult and frustrating. To help you connect the dots, we've identified twelve biblical facts that, when put together, explain why it's necessary for a person to become a Christian. Or, to continue our vegetable analogy, we've sliced the "onion of Christianity" in half in order to look at twelve different layers. We'll start at the center and work our way out.

### *1. God is holy.*

Everything about salvation and Christianity starts with God—who He is and what He's like. We're going to start with His holiness. You can't swing a stick in the Bible without hitting a verse that talks about God's holiness:

- "There is no one holy like the LORD" (1 Samuel 2:2).
- "The LORD our God is holy" (Psalm 99:9).
- "Holy, holy, holy is the Lord God Almighty" (Revelation 4:8).

*Holy* isn't some vague compliment, though ("You look very holy today, God"). It's a word that reveals precisely what it means to be God.

The fact that God is holy means He can have *nothing* to do with sin (or anything sinful). We're not talking about some kind of divine "fussiness," either. It's not like God gets uptight and has to excuse Himself whenever something sinful happens. We're talking about *complete separation.*

God and sin are mutually exclusive. Where God is, sin cannot be. Where sin is, God cannot be. Just as darkness can't exist near the sun, sin can't exist near God. It's impossible.

Needless to say, God can't have a personal relationship with anyone tainted by sin. And that's where the need for salvation begins.

### 2. God created humans with free will.

Go ahead; ask the obvious question: If God can have nothing to do with anything sinful, why did He create us with the potential to sin? Why didn't He just take sin out of the equation altogether, so we wouldn't have to worry about it?

God certainly *could* have created us without the ability to sin. (He's the Creator—He could have designed us so that we sing the "Barney" theme song every hour on the hour, if He'd wanted.) He could have programmed us so that we had no choice but to obey His every command and love Him unconditionally. But how meaningful would that have been for Him?

What God wanted was people who would love and obey Him because they *chose* to, not because they *had* to. He didn't want robots; He wanted people who could think and decide for themselves. So God gave us free will, the freedom to do as we choose.

The downside of free will is obvious: Freedom of choice means the freedom to ignore God and disobey Him. In other words, our free will is what makes us capable of sin. As far as God is concerned, though, the risk of our choosing to disobey Him was worth the reward of what life would be like if we chose obedience.

### *3. God had a perfect plan for the human race.*

God wasn't satisfied with 50-50 odds when it came to our using our free will. He didn't just leave our obedience to chance ("Maybe they'll do what I say, maybe they won't"). Instead, He stacked the deck in His favor.

He did that by creating a plan for the human race that would meet our every need and bring us happiness, satisfaction, and fulfillment beyond our wildest dreams. Evidence of His plan can be found in Genesis 1:27–2:25, as well as a few other passages scattered throughout the Bible. Those verses read like some kind of fairy tale. You've got a garden paradise (called Eden), trees filled with every fruit imaginable, a beautiful river to keep everything fresh and fertile, and every animal in creation living together in peace. Apparently, life in the Garden of Eden was like the world's greatest camping trip and jungle safari rolled into one.

On top of all that, you've got *God Himself* dropping by for visits (Genesis 3:8). Not some angel representing God. Not some bush with God's voice coming out of it. God Himself. We're talking about quality one-on-one time with the Creator of the universe! That's the kind of relationship God envisioned between Himself and His human creation.

**JUST WONDERING**

**What was so special about the Tree of the Knowledge of Good and Evil?**

God's plan was for Adam and Eve to rely on Him for information about what was right and what was wrong. "Good" was whatever He determined to be good, and "evil" was whatever He determined to be evil. By eating the fruit of the tree themselves, Adam and Eve were hoping to "cut out the middleman," acquire their own knowledge of good and evil, and become independent of God.

Talk about a perfect strategy! By giving us paradise and perfection, God made sure that we—the human race, represented by Adam and Eve—would have no reason to ever disobey Him.

### *4. Humans are sinful.*

As far as we know, God's original perfect plan for the human race included just one rule: Don't eat from the Tree of the Knowledge of Good and Evil or you will die (Genesis 2:17). That's it—the only restriction that Adam and Eve had in the Garden of Eden.

They were free to eat from any other plant and tree in the garden, including the Tree of Life, which would make them live forever; explore every square inch of Eden; play with any animal they chose; even hang out with God Himself. With so much to do, you wouldn't think that Adam and Eve would mind not being able to eat from one little fruit tree.

But, of course, if that were true, we'd be living with Adam and Eve in the Garden of Eden right now. That was God's original plan.

So what went wrong?

Genesis 3 tells us that it all started with a little trash-talking from the devil. That's right—as strange as it may seem, the devil actually hung out in the Garden of Eden with Adam and Eve. (If you're wondering where he came from and what he was doing there, flip ahead to chapter 6.)

Disguised as a serpent, the devil slithered over to Eve one day and said something to the effect of "What's the deal with all these rules you have to obey? God must have you on a pretty short leash, huh?"

Even though Eve knew she had only one rule to obey, the devil's question was enough to plant some doubt in her mind.

The devil slithered a little closer and said, "By the way, you won't really die if you eat from that forbidden tree. God just said that because He knows that as soon as you eat it, you'll become as wise and powerful as He is. He's just trying to keep you down."

That was all Eve needed to hear. Genesis 3:6 says, "When the woman saw that the fruit of the tree was good for food and pleasing to the eye, and also desirable for gaining wisdom, she took some and ate it. She also gave some to her husband, who was with her, and he ate it."

And, with that one decision, Adam and Eve put an end to God's original perfect plan for the human race. Using the free will that God had given them, they chose to disobey Him. And, in the process, they brought sin and death into the world.

Remember, God's original plan was for humans to live *forever*, but that plan was for *sinless* humans and had to be scrapped after the forbidden-fruit meal.

Obviously, the death penalty wasn't immediate; Adam and Eve didn't keel over the moment their teeth hit the fruit. However, after their sin, they were booted out of Eden and cut off from the Tree of Life. Without the Tree of Life, death became a reality for them—and for the entire human race.

With a couple bites of fruit, Adam and Eve managed to ruin practically everything that was good in the world. What's more, they started a legacy of sin that would be passed on to their kids, grandkids, great-grandkids, and every generation that followed.

Romans 5:12 puts it this way: "Sin entered the world through one man, and death through sin, and in this way death came to all men, because all sinned."

So does that make us descendants of Adam and Eve innocent victims, unfairly condemned for something that happened thousands of years before we were born? We could probably make a case for that—if it weren't for the impressive collection of personal sins that each of us has managed to accumulate in our lifetime.

You know the old saying, "Don't do anything I wouldn't do"? The Bible makes it clear that Adam and Eve didn't do anything we wouldn't have done. Romans 3 hammers that point home in a couple different ways. Verse 12 says, "All have turned away, they have together become worthless; there is no one who does good, not even one." Verse 23 is a little more succinct: "All have sinned and fall short of the glory of God."

**NOTABLE QUOTABLE**

Heaven goes by favor; if it went by merit, you would stay out and your dog would go in.

—MARK TWAIN

We are all tainted by sin, not only because of our association with Adam and Eve, but because of our own actions and disobedience.

### *5. Sin separates us from God.*

The only distinction that Adam and Eve can claim in the sin department is seniority. They misused their free will before the rest of us had a chance to misuse ours. As a result, it was their disobedience that put us on the business end of God's holiness. Remember, because God is holy, He can have nothing to do with anyone or anything tainted by sin.

Adam and Eve's sin was like a giant meteor that slammed into the ground between humans and God and created a chasm the size of, say, the Grand Canyon—with God on one side and us on the other.

### *6. God is just.*

Being separated from God is not the end of our problems, though. You see, God is not only holy; He's also just. That means He demands punishment for sin. And because He's God—because He's *perfectly* just—His judgment is absolute. In other words, God never just lets things slide. He never turns His head and pretends not to notice when someone does something wrong. He doesn't care about excuses. He doesn't play favorites.

*Everyone* who is guilty of sin automatically receives God's maximum sentence. He doesn't offer parole or time off for good behavior. God's justice cannot be satisfied until the *entire* punishment has been completed.

### *7. The punishment for sin is physical and spiritual death.*

Unfortunately for us sin-stained humans, God's brand of justice makes the state of Texas look soft on crime by comparison. Romans 6:23 delivers the sentence: "The wages of sin is death."

You sin, you die. And not even Johnnie Cochran can get that verdict overturned.

The one bright spot in this whole scenario is that the execution doesn't occur immediately. (If that were the case, the average life expectancy for a human would be about seven years.) Eventually, though, because of our sin, our lives will come to an end. God's perfect justice demands it.

If that's all there were to the story, though, there would be little reason for us to care about sin. Sure, for Adam and Eve, the prospect of death was probably devastating. After all, they had expected to live *forever*. For the rest of us, though, death is just a fact of life. We've always known that eventually we're going to die. So, as punishments go, the prospect of eventual physical death isn't especially worrisome.

**NOTABLE QUOTABLE**

Sin cannot be undone, only forgiven.

—IGOR STRAVINSKY

But physical death is *not* the end of the story. When God created us, He gave us a physical element (our body) and a nonphysical element (our soul and spirit). The physical part of us ceases to exist at death, but the nonphysical part lives on. Forever.

And since the nonphysical part of us is also tainted by sin, it lives forever apart from God. That's *really* bad news, because God is the source of all joy, fulfillment, and peace. To live apart from Him is to be joyless, unfulfilled, and miserable—for eternity. That's called spiritual death.

It's also called hell.

We'll talk more about what hell is and isn't in chapter 6. For now, we'll just call it a place of unimaginable and unending suffering.

### *8. We can do nothing to save ourselves.*

Someone with a positive-thinking, can-do approach to life might say, "All right, I got myself into this mess, and I'm going to get myself out of it. So what can I do to become good again?" The tendency is to believe that if we do enough good things, we might be able to cancel out the bad and get out of God's doghouse.

But that's not how things work. Isaiah 64:6 says that all our righteous acts are like filthy rags to God. You could . . .

- sponsor orphans in a dozen Third World nations,
- open your home to every disadvantaged youth in your neighborhood,
- spend your weekends delivering food to the homeless,
- build enough houses with Habitat for Humanity to populate a small town, and
- vote with the Christian Coalition in every election

. . . but the result would still be the same, as far as God is concerned. When it comes to making up for our sin, God is no more impressed by our good deeds than He would be if we gave Him a basket full of dirty laundry.

Nothing we can do is good enough for God. That's why we sinners—all of us—are powerless to save ourselves.

### *9. God loves us.*

God's holiness and justice leave little hope for a bunch of helpless sinners like us. In fact, we could pretty much write off the entire human race—if it weren't for one other attribute of God: His love. You see, despite the fact that we have . . .

- turned our backs on God,
- done exactly what He instructed us not to do, and
- ruined His perfect plan for the world

. . . God loves us.

If that concept doesn't amaze you to the point of short-circuiting synapses in your brain, you may not be fully grasping what it means.

God *loves* us.

We're not talking about the fickle emotion that we call love. God's love for us isn't based on how He feels on a particular day or whether we've done anything to make Him mad recently. His love, like His holiness and justice, is perfect. Not even our sin can diminish it.

But God's love can't be separated from His other attributes. He can't just "switch off" His holiness and justice and forget about our sin because He loves us. Instead, as a result of His love for us, God created a new plan for the human race—one that would satisfy His holiness and justice. The details of that plan, and the unimaginable sacrifice it involved, reveal just how much God loves us.

The most famous words in the Bible spell it out: "For God so loved the world that he gave his one and only Son, that whoever believes in him shall not perish but have eternal life" (John 3:16).

Romans 5:8 offers a little more detail about what God's "gift" to us actually meant for His Son: "But God demonstrates his own love for us in this: While we were still sinners, Christ died for us."

Jesus is God's ultimate gift of love to the human race. God said to us, "Here's how much I love you: I'm going to sacrifice the life of My only Son to keep you from being separated from Me forever."

### *10. Jesus defeated sin.*

Remember, sinful people can do nothing to change their status before God. The only chance we have of escaping God's punishment—including eternity in hell—is to be *saved* by someone who hasn't been tainted by sin. Only someone *perfect* could bridge the gap between us and God.

Since there was no hope of finding anyone perfect among His creation, God sent Jesus to achieve perfection for us. As part of God's plan, Jesus left His home in heaven to come to earth as a human being. During His time on earth, Jesus faced the kind of daily temptations and frustrations that we face. Unlike us, however, He resisted every temptation and lived a perfect, sinless life for His entire thirty-three years on this planet.

In other words, He defeated sin on sin's home court. And what a victory it was! The fact that Jesus lived a life completely untainted by sin qualified Him to bridge the gap between the human race and God.

**NOTABLE QUOTABLE**

Faith is to believe what you do not yet see; the reward for this faith is to see what you believe.

–St. Augustine

But that's not the end of the story.

### *11. Jesus paid the price for our sin.*

God's requirement of justice didn't just disappear when Jesus came to earth. There was still a penalty to be paid for the sins of the human race. Until that penalty was paid in full, we sinners had no hope of reconnecting with God. The only way *we* could pay that penalty was by dying and spending eternity in hell. That left only one option.

Second Corinthians 5:21 describes it this way: "God made him who had no sin to be sin for us, so that in him we might become the righteousness of God."

Jesus, the only truly innocent person who ever lived, had the sins of the entire world placed on His shoulders. God aimed every bit of His justified wrath—the wrath that we earned with every sin ever committed—at His own Son. He allowed Jesus to be mocked, ridiculed, abandoned, tortured, and killed for the things we did.

The final day of Jesus' earthly life is almost too painful and horrifying to describe. However, it's important that we understand what happened to Him because of *our* sins. After being arrested on trumped-up charges, Jesus was used as a human punching bag by a gang of Roman soldiers. He was spat on. He was beaten with a large wooden staff. He was flogged with a whip designed to tear chunks of flesh from the skin with each lash. He was nailed to a large wooden cross with spikes that were hammered into His hands and feet. Then He was left to hang until the weight and position of His body on the cross squeezed off His airflow and suffocated Him.

God demanded the ultimate punishment for sin, and Jesus paid it.

But that's still not the end of the story.

### *12. Jesus defeated death.*

Jesus died to pay the punishment for our sin. But what good is a dead savior?

Remember, Adam and Eve's original disobedience in the Garden of Eden brought sin *and* death into the world. Jesus destroyed the power of sin by living a perfect life. But if death had been the end of the line for Him, it would have been "game over" for the human race. We would have been left with no way to defeat death ourselves.

Fortunately for us, death was not the end for God's Son. Three days after Jesus' corpse was taken down from the cross and placed in a tomb, God brought Him back to life.

And that changed everything.

"He arose a victor from the dark domain" is the way an old hymn writer described it. Jesus walked out of His tomb the reigning champion over sin and death. By defeating those two forces—the human race's most powerful enemies—Jesus gave us more than hope. He gave us, the entire human race, a way to be reconciled with God once and for all.

There you have it: the story of salvation—or the CliffsNotes version of it, at least. Until we respond to it, though—until we take it personally—that's all it is, a story.

## Classic R&B (Repent & Believe)

That brings us to our second question: How exactly does a person become a Christian?

Let's say you decide that . . .

- being separated from God isn't the way you want to live your life.
- God's sacrifice of His Son is the most incredible thing anyone's ever done for you.
- you don't want hell to be your permanent mailing address after you die.

What do you do?

According to Jesus, you "repent and believe the good news!" (Mark 1:15). That's all a person has to do in order to receive God's salvation and become a Christian. "Repent and believe."

What could be easier? "Repent and believe."

What does that mean?

## R-E-P-E-N-T-A-N-C-E, Find Out What It Means to . . . You

In order to understand repentance, we first have to understand that, as far as God is concerned, Jesus' death paid for *everything*—all the sins of the past and all the sins of the future, as well as any sins that are being committed at this exact moment.

Many Christians prefer to say that "our sins are covered by the blood of Christ." The idea is that when God looks down at Christians, He doesn't see our disobedience and sins anymore; He sees only the blood that came from Jesus' sacrifice on the cross. Anyone whose sins are covered by Jesus' blood is sinless in God's eyes. And anyone who's sinless is welcome in God's presence—and will be welcome forever. In short, you can think of repentance as washing your sins away with Jesus' blood.

There are three things you need to do in order to repent.

### *1. Admit that you're a sinner.*

In order to have your sins wiped clean, you first have to honestly confess to God that you *have* sin in your life. You can do this as simply ("Lord, I am a helpless sinner") or in as much detail ("How have I disobeyed Thee? Let me count the ways") as you prefer. More important than the *length* of your confession is your *attitude*.

Are you genuinely sorry about the sin in your life and what it's done to your relationship with God? Are you willing to acknowledge that you've created a mess for yourself that you can't get out of? If so, then proceed to step 2.

### *2. Ask for forgiveness.*

There are two things you need to know about God's forgiveness: 1. You don't deserve it. 2. God gives it anyway.

Asking for forgiveness means appealing to God's mercy. It means saying, "God, I know I've done nothing to deserve a personal relationship with You, but I'm asking You to cover my sins with Jesus' blood so that I can be reconciled with You forever" (or words to that effect).

### *3. Start anew.*

Repenting is more than a verbal exercise, however. The word *repent* implies a change of direction. Think of it as turning *away* from sin and *toward* God.

Second Corinthians 5:17 takes the idea of change one step further: "Therefore, if anyone is in Christ, he is a new creation; the old has gone, the new has come!" We're not talking about a simple switch of religious affiliation; we're talking about a transformation that affects every area of your life.

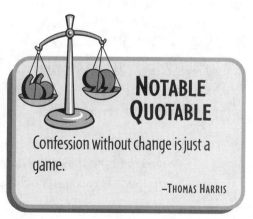

**NOTABLE QUOTABLE**

Confession without change is just a game.

—Thomas Harris

Jesus called it being "born again" (John 3:3)—starting from scratch with a clean slate and a new purpose. Instead of continuing to pursue your own sinful instincts and pleasure, you begin to pursue God and His ways.

## Can You Believe This?

The second part of Jesus' instruction in Mark 1:15—His blueprint for becoming a Christian—is to "believe the good news!" But what is the "good news"? Paul's words in Acts 16:31 narrow it down a little: "Believe in the Lord Jesus, and you will be saved."

### Just Wondering

**Where does faith come in?**
Salvation without faith is impossible. Legally speaking, Christians have little physical evidence to prove that what we believe is true. None of us was an eyewitness to Jesus' miracles. We don't have any audiotape of His sermons or videotape of His resurrection. In order to believe in Jesus, we must rely on the fact that what God's Word says about Him is true. That's faith–placing our complete belief, confidence, and trust in God's Son, sight unseen.

But what is it that we need to believe about Jesus?

- That He's God's Son?
- That He lived a perfect life as a human?
- That He died to take the punishment for our sins?
- That He rose from the dead?

Yes, yes, yes, and yes—along with everything else the Bible says about Him.

However, believing in Jesus isn't simply a matter of knowing the right facts about Him. God's not going to give us a true-false test about His Son to determine whether we get into heaven. The kind of belief we're talking about goes much deeper than surface knowledge.

Believing *in* Jesus, as Paul instructed, means putting all your eggs in one basket. Jesus said, "I am the way and the truth and the life. No one comes to the Father except through me" (John 14:6). That doesn't leave a lot of options. You either believe that . . .

- Jesus' sacrifice is our only hope for salvation,

- His truth is absolute, and
- the life He offers is best

. . . or you don't.

If you sincerely choose to believe those truths, it's going to show up in the way you live. That's just inevitable. You can't legitimately claim to believe that the life Jesus offers is best and then go on living your own life the way you want. Believing in Jesus means putting your money where your mouth is—committing yourself to Him, doing what He says, and trusting that He can and will meet your every need.

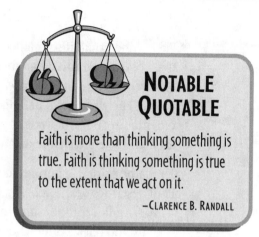

**NOTABLE QUOTABLE**

Faith is more than thinking something is true. Faith is thinking something is true to the extent that we act on it.

—Clarence B. Randall

Believe and repent. That, according to Jesus, is how a person becomes a Christian. That means the answer to our million-dollar question at the beginning of this chapter—"At what point in your life did you become a Christian?"—is . . .

The moment you repented of your sin and put your faith in Jesus.

## Membership Has Its Privileges—Not to Mention Its Responsibilities

All right, now you know *why* it's necessary to become a Christian and *how* to become one. Our final question is, what happens when you become a Christian? In other words, what's in it for you—and what are you in for—after you repent and believe in Jesus?

At the very least, you can expect four major changes in your life when you become a Christian.

### *1. You get a new eternal future.*

Gone is the prospect of hell, the lake of fire, and nonstop suffering. In its place is the guarantee of paradise, heaven, and everlasting happiness. We'll get into the specifics of the afterlife in chapter 7. For now, though, we want to emphasize two things about the "long-range forecast" for all believers that you should be aware of.

First, our eternal life benefit kicks in *immediately* upon death. While Jesus was on the cross, the criminal hanging next to Him realized who Jesus was, repented, and believed in Him. In response, Jesus said to the man, "I tell you the truth, today you will be with me in paradise" (Luke 23:43). One simple confession of repentance and belief was enough to guarantee the man a spot in Jesus' presence for eternity, effective the day of his death.

The same principle applies to all believers today. In 2 Corinthians 5:8, the apostle Paul describes death as being "away from the body and at home with the Lord." We're talking about same-day delivery here. There's no trial period, no waiting list, no background check. The moment we cease to exist on earth, we begin to live in God's presence.

> **NOTABLE QUOTABLE**
>
> Salvation is moving from living death to deathless life.
>
> –Jack Odell

Second, the future is *guaranteed* for all believers. Romans 8:38–39 says, "Neither death nor life, neither angels nor demons, neither the present nor the future, nor any powers, neither height nor depth, nor anything else in all creation, will be able to separate us from the love of God that is in Christ Jesus our Lord."

You could add doubts, questions, mistakes, and moments of weakness to that list, too. When we put our faith in Jesus, we put our eternal destiny in God's hands. And there's nothing in the world strong enough to break His grasp.

### *2. You get a new leader.*

This is the change of direction that comes with repentance. Romans 8:5 spells it out this way: "Those who live according to the sinful nature have their minds set on what that nature desires; but those who live in accordance with the Spirit have their minds set on what the Spirit desires."

Instead of pursuing sin and selfish interests, a Christian sets his or her mind on what the Spirit of God wants. The most obvious way of doing that is by following the example Jesus set during His time on earth.

We'll get into the specifics of how to live a "Christian life" in the chapters that follow. For now, though, we need to understand that for Christians, Jesus is not just Savior; He's Lord. That means He dictates how we . . .

- talk,
- act,
- spend our time,
- treat the people around us, and
- even respond to our enemies.

If that sounds suspiciously like having a "master" to you, well, you're starting to get the idea (look at Colossians 4:1; 2 Timothy 2:20–21). The good news, though, is that our Master not only wants what's ultimately best for us, He also knows exactly how we can achieve it.

### *3. You get a new responsibility.*

Just before Jesus left for heaven, He gave His followers one last instruction—one that still applies to all believers today: "Go and make disciples of all nations, baptizing them in the name of the Father and of the Son and of the Holy Spirit, and teaching them to obey everything I have commanded you" (Matthew 28:19–20).

You'll notice that Jesus didn't set any criteria for who should be making disciples. He didn't say, "Go, if you're good at communicating with people," or "Go, if you've been a Christian for most of your life," or "Go, if you've had some evangelism training." He just said, "Go." And His command applies to everyone who calls himself or herself a Christian.

Jesus expects His followers to share what has been given to them. Someone once described the process as one beggar telling another beggar where he can find food. The idea is that we have a responsibility to make others aware of the good news of Jesus by telling them what it's done for us personally. (We'll explore the specifics of how to share our faith in chapter 12.)

### *4. You get a new enemy.*

His name is Satan (which actually means "adversary"), and he opposes everything related to God and His work. Satan couldn't stand seeing Adam and Eve's close relationship with God in the Garden of Eden, so he tempted them to sin and destroy it (Genesis 3:1–6). Unfortunately for us, his feelings haven't changed much in the millennia since then.

Satan still can't stand seeing people have fellowship with God. That's why he's committed to doing whatever he can to disrupt believers' relationships with Christ and neutralize our impact on other potential believers. He can't change our eternal destination (remember, that's in God's hands), but he can do serious damage to our effectiveness by appealing to our doubt, fear, lust, resentment, laziness, indifference, or any other weakness he spots in us.

We'll get into the specifics of how Satan works in chapter 6. For the purpose of this chapter, though, you need to understand two things about him. First, his opposition is real. If you commit yourself to making Jesus Lord of your life and following His example in the way you live, you might as well paint a big ol' bull's-eye on your back because you will become a target of Satan.

**ON A PERSONAL NOTE**

Start a list of questions that you have about the Christian faith. Think about Bible passages you don't understand, concepts that don't make sense to you, uncertainties about how to apply certain principles to your life, and doubts that you just can't shake. Keep your list handy, so that you can add to it as ideas occur to you. The goal of this book is to address as many of those questions as possible. If, however, you still have unanswered questions after reading this book, you have a responsibility to get those questions answered (1 Peter 3:15) by a mature, trustworthy Christian—preferably your pastor.

Second, the only power Satan can have in our lives is the power we give him. He can use temptation, fear, and discouragement to distract us from our responsibilities as Jesus' disciples, but he can't *make* us give in to them. Only *we* can make that decision. That makes our battle plan pretty obvious: "Resist the devil, and he will flee from you" (James 4:7).

## In a Nutshell

Christianity is the world's least exclusive club. Not only can anyone join at any time, but current members are encouraged to recruit everyone they can find to join, too. The benefits and privileges that come with membership are too numerous to list (though we've covered some of them in this chapter and will explore others in the chapters that follow).

However, in order to enjoy those benefits and privileges, a person must take the necessary steps to join the club. Pretend affiliation just won't cut it.

God's requirements for membership are simple, but absolutely necessary.

Joining the club means taking on the responsibilities and challenges that go along with being a club member. It also means submitting to the leadership of the club "president."

Now that we're on the same page regarding what it means to be a believer (or Christian), we can focus our attention on the specifics of the Christian life.

## Know What You Believe

How much do you know about what it means to be a Christian? Here's a quiz to test your knowledge.

1. Why is it important for Christians to define our beliefs?
   a. God has a tricky vocabulary test waiting for anyone who expects to get into heaven.
   b. If we don't do it, we may be tempted to rely on other people's definitions.
   c. It gives us a decided advantage in Bible trivia games.
   d. It keeps our minds occupied so that we don't have time to think about sin.

2. Which of the following is not an essential fact in explaining why it's necessary to become a Christian?
   a. God is holy.
   b. Humans are sinful.
   c. Church membership has declined steadily over the past quarter century.
   d. We can do nothing to save ourselves.

3. What two things did Jesus say are necessary in order for a person to become a Christian?
   a. Repentance and belief
   b. Good works and a loving spirit
   c. A love for God and a hatred of Satan
   d. Church membership and a weekly tithe

4. What does it mean to believe in Jesus?
   a. Accepting that Christianity makes more logical sense than any other major religion
   b. Acknowledging that many of Christ's philosophies and teachings are still relevant today
   c. Admitting that Jesus lived a much holier life than anyone else in human history
   d. Putting your faith in the fact that Jesus' sacrifice is our only hope for salvation

5. Which of the following is not one of the major changes that occurs when you become a Christian?
   a. You get a new leader.
   b. You get a new enemy.
   c. You get a new nickname.
   d. You get a new eternal future.

*Answers: (1) b, (2) c, (3) a, (4) d, (5) c*

CHAPTER 2

# Yahweh Is My Way

## SNAPSHOT

Chip threw down the nine of hearts in disgust. "Aw, come on, not *God,*" he said.

"What's wrong with talking about God?" Whitey asked as he sat back in his chair and watched Lorne collect the cards and Chip and Otto add up their points for the round.

"I've lost the past three hands," Chip complained. "The last thing I need is to be distracted by you guys talking about abstract concepts."

"I don't think God is an abstract concept," Whitey objected.

"Oh, come on," Chip said. "Nobody knows anything about Him."

"You didn't seem to know anything about the queen of spades Otto was holding last hand," Lorne said with a grin. "Does that make the card an abstract concept?"

"Hey, less talking and more shuffling from you,"

### SNEAK PREVIEW

1. If God hadn't chosen to reveal Himself, we could know nothing about Him.
2. The primary, and most reliable, source of information about God is the Bible.
3. The more we understand about what God is like, the closer our relationship with Him will be.

Chip growled. "And do you think you could deal me a hand that's not all sevens, eights, and nines this time?"

"Why do you say nobody knows anything about God?" Whitey asked. "The Bible tells us a lot about Him."

"The *Bible*," Chip scoffed.

"Yeah, the *Bible*," Whitey emphasized. "God gave it to us because He wanted us to know Him."

"So you think that just because you've read the Bible you know what God is like?" Chip asked. "With no doubt in your mind?"

"Well, yeah," Whitey replied.

"You're wrong, and I can prove it," Chip said. "Do you believe that God created all living creatures?"

"Yeah," Whitey said with a slight hesitation.

"Okay," Chip said, "tell me, what have we been talking about for the past half hour?"

"Girls," Whitey replied.

"How hard it is to get a date," Lorne added.

"What losers we are," Otto chimed in.

Chip nodded. "We all agreed that we're pretty clueless when it comes to women, right?"

"Yeah, but what's that have to do with God?" Whitey asked.

"Think about it," Chip said. "If we can't figure out women, how can we even *hope* to understand the One who made them the way they are?"

* * * * * * * * * * * * * * * *

Contrary to popular opinion, there's nothing inherently Christian or even religious about believing in God. Genesis 1:1, the first verse of the Bible, treats

God's existence as a foregone conclusion ("In the beginning God . . ."), a fact that everyone is aware of. Granite is solid, fire is hot, toupees are obvious, and God exists. Big deal.

James 2:19 says that even *demons* believe in God. So, technically, simply acknowledging that there is a God makes a person about as spiritual as one of Satan's minions.

What separates believers from students of the obvious and God-fearing demons is the desire to *know* God, to discover what He's like, to grow closer to Him, to learn to relate to Him on a personal level. That's what this chapter is all about.

## Brought to You by God

Let's get one thing straight from the start. The only reason that knowing God is even a possibility for us is that God has *made* it possible. He has taken the initiative in revealing Himself to us. Without His self-revelation, we'd be clueless as to what God is really like. Trying to understand who God is and what He does without His help would be like a preschooler trying to grasp quantum physics. Our brains just aren't up to the task.

The only things we're capable of understanding about God are the things that He makes known to us. When it comes to gaining insight into who He is, we are completely at His mercy. Fortunately for us, God is extremely generous in sharing information about Himself.

Generally, God makes Himself known to us in three ways: through nature, through personal experience, and through His Word, the Bible. Let's take a look at what we can learn from each of those sources.

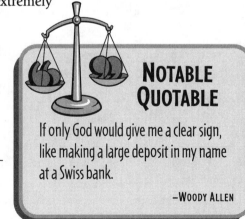

**NOTABLE QUOTABLE**

If only God would give me a clear sign, like making a large deposit in my name at a Swiss bank.

—WOODY ALLEN

## Nature Calls

God is the creator of the universe. We know this because the Bible says so (Genesis 1:1) and because God left His fingerprints all over His work. By looking at the world around us, we can pick up clues as to what God Himself is like.

For example, when we see the immensity of Niagara Falls or the Grand Canyon and realize that God simply spoke them into existence, we get a sense of His power. When we see the stunning spectacle of the Painted Desert—or any given sunset, for that matter—we get a sense of God's love of beauty. When we consider the complex design of the human body or the interconnectedness of life on this planet (including the food chain, the water cycle, and all those other scientific processes that we've forgotten since high school), we get a sense of God's wisdom and His perfect design.

**ON A PERSONAL NOTE**

If you've never considered nature as a way of getting to know God, do yourself a favor and start investigating the physical world around you. Keep a notebook of "evidence" that reveals the nature of the Creator. A little research should yield some intriguing information about how perfectly designed our earth is. For example, scientists have concluded that if the earth's angle of rotation were off even by a couple of degrees, the planet couldn't sustain life. The same is true with the content of our atmosphere. If the elements that comprise it were changed even slightly, there would be no life on the earth.

We must be careful not to make too many assumptions based on nature, however, because nature—not to mention our understanding of it—is flawed. For example, we might say, "God created mosquitoes, skunks, and game-show hosts, so He must enjoy annoying us."

Not true. The fact is, we live in a fallen state. The natural world was once ideal, but it's been affected by sin. The curse that God handed down after Adam and Eve's sin in the Garden of Eden affected the earth itself as well as its inhabitants. (Check out Genesis 3:17–19 for more details.)

When we look at nature now, we can still see *remnants* of God's perfect design, but it's been marred by our own imperfection. For that reason, nature is a useful, but imperfect, tool for discovering what God is like.

## Personally Speaking

Sometimes God reveals Himself in more dramatic ways. Occasionally He performs specific, obvious works in people's lives that demonstrate who He is, what He's capable of, and what He wants from us.

If you think hard enough, you can probably recall an experience in your own life that can only be explained by God's work, whether it's . . .

- a well-timed, unexpected source of income,
- an injury or illness that should have been more serious than it was, or
- any obvious answer to prayer.

Regardless of the specifics, it's safe to say that there are times when God demonstrates His power, protection, and love for us in ways that leave us slack-jawed. God can speak personally and dramatically.

However, we need to be careful about confining our search for God in our lives to "big things." The Old Testament prophet Elijah learned this lesson in an extraordinary way.

Elijah was depressed and scared because he thought he was going to be put to death for doing what God wanted him to do. To bolster the prophet's spirit, God told Elijah to go get a front row seat on Mount Horeb because He, the Lord, was going to pass by—in person. While Elijah watched, a powerful wind tore the mountain apart and shattered the rocks around him. Elijah looked for God in the wind, but He wasn't there.

Next came a devastating earthquake that shook the mountain to its core. Elijah looked for God in the earthquake, but He wasn't there.

After the earthquake came a roaring fire that consumed everything in its path. Elijah looked for God in the fire, but He wasn't there.

In the wake of the fire's roar, after arguably the most awesome parade of natural phenomena ever witnessed, Elijah heard a gentle whisper. First Kings 19:13 says, "When Elijah heard it, he pulled his cloak over his face." Why? Because God was in the whisper.

God certainly could have made Himself known in the wind, the earthquake, or the fire. He's done it before. But this time He made Himself known in a gentle whisper. And if Elijah had only focused on the blockbuster stuff, he would have missed a meaningful interaction with God.

The same thing goes for us. If we confine our search to the kinds of things that make headlines, we're going to miss many important facts about God. We need to look and listen carefully to the things that go on in our lives, and search for evidence of His work, guidance, and love. The better we get at learning to hear His gentle whispers, the better idea we'll have of what God is really like.

Keep in mind that God does not often reveal Himself through "big things" and personal revelations. They remain the exception, as He calls on us to trust Him.

### Just Wondering

**What does it mean that God is our "heavenly Father"?**

When we repent and believe in Jesus, we become the children of God. We are adopted into His family. Not only does that give us the right to call Him "Father," it also means we can expect to be treated like His beloved children. We can take all of our needs and concerns to Him and receive the comfort, love, and sense of importance that a loving Father provides. (For more information on what it means to have a heavenly Father, check out Matthew 7:9-11; Romans 8:14-17; Hebrews 12:5-11.)

## Abandon All Preconceptions, Ye Who Enter

As is the case with nature, we need to be careful about relying too heavily on personal experience in trying to determine what God is like. The problem is that it's difficult for us to separate our actual experiences from our wishful thinking. For example, we might convince ourselves that God is all-loving if we don't want to face the prospect of His justice.

We must not allow our personal beliefs and biases to dictate what we believe about God. The brutal truth is that our beliefs have no bearing on reality. What's more, it's pretty conceited to believe that they do.

You've probably heard all kinds of reasons for why people won't accept or believe in God.

- "I just can't believe in a God who considers homosexuality a sin."
- "I refuse to believe in Someone who would allow thousands of innocent people to die in the World Trade Center attacks."

- "I believe in a God who cares about His people, not one who sends people to hell for disagreeing with Him."

All of these statements reflect a misunderstanding of what God is like. But they also reflect a dangerous attitude—one that says, until God meets certain preconceived notions of what He should be like, until He conforms to what we want Him to be, He can be dismissed.

But that makes absolutely no sense at all. It's like taking a bold stand against gravity ("I just can't believe in a force that would cause elderly people to fall to the ground when they lose their balance"). Gravity exists, regardless of whether or not we believe in it or understand it completely. And so does God.

You can choose not to believe in gravity, but that doesn't mean you won't pay the price for trying to defy it. Likewise, you can choose not to believe in God, but that doesn't mean you won't ultimately pay the price for your decision.

## God: The Authorized Biography

Nature won't give us an accurate picture of what God is like, and neither will our personal experiences. If we want absolutely trustworthy information about who God is, we need to go straight to the Handbook.

The Bible is ground zero for information about God. It's safe to say that everything God wants us to know about Him can be found in His Word.

For starters, there's the name He chose for Himself: "I AM" (Exodus 3:14). Though those two words may seem vague at first ("I am . . . what?"), they actually provide the framework with which to explore God. God is saying, "Regardless of whatever else seems real or logical to you, I am."

Others pretend; God is. Other things "give the appearance of"; God is. Others claim; God is. So when we answer the question, "What is God like?" the only information we can rely on is that which comes from the source—"I AM" Himself.

The ancient Hebrew name for God, *Yahweh* ("I am the One who is"), reflects this concept of absolute existence and identity. In most Bibles, *Yahweh* is translated as "the LORD," with the word in small capital letters: *LORD*. (See Exodus 3:15 for an example.)

## Attributes and Perfections

There's a nagging theological issue that we need to take care of before we start seriously talking about what God is like. Strictly speaking, God doesn't have "characteristics" or "personality traits." He has *perfections*.

Humans have personality traits. For instance, in describing a potential blind date, a friend might say, "She's a little shy, but she has a great sense of humor. She can be a little bossy and demanding sometimes, but if you're patient with her, you'll see how caring she can be." *Shy, humorous, bossy, demanding,* and *caring* are all descriptive characteristics that help us understand what someone is like.

But in our understanding, we recognize that those characteristics exist in moderation. If you heard that someone is shy, you wouldn't expect her to cower under a table all night. If you heard that someone has a great sense of humor, you wouldn't expect him to do a fifteen-minute stand-up routine. We understand that a person can be a little this and a little that.

Not so with God. When characteristics or attributes are applied to Him, they become perfections. You see, there's nothing "halfway" or "occasional" about God. He's not somewhat merciful; His mercy is perfect. He doesn't "become" just when the mood strikes Him; His justice is complete. He isn't "kind of" loving; His love is the standard against which all other love is measured.

What's more, His perfections exist in complete harmony. God's love never cancels out His mercy, and His justice never interrupts His love. He is always completely loving, completely merciful, completely just, and so on.

### Just Wondering

**What does it mean that God created us in His image?**
The statement in Genesis 1:27 isn't referring to a physical likeness. Remember, God is a Spirit. We don't have "His eyes" or "His hairline." Instead, our likeness to God has to do with our intelligence and personality. Unlike animals, humans are capable of distinguishing between right and wrong, as God is. Emotions such as joy, concern, and sorrow are also part of our likeness to God. Perhaps it's our likeness to God that makes us capable of understanding Him (at least to a limited degree).

If that seems impossible, it's because we don't have the brain power to understand God fully. That's one of the problems with being finite—we have no grasp of the infinite. Our only option, then, is to take God at His word when He describes Himself.

# Name Them One by One

But where do we begin? Trying to nail down God's attributes and perfections is like trying to take a picture of the entire Great Wall of China. There's no way you can get everything into focus and give the details the attention they deserve.

With that in mind, we've chosen to narrow our focus to ten of God's perfections. They will give us a good starting point in learning what our heavenly Father is like, and a good jumping-off point for further study. Since none of God's attributes is more important or prominent than another, we've arranged them in alphabetical order.

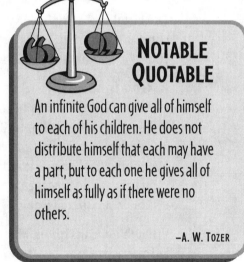

> **NOTABLE QUOTABLE**
>
> An infinite God can give all of himself to each of his children. He does not distribute himself that each may have a part, but to each one he gives all of himself as fully as if there were no others.
>
> —A. W. TOZER

### *1. God is eternal.*

This can be a tough concept to grasp in a world where the words "long lasting" are used to describe everything from breath mints to deodorant. Our problem is that we're bound by our concept of time. It's hard for us to consider anything beyond "a long, long time ago."

Time, however, doesn't apply to God. Trying to measure God with human concepts such as years, centuries, and millennia is like trying to measure the cosmos with a ruler. It just won't work. God had already existed forever before we started keeping track of time and He will exist forever after time ends. For God, time is like a scroll rolled out on a table. He can see the past, the present, and the future all at the same time, because He's above it all.

The fact that God is eternal means there's never been a time when He didn't exist, and there will never be a time when He doesn't exist. If you want to get technical about it, you could say that God is *self-existent.* Unlike everything else in the universe, God was not created. That means you'll never see His name on a list of celebrity birthdays. ("Best wishes go out to the Almighty, who's celebrating His 1,176,809,311,021st birthday today.") More importantly, it means that He's not dependent on anyone or anything for His existence. We are alive because God created us. God is alive because He *is* life.

Check out the translation of God's Hebrew name *Yahweh* again: "I am the one who is." That title has applied forever and it will continue to apply forever. God is the only Being who can claim complete independence.

People in Bible times found comfort in the fact that God is eternal. Psalm 90:1–2 is a great example: "Lord, you have been our dwelling place throughout all generations. Before the mountains were born or you brought forth the earth and the world, from everlasting to everlasting you are God."

The fact that God will always be around to protect and guide us should bring us comfort, too. When He says, "I will be with you always" and "I will never forsake you," He has the credentials to back it up. In other words, God will always be God.

### *2. God is holy.*

We talked about the implications of God's holiness—the fact that sin can't exist in His presence—in chapter 1. But there's another element that we need to look at. The fact that God is holy means that everything about Him is good and right. Everything God does is good because He does it. Everything He commands is the right thing to do, because He commands it. One who is truly holy cannot commit evil or do anything wrong.

What that means for us, His servants, is that we never have to worry about being led astray by God. If we follow His instructions and obey His commands, we are guaranteed to do the right thing.

Holiness is more than just a quality to admire in God, however; it's one to work toward in our own lives. First John 1:6–7 makes it clear that God expects us to reject sin as He does. That's not to say He demands perfection and sinlessness from us. He knows that we will fail occasionally. But that shouldn't keep us from striving to achieve God's high standard of holiness.

### 3. *God is immanent.*

Immanent? The idea here is that God is a hands-on manager. He didn't just create the world and then walk away, leaving us to fend for ourselves. He doesn't rely on angels to bring Him monthly progress reports regarding the human race. He's right here with us, always present, always near. His Being permeates the universe.

God's immanence is closely related to His *omnipresence,* the fact that He's everywhere at once. There is no place we can go where God is not. That's bad news for people who would prefer to operate behind God's back, but it's good news for anyone interested in His constant protection and companionship.

We need to emphasize a point here. God is everywhere, but He's not *everything*. And everything is not God. This is an important distinction to understand. As we'll see when we discuss God's transcendence, God is intimately involved in His creation, but He is not part of His creation.

What God's immanence means for us is complete access, round-the-clock, 24/7. When God says "I am with you" (see Isaiah 57:15), He's not talking about support from afar. He's not saying, "I'll be rooting for you" or "I'll be watching you." He's saying, "No matter where you go or what you do, I will be there."

### 4. *God is just.*

This is the attribute that keeps us from overemphasizing God's other perfections —namely, His love and mercy. It's also the attribute that answers the age-old question, "How can a loving God send people to hell?" God is perfectly loving, yes. However, He is also perfectly just. Habakkuk 1:13 says that God "cannot tolerate wrong." That means He cannot allow sin to go unpunished.

No one who believes in Christ will have to face God's ultimate justice. Christ already faced it for us. What's more, we can take comfort in God's justice because it ensures that one day everyone will get what he or she deserves. While it may often seem as though evil people prosper in this world while good people suffer, someday God will make everything right.

### 5. *God is loving.*

Time for a quick perspective check. God's love is *perfect,* the standard against which all other love is measured. If we see something in God's love that doesn't

**NOTABLE QUOTABLE**

A God all mercy is a God unjust.

—EDWARD YOUNG

match our opinion of what love should be, it's our problem, not His.

Dismissing, or even questioning, God's love on the basis of how it compares to our ideal is like estimating that a piece of plywood is 48 inches long and then questioning the tape measure that says it's actually 62 inches long.

Recognizing the perfection of God's love can help us work through tough questions like these (fill in the blanks yourself):

- "If God loves us, why does He ______________?"
- "How could a loving God allow ______________?"
- "How can you say God is loving when He's responsible for ______________?"

The fact is, God's perfect love involves instruction, correction, discipline, and allowing us to face the consequences of our actions. Hebrews 12:5–6 makes that quite clear: "My son, do not make light of the Lord's discipline, and do not lose heart when he rebukes you, because the Lord disciplines those he loves, and he punishes everyone he accepts as a son."

The fact that God loves us means that He wants only what's best for us. More than that, though, it means He will do whatever is necessary to make sure that we recognize and pursue what's best for us. His methods may seem harsh or disagreeable to us, but that's only because we don't understand the depths of His love for us.

First John 4:7–9 spells out what God's love means for us. First of all, it means eternal life. God's love for us is what prompted Him to send His Son to take the punishment for our sins.

Second, God's love for us makes it possible for us to love others. It's like a garden fountain that has a series of basins; when the top one is full and the water continues to flow, it spills over into a second basin, and then a third and a fourth.

God's love should overflow from us into many more basins—er, lives.

If you want another outdoor analogy, we could say that God's love is like a tree branch and we are like wood chippers, taking it in, processing it, and then firing it out in all directions. Take your pick.

Either way, the implications are the same for us. Because God has shown His love to us—His undeserved, active, selfless, serving love—we have the responsibility to show that same kind of love to others.

### *6. God is omnipotent.*

The common shorthand definition of *omnipotent* is "all-powerful." But that's a little vague, don't you think? The question that invariably arises when people discuss God's power is, Can God do anything? And the answer, strictly speaking, is no.

**NOTABLE QUOTABLE**

One on God's side is a majority.

—Wendell Phillips

God has what are called natural limitations, things He can't do because they go against His nature. Among other things, God can't lie (Titus 1:2), be tempted to sin (James 1:13), or deny His nature ("disown himself"; 2 Timothy 2:13). Those limitations don't make Him any less powerful; they simply make Him true to His nature.

So let's put it this way: God can do anything that is within His nature. His power over the universe is limitless. Exhibit A is the very existence of the physical world itself. The world exists—we exist—because God decided that that would be a good thing. One word from Him brought the universe, in all of its unimaginable complexity, into being.

What's more, God has demonstrated His awesome power throughout history by defying, suspending, or overpowering natural laws in ways that can only be explained in terms of the miraculous. The Bible records hundreds of such demonstrations. For example . . .

- In Genesis 21:1–7, God caused a ninety-year-old woman to become pregnant and give birth to a son.

- In Exodus 14:10–31, God held back the waters of the Red Sea so that the

Israelites could walk across on dry ground.

- In Joshua 10:1–15, God made the sun stand still so that the Israelites could win a military battle.
- In Daniel 3, God allowed three of His servants to walk around unharmed inside a fiery furnace.
- In Jonah 1:17 (and 2:10), God kept Jonah alive in the stomach of a giant fish before causing the fish to vomit the prophet onto shore.

The implications for us are obvious. God is all-powerful, and He loves us! What could be better than that? The same hands that held back the Red Sea are now holding us in their grasp. And nothing can pry us from them. That's why the apostle Paul was so confident when he wrote: "For I am convinced that [nothing] . . . in all creation, will be able to separate us from the love of God that is in Christ Jesus our Lord" (Romans 8:38–39).

### *7. God is omniscient.*

God knows everything. He knows everything that's happened in the past. He knows everything that's happening at this moment. He knows everything that will happen in the future. He knows every choice we will ever face. He knows the consequence of every possible decision we will ever make. He knows how everything in the universe works. He knows why everything happens.

God knows our true motives. He knows our deepest feelings. He knows how we can find ultimate fulfillment and happiness. He knows how we can be most effective in serving Him and doing His work.

The greatest human achievements and the highest levels of human thought are foolishness compared to God's wisdom, the Bible declares (1 Corinthians 3:18–20). Fortunately for us, God isn't content to leave us to our "foolishness." That's why He makes His wisdom, knowledge, and expertise available to all who ask. God can and will give us the guidance we need to live our lives wisely.

### *8. God is sovereign.*

God has no boss and does not answer to anyone. He is the ultimate authority, no matter what the subject is. He's not obligated to do anything. He doesn't rely on advisors, focus groups, image handlers, or marketing surveys. He's not motivated by popularity or politics. He does what He wants, when He wants. What's more, everything He does is right and perfect simply because He does it.

From time to time in our Christian walk, it may seem as though God asks a lot from us. One of the best ways to regain focus during those times is to remind ourselves that God doesn't *need* us. He's sovereign, after all. For that reason, we should consider it an honor to be included in His will and His plans at all.

### 9. *God is transcendent.*

Being transcendent is the flip side of being immanent. The idea here is that God is not contained by the universe or anything in it. He's distinct from His creation. He's not subject to the laws of physics or any other constraints in our world.

> **JUST WONDERING**
>
> **If God is so powerful, why doesn't He destroy all evil in the world?**
>
> God certainly has the power to destroy evil. In fact, one day He will. (The book of Revelation promises it.) But, for now, His mercy causes Him to withhold His judgment and His destructive powers, so that as many people as possible will have an opportunity to repent and believe in His Son.

The fact that God is immanent also means that He's beyond the grasp of our intellect. If He hadn't taken the initiative in making Himself known to us, we would have no hope of understanding Him. In Isaiah 55:9, God explains His transcendence this way: "As the heavens are higher than the earth, so are my ways higher than your ways and my thoughts higher than your thoughts."

What it boils down to is this: God is intimately involved in the everyday workings of the world because He *chooses* to be. He's not compelled to be part of our lives; He *wants* to be part of them.

### 10. *God is unchanging.*

Numbers 23:19 says, "God is not a man, that he should lie, nor a son of man, that he should change his mind." James 1:17 tells us that our heavenly Father "does not change like shifting shadows."

Fashions change. Clothes once considered scandalous would barely draw a second look today. Laws change. Once upon a time, selling liquor was illegal in the United States. Now liquor ads are everywhere. Society's standards change. Words that were once considered offensive are now commonplace.

**NOTABLE QUOTABLE**

Don't try to defend what God does. What He does is right because He does it.

—HENRY JACOBSEN

God, however, doesn't change. Never has, never will. Furthermore, His promises will never fail. We can always count on God to be just who He says He is and do just what He says He will do.

## Responding to God's Perfections

If knowing what God is like and understanding His perfections were an intellectual pursuit, we could end the chapter right here. But simply having information about Him isn't enough. As we suggested earlier in this chapter, there are quite a few demons who could probably do well in a trivia quiz about God.

We as believers need to take the next step and incorporate what we know about God into our everyday lives—specifically, into our everyday interaction with Him.

Because God is who He is, we should respond to Him in several specific ways.

### *1. Respond with a sense of wonder.*

David was chosen by God to lead God's people. He was a committed prayer warrior. (You know those 150 psalms in the middle of your Bible? David wrote most of them.) As far as we can tell, he spent a good chunk of each day in direct communication with his heavenly Father. Few people in history have ever been closer to God than David was.

Despite his tight friendship with God, however, there were still moments in David's life when he practically had to pinch himself to make sure that he wasn't dreaming. Deep down, David was amazed at his good fortune. You can almost hear the incredulity in his words in verses like Psalm 8:4: "What is man that you are mindful of him, the son of man that you care for him?" In other words, David wanted to know, "Why in the world would God want a personal relationship with someone like me?"

It's a legitimate question—and a good attitude to maintain. The opportunity of having a personal relationship with God should never seem commonplace or deserved to us. There should always be a part of us that's a little overwhelmed by the privilege of calling God "Father."

### *2. Respond with frequent praise.*

When we see a great play at a baseball game, we cheer. When we see a moving performance at the theater, we applaud. It only makes sense, then, that when we come face-to-face with God's perfections, we respond by showing our appreciation and awe for who He is and what He's done.

As we'll see in chapter 10, praise and worship are vital elements in the life of a believer. The more specific we can be in our praise—the more we recognize God's individual attributes and His work in our lives—the more sincere our worship will be.

### *3. Respond with boldness.*

Jesus' sacrifice and the salvation it brought means that those of us who believe in Him don't have to cower in the presence of God the way Adam and Eve did after their sin in the Garden of Eden (Genesis 3:7–10). God welcomes everyone who claims the gift of salvation offered by His Son. For that reason, we can approach God in the same way a child approaches his or her father—with love and affection and without fear of being turned away.

Hebrews 4:16 puts it this way: "Let us then approach the throne of grace with confidence, so that we may receive mercy and find grace to help us in our time of need."

When it comes to approaching God, there is no need for us to feel self-conscious, or as though we're imposing on Him. We can take Him our boldest requests without having to worry about being tossed out of His presence.

### *4. Respond with a desire to put His power to work.*

We'll be examining the topic of prayer in detail in chapter 9. For now, though, we need to understand that God hears our prayers—all of them. What's more, He *responds* to our prayers. John 14:13 says, "I will do whatever you ask in my name."

Imagine the possibilities. God knows all and sees all. He can do anything. On top of all that, He loves us and wants the very best for us. Think of the changes He can make in our lives, our families, our communities, and our world. He's ready, willing, and able to unleash His power and His goodness for His purposes. And He wants us to be a part of His work. Can't you just picture Him in heaven, with a big smile on His face, inviting us to make our requests known, saying, "Come on, just ask Me"?

### *5. Respond with closeness.*

Hebrews 10:22 urges us to draw near to God. We do that by . . .

- studying His Word,
- learning more about Him, and
- following the example of His Son.

In return, God will draw near to us by giving us His love, strength, support, encouragement, guidance, wisdom, discernment, peace, and fulfillment. That's quite a deal.

### *6. Respond with obedience.*

If we truly believe that God knows everything, including the consequences of every possible action we might take, it only makes sense to rely on His guidance and follow His instructions for our lives.

Imagine that life on this planet is one enormous maze, with hundreds of thousands of possible turns and choices. Unlike traditional mazes, however, this one has a different starting point and a different finishing point for everyone. In other words, everyone has a unique path to discover in the maze. Because our minds are finite, we have no idea what lies around the next corner of the maze or what will happen as a result of our next choice.

God, on the other hand, stands above the maze, looking down over all of it. He can see every individual path. He knows which turns we should make and which ones we should avoid. He knows exactly where we are at any given moment, not to

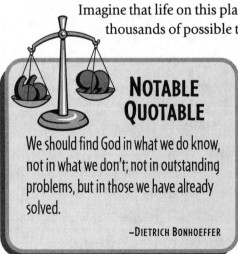

**NOTABLE QUOTABLE**

We should find God in what we do know, not in what we don't; not in outstanding problems, but in those we have already solved.

–DIETRICH BONHOEFFER

mention what lies ahead for us.

What's more, God has given us written instructions on how to work our way through the maze. It's called the Bible, and it's a surprisingly helpful resource for navigating the various turns, intersections, and dead ends we'll face in this maze of life. On top of all that, Gods runs a twenty-four-hour hot line, called prayer, for anyone who ever feels lost or in need of direction.

All we have to do is follow His directions and obey His instructions.

Sometimes His commands may not seem right to us. They may not be what we want to hear. We may be tempted to question them. But we need to ask ourselves, Who has the better perspective on where we're at and where we need to be—God or us?

### On a Personal Note

Throughout Scripture, God is referred to by many different names. Each name emphasizes a specific element of His nature. For example, "I am who I am" (Exodus 3:14) emphasizes God's self-existence; "God Almighty" (Genesis 35:11) emphasizes the fact that He has guided His people throughout history; "Lord" emphasizes His command over everything; "LORD Almighty" (Psalm 24:10) emphasizes His heavenly kingship. You can follow the example of the Bible writers–and personalize your communication with God in the process–by incorporating different names of God into your prayer life. The names you choose to use in a particular prayer will depend on which characteristics you want to emphasize at that moment.

## You Make the Call

As we mentioned earlier in this chapter, our beliefs and wishful thoughts about what God is like have no bearing on what He's actually like. God is not interested in making Himself what we want Him to be.

That leaves us with a choice. We can . . .

- cling to our fantasies and choose to live in an imaginary spiritual world in which God exists to fulfill our wishes and accept us on our own terms,
- allow ourselves to become bitter about God's failure to live up to our expectations and refuse to pursue a personal relationship with Him, or
- work to learn everything we can about what God is really like so that we can take advantage of the personal relationship He so graciously offers.

Before you make your decision, consider one more thing about God. He didn't have to reveal anything about Himself. He could have left His nature a complete mystery to us. He could have forced us to guess at what's He like and then punished us for getting it wrong. He could have had us walking around on pins and needles, always worried about offending Him and being struck by a bolt of lightning from the heavens.

But that's not what God chose to do. Instead, He gave us a guidebook, a written document that contains everything we need to know in order to have a Father-child relationship with Him. He gave us the Bible and said, "Here; if you're interested in learning about Me, check this out."

The obvious question is, What could be *more* interesting, or more important, than learning everything we can about Him?

## Know What You Believe

How much do you know about God? Here's a quiz to test your knowledge.

1. Which of the following is not a potential source of legitimate information about God?
   a. The Bible
   b. Personal experience
   c. Tabloid newspapers
   d. Nature

2. What's wrong with a statement such as, "I refuse to believe in a God who lets good people go to hell because they didn't believe the right way"?
   a. It's grammatically incorrect.
   b. It's theologically incorrect; God will never let anyone go to hell.
   c. It assumes that our beliefs dictate what God is like.
   d. It refers to the Muslim God, Allah, and not the God we worship.

3. Which of the following is not one of God's perfections?
   a. Holiness
   b. Transcendence

c. Immanence
d. Malleability

4. Based on what we know of God's perfections, how should we not respond to Him?
   a. With frequent praise
   b. With fear and trembling
   c. With a desire to put His power to work
   d. With a sense of wonder

5. Which of the following is not true of God?
   a. He occasionally gets tired of humans trying to figure out what He's like.
   b. He took the initiative in making Himself known to us.
   c. He hears our prayers.
   d. He will never change.

*Answers: (1) c, (2) c, (3) d, (4) b, (5) a*

CHAPTER 3

# Here Comes the Son

## SNAPSHOT

"Well, if it isn't my Christian coworkers," Kevin said as he set down his food tray and pulled up a chair. "Shouldn't you guys be at a lunchtime prayer meeting somewhere, weeping over lost souls?"

"How many times do we have to tell you, Kevin?" Andy asked. "*Tuesday* is weeping, Wednesday is teeth gnashing, and Thursday is Italian beef at the food court."

"It's all right there in the New Testament," Don chimed in.

Kevin smirked. "You guys should have come to that marketing seminar last weekend," he said. "The speaker had some interesting things to say about your religion."

"For instance?" Don asked.

Kevin smiled. "He said the only reason that we know anything about Jesus today, instead of the other rabbis and teachers who were around during

### SNEAK PREVIEW

1. Believing that Jesus is who He claims to be should change our lives completely.
2. Popular notions of Jesus hardly scratch the surface of who He really is and what He's done for us.
3. Jesus modeled the life He wants His followers to live.

that time, is that Jesus and His followers understood the value of publicity and marketing."

"Yeah, those two semesters at Nazareth Business College really paid off," Andy said.

Kevin ignored him and continued. "That got me thinking about whether someone could do the same thing today."

"Do what?" Don asked.

"Start a new religion and make a name for himself the way Jesus did," Kevin replied.

"Someone like *you*, you mean?" Andy asked.

"Sure, why not?" Kevin said. "If there's anything I know, it's marketing. Here's how I'd do it. First, I'd recruit Artie and Lew, the two best copywriters in the firm, to start keeping journals about me. I'd have them make up stories about my going to hospitals and healing sick people just by touching them or about my going to funerals and raising people from the dead. Only I'd have them write about it in a real believable way, you know?"

Andy and Don nodded but said nothing.

"I could even have them take it to the extreme, if I wanted," Kevin continued. "I could have them write that I was actually God's youngest son, and that I was sent to bring a new message to the world—maybe 'Do whatever feels good.' I could have them write that my mother was a virgin when I was born, that I lived a perfect life, that I was put to death by the government, and that I came back to life—just like your guy."

"What would you do with the journals after your writers got done with your story?" Andy asked.

"I'd hide them someplace where they wouldn't be found for hundreds or even thousands of years," Kevin answered. "When people finally discover them, they'll look at the stories and say, 'Wow, this Kevin Mushnick guy was incredible. Look at all the miraculous things he did! He really was the son of God. Let's obey his command and do whatever feels good.' And, before you know it, I'd have a religion just like Christianity."

"And you'd be worshiped by Mushnickians all over the world," Don added.

"Exactly," Kevin said with a big grin.

"Of course, it wouldn't be *just like Christianity,*" Andy pointed out.

"Why not?" Kevin asked.

"Well, if you want it to be like Christianity," Andy said, "you'd have to make sure that the journals would be made public about twenty years after you died. That's how soon the earliest books of the New Testament started showing up after Jesus left the earth."

"And the problem with that," Don added, "is that there would still be people alive who knew you personally. And if your journals started to get popular, those people would write books of their own, saying, 'I knew that guy. He could barely open a Band-Aid, let alone heal sick people in the hospital.'"

Andy continued the thought. "Or they'd say, 'Kevin Mushnick lived a perfect life? No way. I was at a convention in Vegas with him one time, and I saw him—'"

"Okay, okay, skip the part about the perfect life," Kevin interrupted.

"That's the point," Andy explained. "Jesus' enemies *tried* to find people who could tell stories like that about Him. They tried to find someone who could accuse Him of sin at His trial. But they couldn't find anyone. No one could think of anything that He'd done wrong. So they had to lie about Him."

"And if you're going to say that you rose from the grave," Don added, "you'd better make sure you do it. Otherwise, some tabloid newspaper will come along and have your grave opened to prove that your body—or what's left of it—is still there."

"Oh, and if you want your religion to be like Christianity, there's one more thing you have to do."

"What's that?" Kevin asked.

"You have to make sure that Artie, Lew, and everyone else involved in your scheme are willing to be tortured and killed for keeping your secret."

"What?" Kevin asked.

"That's what happened to almost all of Jesus' disciples, the ones who spread the word about Him," Andy explained. "The Jewish leaders and Roman officials wanted to put an end to all the talk about Jesus, so they arrested His followers and gave them a choice: Deny what you've been saying about Jesus or die. And His disciples chose death."

Kevin nodded his head. "That might be a problem with Artie and Lew," he acknowledged. "I can't even get them to work weekends for me."

* * * * * * * * * * * * * * * *

"I am the way and the truth and the life. No one comes to the Father except through me" (John 14:6).

"The woman said, 'I know that Messiah' (called Christ) 'is coming. When he comes, he will explain everything to us.' Then Jesus declared, 'I who speak to you am he'" (John 4:25–26).

"I and the Father are one" (John 10:30).

"The high priest said to him, 'I charge you under oath by the living God: Tell us if you are the Christ, the Son of God.' 'Yes, it is as you say,' Jesus replied" (Matthew 26:63b–64a).

Consider the gauntlet thrown down. All four of the previous quotes come from Jesus Himself. You can find them in any New Testament. It's important to recognize these quotes for what they are, because they drastically limit our possibilities and narrow our focus in discussing who Jesus is.

You see, some people try to separate the Jesus of history from the Christ of Christianity. They believe that Jesus was a great philosopher and moral teacher—and nothing more. They suggest that Jesus would actually be appalled and embarrassed if He knew what His followers were saying about Him today. They argue that Jesus never identified Himself as the Son of God, Messiah, or Savior—that those titles were given to Him by wishfully thinking disciples.

## Telling Words

But Jesus' own words, in the previous passages and in dozens of others throughout the Bible, blow that possibility right out of the water. Jesus didn't give us the option of writing Him off as merely a great moral teacher. If He had, we could respond to Him in the same way we respond to most other teachers—with passive indifference.

If Jesus were nothing more than a world-class philosopher, there would be no reason to study the details of His life. We could just leaf through a collection of His greatest sayings whenever the mood struck us. We could place Him in the pantheon of upstanding historical figures, alongside Abraham Lincoln, Mohandas Gandhi, and Mother Teresa, and be done with Him.

But Jesus didn't leave us that option.

Instead, He said . . .

- "I am the Son of God."
- "I am the Messiah."
- "I am your only hope for salvation."
- "I am Lord."

And then He put the ball in our court.

## Evidence That Demands a Verdict; Verdict That Demands a Life

Here's what it comes down to: Either Jesus *is* who He says He is or He *isn't*. Either the Bible is right about Him or it's wrong. The implications of each of those possibilities are staggering.

First, if Jesus *isn't* who He claimed to be, if the Bible's portrayal of Him is a lie, then He has to go down as one of the most despicable characters in human history. That would mean . . .

- He duped billions of innocent people into giving up their pursuit of personal pleasure and obeying His commands.
- He gave the world the worst kind of false hope.
- He called people to live a life that He knew was a dead end.
- His promise of eternal life was sadistic, especially if He knew all along that the ultimate fate of humanity was either eternal suffering or complete obliteration.

**NOTABLE QUOTABLE**

Jesus says, "I love you just the way you are. And I love you too much to let you stay the way you are."

—Chris Lyons

It would be tough, if not impossible, to have a neutral reaction or passive attitude toward someone who was capable of that kind of deception. Such a person would demand our complete opposition. We couldn't stand by and watch others get tricked into believing His lies. We'd have to do whatever we could to put an end to His influence in the world.

If, on the other hand, Jesus *is* who He claims to be—if the Bible's portrayal of Him is accurate—our reaction should be just as extreme. Knowing that the Son of God—the Messiah, the Savior, the only hope for the human race—wants to have a personal relationship with us should rock our world. It should give us hope and meaning in our lives beyond anything we've ever experienced before. More than anything else, though, it should motivate us to action.

The first course of action is accepting Him as Savior. (We talked about that in chapter 1.) The second course is discovering all we can about Him in God's Word. Usually that takes . . . oh, about a lifetime to accomplish. You see, the Bible is written in such a way that it reveals new information each time we read it.

Your first time through the Gospels—the books of Matthew, Mark, Luke, and John, which record the story of Jesus' life on earth—will introduce you to the who, what, when, and where of Jesus' human existence. Your second time through might reveal important details that you missed the first time. Your third time through might reveal connections and recurring themes that will help you see the "big picture" of God's plan of salvation—and so on, and so on.

# Ten Things That May Surprise You About Jesus

To help you in your information gathering, we've come up with a list of ten facts about the Son of God that you may not be aware of—ten pieces of information that will help you . . .

- understand what's going on in the Gospels,
- flesh out your concept of who Jesus is and what He's like,
- deepen your appreciation of what He's done, and
- understand His role in your life.

Let's take a look at them.

### *1. News of Jesus' arrival leaked early.*

Actually, the news leaked several thousand years early. Old Testament prophets often preached about a coming "Messiah," One who would save the people of Israel once and for all. Many prophets offered specific details of what the Messiah would be like and how the people could recognize Him.

For example, Isaiah 7:14, a passage written about seven hundred years before Jesus' birth, predicts that the Messiah would be born of a virgin. Luke 1:26–38, in turn, describes how Mary, a teenage *virgin,* was chosen to give birth to Jesus and how she was supernaturally impregnated by God's Spirit.

Here are some other prophecies guaranteed to raise an eyebrow or two:

- Micah 5:2, which was probably written around 700 B.C., predicts that a ruler of Israel would come from a little village in the region of Ephrathah called . . . Bethlehem. Joseph and Mary were from Nazareth, so many people assumed that that's where Jesus was born. But Luke 2:1–7 describes the sequence of events that put the couple in the town of Bethlehem when Mary went into labor and gave birth.
- Isaiah 53:3, which was also probably written around 700 B.C., offers the stunning prediction that the long-awaited Messiah would ultimately be

rejected by the people He came to save. In the New Testament, John 1:10–11 describes the rejection to Jesus' ministry on earth.

- Zechariah 9:9, which was probably written around 500 B.C., paints the unusual picture of a king riding into Jerusalem on a donkey colt. Would you care to guess how Jesus entered Jerusalem the week before His crucifixion? Check out Matthew 21:1–11 for details.

Skeptics might argue that three or four ancient predictions prove nothing. And they'd be right. Three or four measly fulfilled prophecies could be chalked up to lucky guessing or pure coincidence. Hardly definitive proof of the Messiah's identity.

But when those fulfilled prophecies start numbering in the hundreds, it's time to sit up and take notice. Bible scholars have estimated that Jesus fulfilled over two hundred ancient prophecies during His lifetime. *Two hundred.* So much for lucky guessing and pure coincidence.

Today we don't have the luxury of physically interacting with Jesus. We can't listen to Him speak or watch Him perform miracles. Instead, we must have faith that He is who He claims to be. But that faith doesn't have to be blind.

The Bible doesn't say, "Jesus is the Savior—believe it or else." Instead, it says, "Jesus is the Savior, and here's why." The evidence is there for us to examine. All we need is the initiative to find it.

**JUST WONDERING**

**Why was it important for Jesus to be born of a virgin?**
The fact that the Holy Spirit planted His seed in Mary's womb meant that Jesus was unaffected by the human sin nature that's been passed down from generation to generation since Adam. Unlike every other baby ever born, Jesus came into this world morally perfect and blameless in God's eyes.

### *2. Jesus' sacrifice began at birth.*

When we think of Jesus' sacrifice, we tend to think in terms of the cross, and the suffering and death that He experienced there. But Jesus' sacrifice began much earlier than that. In fact, His sacrifice began the moment He took human form.

In order to understand this, we need to understand who Jesus is. In the Bible, He's called the Son of God. But don't be confused. As we'll see in the next chapter when we explore the concept of the Trinity, Jesus is God. He is equal to—and one with—God the Father and God the Holy Spirit.

Jesus spoke the universe into existence in Genesis 1. He created and breathed life into the human race. He possessed all of the attributes of God we described in chapter 2. His presence dwarfed the universe. His power and knowledge were limitless. He was impassible, meaning nothing could harm Him or inflict pain on Him.

Yet Jesus willingly laid His perfections aside in order to come to earth and dwell among His creation as one of us. He left His idyllic existence in heaven for a life of rejection, ridicule, and betrayal on our sin-ravaged planet. He gave up His autonomy and became a helpless baby, dependent on His human mother for care. He gave up His impassibility and made Himself vulnerable to pain, sickness, exhaustion, torture, and eventually death. He submitted Himself to physical restrictions like hunger and thirst. He squeezed His infinite presence into a container of flesh roughly five and one-half feet high.

Can you imagine how restricting and agonizing that transition must have been for Him? Can you imagine the kind of love that motivated Him to make such a sacrifice?

### 3. *Jesus was opposed from the very beginning.*

You know the Christmas story. The decree from Caesar Augustus that sent Joseph and Mary to Bethlehem. The shortage of hotel rooms there. The birth of Jesus in the stable where the animals were kept. The food trough, or manger, that became a baby bed. The angelic birth announcement. The visit from the shepherds. The chestnuts roasting on an open fire (okay, maybe not).

An event that you probably haven't heard in any retelling of the Christmas story, however, is Herod's "slaughter of the innocents." Herod was the reigning king of Judea when Jesus was born. When he heard from the Magi or "wise men" that the king of the Jews had been born, Herod snapped.

Matthew 2:16 tells us that he ordered the execution of every male child under two years of age in Bethlehem and the surrounding area. The last thing Herod wanted was a challenger to his throne. And since he didn't know who that challenger was

### Just Wondering

**If "B.C." means "before Christ" and "A.D." means "anno Domini" (which is Latin for "in the year of the Lord"), does that mean Jesus was born in the year 0?**

No, strange as it may seem, He was probably born around 4 or 5 B.C. (That's right, historically speaking, Christ was born four or five years before . . . well, Christ.) Modern historians have discovered that the people responsible for creating the Gregorian calendar that we use today were off by about four or five years in their calculations.

or exactly where he lived, Herod killed every possible candidate (or so he thought).

We could write this story off as a disturbing example of how power corrupts. But if we do that, we miss the bigger picture. Ultimately, it wasn't Herod who wanted to prevent a challenge to his authority and protect what was his; it was Satan.

This may come as a surprise to you, but Satan is the ruler of the earth. Jesus Himself called Satan "the prince of this world" (John 12:31). Satan's authority is temporary and exists only because God allows it, but it is real.

The Bible doesn't tell us how much Satan knew about Jesus' earthly mission before it began. But the devil must have sensed that the baby boy born to a teenage mother in that Bethlehem stable was dangerous to him. Perhaps Satan realized that God's plan for saving the human race had begun, and that his days were numbered. The slaughter of the innocents in Jerusalem, then, was a desperate attempt by Satan to prevent his inevitable downfall.

Obviously, God's intelligence network was up to Satan's challenge. The Lord warned Joseph in a dream to move his family to safety in Egypt. Joseph obeyed. Later an angel told them to return to Israel, and Joseph took them to a town called Nazareth. So Jesus, the Messiah, grew up as a Nazarene.

Just like the prophets had predicted He would (Matthew 2:23).

### *4. The majority of Jesus' life on earth is almost a complete mystery.*

We know that Jesus was circumcised when He was eight days old (Luke 2:21). We also know that about forty days later, Joseph and Mary took Him to Jerusalem to dedicate their child to God, according to Jewish tradition (Luke 2:22–39). After that event, the biblical account of Jesus' life fades to black.

When it fades in again, Jesus is almost a teenager. Luke 2:41–50 tells a story about Mary and Joseph finding the twelve-year-old Jesus in a Jewish temple, amazing religious scholars with His understanding of Scripture.

After that incident, the biblical account fades to black again. When it fades in the next time, however, Jesus is *thirty* years old—and ready to start His public ministry.

If the Gospels were a photo album of Jesus' life, they would contain only one snapshot of Him between the time He was two months old and the time He was thirty years old.

That's a pretty big gap, especially when you consider that Jesus lived to be only thirty-three. That means virtually everything we know about Him occurred during the last three years of His life. Think about that. In just over a thousand days, Jesus went from being a relatively anonymous Nazarene (although One with an interesting birth story) to being the central figure in human history. In roughly thirty-six months, He established a future for the human race that did not exist before. Over the course of about twelve seasons, He laid the groundwork for a spiritual movement that continues to thrive two thousand years later.

In the time it takes most people to choose a college major, Jesus radically altered everything, from the way we record time (B.C. and A.D.) to the way we view the world and the people in it.

**JUST WONDERING**

**Did Jesus know who He was and what He was going to do from birth?**

Luke 2:41–50 indicates that Jesus knew by the time He was twelve that He was God's Son. However, Luke 2:52 suggests that that knowledge wasn't something He was born with. The words "Jesus grew in wisdom" indicate that, like us, Jesus had the capacity to learn, which means He wasn't born all-knowing.

### *5. Jesus' appearance was likely rather un-Messiahish.*

Thanks to movies (*The Greatest Story Ever Told, The Last Temptation of Christ*), theater (*Jesus Christ Superstar*), TV (*Jesus*), and Sunday school art, many people have a pretty standard image of Jesus' physical appearance: Caucasian features; a swimmer's build—tall, smooth, and graceful; beautifully moist eyes, perfect for conveying sensitivity and love; long, wavy brown hair, tousled just right; and a nicely trimmed beard. They also picture Him as having the otherworldly demeanor of an elite New Age guru, charismatic yet ultimately unapproachable.

### Just Wondering

**Did Jesus have the same kind of feelings and emotions that other people have?**

Absolutely. When He found sleazy merchants in His Father's temple, He got angry (John 2:13-16). When He saw people mourning for His friend Lazarus, He got sad (John 11:35). When the time came for Him to suffer and die, He got scared (Matthew 26:36-39). He experienced the same kind of emotions and temptations that we experience (Hebrews 2:17). The only difference is that Jesus never let His feelings or emotions get the best of Him.

In short, many people tend to picture Jesus as a Hollywood "leading man" type. There's certainly nothing blasphemous about that. The Bible doesn't indicate that Jesus worried much about what people thought of His looks. In fact, the Bible doesn't say much about Jesus' physical appearance. However, there are some clues that can help us get a fix on how He might have looked and acted.

First of all, His features were most likely Jewish. His mother was Jewish. His extended family was Jewish. People recognized Him as being Jewish. So it's likely that Jesus had the physical characteristics of a Middle Eastern Jew.

Second, Jesus was a working-class guy—a carpenter, to be specific. Chances are, He had the wiry, muscular build common to people of that profession. He was a worker, a doer. He wasn't an "ivory tower" academic who spent all of His time in the temple. He was the kind of guy who liked to get His hands dirty.

Third, apparently there was nothing spectacular about Jesus' appearance or demeanor. Isaiah 53:2 tells us that "he had no beauty or majesty to attract us to him, nothing in his appearance that we should desire him." When the people of Nazareth heard Him speak in the synagogue, they were amazed—and offended (Mark 6:1–6). They said, "This guy was a carpenter, a regular person, just like the rest of us. We watched Him grow up. Who does He think He is, trying to pass Himself off as someone special?"

In short, Jesus didn't have the "star quality" that people expected of the Messiah. Those who came to Him were drawn by His message of love, forgiveness, redemption, and eternal life. But first they had to give up their preconceived notions of what the Savior should be like.

The same principle applies to believers today. Before we can see clearly what Jesus is all about, we need to give up our notions of what He *should* be like.

### 6. Jesus surrounded Himself with unlikely people.

You'd figure that when the Son of God came to earth, the first people He'd hook up with would be priests, religious leaders, scholars, and experts in God's law. You'd figure those would be the people He'd have the most in common with and the ones He would use to spread His message. You'd be wrong.

When Jesus chose His traveling companions—those who would become His closest friends and most trusted followers—He revealed His fondness for underdogs and outcasts, people who were looked down on in society. His hand-picked core of twelve disciples included fishermen, blue-collar workers, and even a hated tax collector. These men were rough, uneducated, impetuous, cowardly, stubborn, weak, competitive, easily confused, and not entirely trustworthy.

On the surface.

But that's not where Jesus was looking. He was looking beyond outward appearance and first impressions. His focus was on the long-term potential of His soon-to-be apostles and not their immediate spiritual maturity. He wasn't looking for pillars of the community or renowned religious experts; He was looking for people who could be molded into what He wanted them to be.

In other words, Jesus wasn't concerned with who His disciples *were*; He was concerned with who they would *become*. Granted, their imperfections made for some rough stretches along the way. Among the incidents you probably won't find on the disciples' résumés:

- James and John trying to weasel their way into prime locations next to Jesus' throne when they all got to heaven (Mark 10:35–45);
- the entire group preventing little kids from seeing Jesus (Mark 10:13–16);
- Peter, James, and John falling asleep on the job on the night Jesus needed them most (Mark 14:32–42);

- Judas Iscariot betraying Jesus and turning Him over to His enemies (Mark 14:43–46);
- the rest of the disciples hiding in fear after Jesus' arrest (Mark 14:50); and
- Peter denying that he knew Jesus—on three separate occasions (Luke 22:54–62).

As rookies, Jesus' disciples weren't much to speak of. But you should have seen them at the end of their careers.

All but two of Jesus' original disciples died as martyrs—meaning they were executed because of their faith. (The two exceptions were Judas Iscariot, who committed suicide after betraying Jesus, and John, who died of natural causes after being exiled to an island because of his Christian beliefs.) Before their deaths, they spread the good news of Jesus across the Middle East. They multiplied the number of Christian believers in the world from dozens to thousands. They trained new believers to take the message of Christ to countries around the world. They were largely responsible for creating the church as we know it today. At least three of them—Matthew, John, and Peter—were used by God to write books of the Bible.

That was the potential Jesus saw when He chose them to be His disciples.

Fortunately for us, Jesus' vision hasn't changed in the past 2,000-plus years. When He calls people to Himself today—people like us—He doesn't look at what we are. He looks at what we can become, what He can make us.

Jesus doesn't say, "Get your act together and then come see Me," or "If you quit those nasty habits of yours, you can be My disciple."

He says, "Follow Me."

Those who accept His invitation—those who pursue Him with all of their heart, soul, and mind (Matthew 22:37)—will be transformed as completely (though perhaps not as famously) as the disciples were. Jesus has that effect on people.

### *7. Jesus is not one to spoon-feed.*

If someone had asked Jesus' disciples about the most frustrating part of their lives with Christ, a couple of them might have mentioned the constant travel. A few others might have objected to the large crowds that followed them everywhere. One or two others might have brought up the fact that none of them knew how things were going to end.

But, chances are, all twelve of them would have cited one particular frustration that drove them absolutely nuts: parables.

**NOTABLE QUOTABLE**

What Christ had to say was too simple to be grasped, too truthful to be believed.

—MALCOLM MUGGERIDGE

Often when Jesus spoke to His followers, He used stories, called parables, to get His point across. For example, He would say things like . . .

- "The kingdom of God . . . is like a mustard seed, which a man took and planted in his garden. It grew and became a tree, and the birds of the air perched in its branches" (Luke 13:18–19).
- "The kingdom of God . . . is like yeast that a woman took and mixed into a large amount of flour until it worked all through the dough" (Luke 13:20–21).
- "No one sews a patch of unshrunk cloth on an old garment. If he does, the new piece will pull away from the old, making the tear worse" (Mark 2:21).

Many times He left His listeners wondering what, exactly, He was talking about. The Bible records a couple of incidents in which the disciples went to Jesus and said, "What was that last story all about? What was it supposed to mean?" For the most part, though, they seem to have been clueless about many of the things Jesus talked about.

The question is, Why did Jesus use parables to teach? Why didn't He just come right out and tell His disciples exactly what they needed to know?

One possibility is that Jesus understood that parables are more memorable than straight teaching, that stories can make a point more vividly than dull old preaching can. After all, it's one thing to say that God cares about people. It's another thing to say that He searches for them like a shepherd looks for a lost sheep (Matthew 18:12–14). That's a vivid image—and a memorable one, as well.

Another possibility is that Jesus understood human nature enough to know that if His message was too straightforward and simple, it wouldn't have seemed as profound to His listeners. In other words, Jesus knew that the parables gave His message an air of mystery that would have been intriguing to His listeners.

Perhaps the best explanation, though, is that making things easy or convenient for His followers is not a high priority for Jesus. Don't misunderstand. Insight into Christ's kingdom and countless other Bible topics is ours for the taking. But Jesus isn't handing it out on flash cards.

Take another look at Matthew 22:37, the verse we quoted in the previous point: "Love the Lord your God with all your heart and with all your soul and with *all your mind*" (italics added). Check out those last three words again: all your mind. When it comes to His words, Jesus wants our brains engaged.

Working to figure out the meanings of Jesus' parables is a way of showing Him love. The more effort we put into it, the more love we demonstrate. What's more, there's a "treasure hunt" element to all of Jesus' teachings. The deeper we dig, the more valuable our find will be.

Ultimately, it doesn't matter why Jesus used parables to communicate. The fact is, He did. What we're talking about are the words of Christ Himself—information so important that God made sure it was featured prominently in His Word.

As Christ's followers, we can either . . .

- dismiss those teachings because their meanings aren't obvious enough at first glance and then complain about how hard it is to read the Bible, or
- pray, study, ask questions, and do whatever else we need to do in order to understand what Jesus meant and why it's important to us.

If you're having a hard time deciding, consider this encouragement from Jesus: "Ask and it will be given to you; seek and you will find; knock and the door will be opened to you" (Matthew 7:7). The thing is, if you're serious about discovering the meaning of Jesus' teachings, He will reward your effort. That's a promise.

### *8. Jesus wasn't big on religion.*

Religious leaders weren't exactly lining up to join Jesus' fan club, either. If that surprises you—if you assumed that Jesus would have been a big hit with the religious leaders of His day—you need to understand what religion had become at the beginning of the first century A.D.

God's laws—the Ten Commandments and other instructions that He had given His people to guide their everyday lives—had been rendered almost unrecognizable. You see, the religious leaders of the day weren't content with God's words. So they added their own interpretations to His laws. Then the next generation of religious leaders tacked on codicils and amendments to those interpretations, and so on, and so on.

The result was that God's law, originally just a few score or so short commandments, grew into an absurdly complex and enormous catalog of dos and don'ts, guaranteed to confound all but the most rigorous religious scholars.

Here's an example of what the God-loving people of Jesus' day were up against. In the Ten Commandments, God gave this instruction: "Remember the Sabbath day by keeping it holy. Six days you shall labor and do all your work, but the seventh day is a Sabbath to the LORD your God. On it you shall not do any work" (Exodus 20:8–10a). That wasn't good enough for the Jewish religious leaders. They thought the people needed more specific guidance, so they came up with a series of rules about what constituted "work"—in other words, what people could and couldn't do on the Sabbath.

To call these rules nitpicky would be an understatement. Religious leaders created laws about how far people could walk on the Sabbath, what objects they could lift, and what physical movements they could make.

Even worse, the religious leaders treated their own interpretations and amendments —over *six hundred* of them in all—as being equal to God's original commandments. So if a person traveled a certain number of miles or lifted an object heavier than a certain number of pounds on the Sabbath, he was judged to be a sinner.

The problem was normal people couldn't keep track of the hundreds of laws on the books, so they relied on the religious leaders and scholars to tell them what they could and couldn't do. Obviously, that gave the religious leaders an enormous amount of power and influence in Jewish society. And they ate it up.

For the people, however, the Law was a source of constant frustration. With so many rules to think about, they must have felt like they couldn't scratch their noses without committing seven major violations. In other words, they were prisoners of the Law.

When Jesus arrived on the scene, however, He wasted little time putting things straight. He said, "You guys have got it all wrong. God didn't give you His law to make you slaves to a bunch of rules and regulations. He wants you to be free." And then He beat the religious leaders at their own game. He took their extreme rules one step further to show them how foolish it is to try please God through works and actions.

For example, the Law said, "Love your neighbor as yourself" (Leviticus 19:18); Jesus said, "Love your enemies and pray for those who persecute you" (Matthew 5:44). The Law said, "You shall not commit adultery" (Exodus 20:14); Jesus said, "Don't even look lustfully at a woman" (see Matthew 5:28).

Jesus' purpose was not to make things harder for us, though. He was saying, "If you want the Law to save you—to reconcile you with God—you're going to have to be a whole lot better than the Pharisees." For the people of the first century, though, that prospect was hopeless. The Pharisees were on the top rung of the religious ladder. They were the cream of the crop when it came to obeying the Law.

Fortunately, Jesus had an alternate plan. "You could believe in Me and the sacrifice I'm going to make for you on the cross," He offered, "and allow God's grace to save you."

The choice is this: Either knock yourself out trying to do everything perfectly, or believe in Jesus. If we try to rely on our religiousness—how often we go to church, how nice we are to people, how much time and money we dedicate to charity—to save us, we're doomed.

### *9. Jesus was rejected, for the most part.*

Jesus healed blind people, deaf people, lepers, and people with blood disorders. He fed a crowd of over 5,000 with the contents of a young boy's lunch box. He turned water into wine. He walked on water. He raised people from the dead. Three days after He was nailed to a cross and executed, He walked out of His tomb in perfect health. What's more, He did these things in front of hundreds, sometimes even thousands, of witnesses. These weren't tricks or illusions. They were genuine miracles.

Yet most of the people who encountered Jesus during His lifetime ultimately refused to believe that He was who He said He was.

The obvious question is "Why?" Why would the people who heard Jesus' teachings and witnessed His miracles firsthand reject what He had to say? As hard as it may be to imagine, there are a few explanations for people's stubborn refusal to believe Jesus' claims.

For one thing, Jesus wasn't what they had in mind when they pictured the Messiah. The Jewish people, including Jesus' disciples, expected a religious and political leader who would lead an uprising against the Roman government that ruled over them. They expected Rambo, not a Redeemer. They certainly didn't expect a humble carpenter from Nazareth.

They saw flashes of promise and hope in Jesus, but when He ultimately failed to live up to their expectations, things got ugly. Check out the about-face the people did when Jesus entered Jerusalem during the last week of His life. They welcomed Him with palm branches and cheers, figuring He was getting ready to put the hurt on their Roman enemies (Matthew 21:1–11). A few days later, when they discovered that a revolt wasn't in the cards, they started calling for His execution like a bloodthirsty lynch mob (Matthew 27:11–26).

It didn't matter to the Jewish people who Jesus was or what He had done. They couldn't get past what He *wasn't* going to do.

It's also safe to say that Jesus' message had a lot to do with His rejection. It was just too radical. Calls to deny yourself, to put other people first, and give up everything to follow Jesus weren't any more popular 2,000 years ago than they are today.

Those weren't the kind of things people wanted to hear. So they refused to listen.

There may have been some who wanted to believe in Jesus but were too afraid of stepping away from the status quo. As we pointed out in the previous section, Jesus' message was radically different from what the religious leaders of the day were teaching. Choosing to follow Him would have been like painting a target on your back. At the very least, it would have meant taunting and rejection. In some cases, it would have meant torture and death.

Other people may have been put off by Jesus' rigid stance. The fact is, Jesus didn't leave people a lot of options. He said, "I am God. I am the way, the truth, and the life. If you believe in Me, you will be set for this life and the afterlife. If you don't believe in Me, you will suffer the consequences for eternity." (See John 14:6; 3:16–18.) Those are all bold statements—too bold for most people. It's one thing to say, "Here are some beliefs that you might want to consider, some ways of living that might improve your life." It's another thing to say, "Your eternal fate rests on what you believe about Me."

In fact, coming from anyone but the Son of God, those words would have been blasphemous. But Jesus backed up His every claim with His actions.

Christians today tend to assume that having faith in Jesus would be a lot easier if we could just see or hear Him in person. Based on the response of the people He encountered in His lifetime, however, that's not necessarily the case. The truth is, once a person makes up his or her mind not to have faith in someone or something, no amount of evidence is going to change that decision.

### *10. Jesus is going to shock a lot of people the next time He comes back.*

The book of Revelation is full of unsettling images of the future, including a seven-headed beast, a carnivorous dragon, and a lake of burning sulfur. One of the most startling images, however, is that of the "rider on the white horse" described in Revelation 19:11–21. The eyes of this rider are like blazing fire. On His head are many crowns. He's wearing a robe that's been dipped in blood. Out of His mouth comes a sharp sword that He uses to kill entire armies. The identity of this rider is made clear by the words inscribed on His robe and on His thigh:

"King of Kings and Lord of Lords."

The rider on the white horse is Jesus, and the battle described in Revelation 19 will take place when He returns to earth, as He promised in Matthew 24:29–30. The first time Jesus came to our planet, it was as a tiny baby. Next time, it will be as a conquering Warrior-King.

And at that time, everyone who rejected Him, everyone who wrote Him off as a mere teacher or moral philosopher, will see Him in all of His majestic glory and power—and will realize what a tragic mistake they made.

We'll explore the events that accompany Jesus' return in chapter 7. For now, note that when Jesus returns, it will be to take care of some unfinished business—namely, putting an end to Satan and his forces.

Here's the deal. Satan's war against God was lost the moment Jesus rose from the dead and completed God's plan of salvation. Christ's resurrection—which sealed His victory over death—was Satan's defeat. However, while the war is technically over, Satan is still free to do battle against believers. And, for 2,000-plus years, that's what he's been doing, as a lame-duck ruler of the earth. All of that will end when Jesus returns.

**JUST WONDERING**

**Is "Christ" Jesus' last name?**
No, Jesus' earthly parents were not named Joseph and Mary Christ. Christ comes from a Greek word meaning "anointed one." It's a title designed to show that Jesus is the Messiah, the one God promised to send to save the world.

Jesus' second coming will begin the final battle between good and evil. Jesus, the Warrior-King, will lead His army against Satan's forces. When the dust clears, Jesus will be the undisputed champion—the King of Kings and Lord of Lords. Satan, defeated once and for all, will be thrown into the lake of fire, where he "will be tormented day and night for ever and ever" (Revelation 20:10).

## Three Little Letters

Before we wrap up this chapter on Jesus, there are three letters of the alphabet that we need to consider. The first letter is *I*, the second is *A*, and the third is *N*.

Together they form the popular suffix *-ian*, which means "characteristic of or resembling."

Tack those letters onto the word *Christ*, and you've got *Christian*, meaning "characteristic of or resembling Christ." Talk about daunting expectations! To call yourself a Christian is to say, "I have the characteristics of Christ," or, more significantly, "I resemble Christ in the way I live." Either way, it's a bold statement—and one that invites scrutiny.

> **JUST WONDERING**
>
> **Where is Jesus now, and what's He doing?**
>
> Passages such as Hebrews 7:25 and 1 John 2:1 suggest that Jesus acts as a priest/defense attorney for us before God. The idea is that Jesus intercedes for us; He defends us and speaks on our behalf to God the Father. In other words, He keeps us on good terms with God. John 14:1-3 indicates that Jesus is also doing some architectural work on our behalf. Specifically, He's preparing our permanent residences, our heavenly homes.

Jesus' desire is for His followers to be immediately recognizable because of our resemblance to Him in the way we live, the priorities we demonstrate, and the manner in which we interact with others. Toward that end, Jesus gave His followers specific instructions to follow. You'll find them in passages like . . .

- ➤ Matthew 5:42 ("Give to the one who asks you, and do not turn away from the one who wants to borrow");
- ➤ Luke 20:25 ("Give to Caesar what is Caesar's, and to God what is God's"); and
- ➤ Matthew 28:19–20 ("Go and make disciples of all nations, baptizing them in the name of the Father and of the Son and of the Holy Spirit, and teaching them to obey everything I have commanded you").

More than that, however, Jesus gave us His *life* as an example to follow and a model to pattern our own lives after. With only a few pages remaining in this chapter, we don't have room to explore Jesus' every action, looking for ways we can emulate it in our own lives.

# Five Key Qualities

What we *can* do is highlight five qualities that Jesus demonstrated over and over again during His lifetime—characteristics that He also expects from His followers.

### *1. Commitment*

Despite the distractions that the world threw His way, Jesus never lost sight of His ultimate goal. (Check out His stunning words for Peter in Matthew 16:23, after Peter tried to talk Him out of what Jesus knew had to be done.) Jesus devoted His entire life to fulfilling God's plan. Satan's temptation couldn't keep Him from it; the people who tried to make Him a celebrity couldn't keep Him from it; even the prospect of torture and death couldn't keep Him from it.

Jesus expects the same kind of commitment and devotion from His followers. If we're going to follow Christ, our commitment to Him must come before everything, including family, friends, and career. Jesus outlined the kind of devotion He expected to a man who wanted to wait until after his father died to follow Jesus. Jesus said, "Follow me, and let the dead bury their own dead" (Matthew 8:22).

If that seems incredibly insensitive, it's because we don't understand how important complete devotion is. Once Jesus is installed as the number one priority in our lives, everything else, including family, friends, and career, will be taken care of.

### *2. Compassion*

If anyone in history ever has had a right to wield a holier-than-thou attitude, it's Jesus. He truly is holier-than-thou. But that's not how Jesus responded to the people who needed Him.

Instead of giving them attitude, Jesus gave them compassion—no matter who they were. Jesus gave hope to prostitutes, adulterers, tax collectors, even hated foreigners. He didn't reject them for who they were; He encouraged them to become better. He

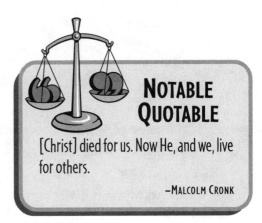

**NOTABLE QUOTABLE**

[Christ] died for us. Now He, and we, live for others.

—Malcolm Cronk

empathized with their pain and struggle. He got up close and personal with them to discuss their needs. Finally, He did what He could to meet those needs. Sometimes He healed people. Sometimes He let people know that their sins were forgiven. Sometimes He gave people much needed words of encouragement. Regardless of what they received from Him, no one came away from a personal encounter with Jesus unchanged.

That's the kind of effect Jesus expects His followers to have on people as well. Obviously none of us has the healing power of Jesus. But we do have a capacity for compassion and concern. We have the ability to treat people kindly. With practice, we can learn to empathize with others and respond to their needs—like Jesus did.

**ON A PERSONAL NOTE**

Think of three recent conversations, disagreements, or interactions you had with friends, acquaintances, or strangers. Write in your journal a brief description of each encounter–what happened, what you said, and how the other person responded. Then write a brief description of how Jesus might have handled each encounter–what He might have said and how the person might have responded. Compare the two sets of scenarios. Write down what you could have done (or could do in the future) to be more like Christ in your personal encounters.

### 3. *Dependence on God's Word*

When Satan challenged Jesus to a one-on-one showdown in the wilderness, Jesus came packing the most powerful weapon at His disposal: God's Word. Three times the devil tried to tempt Jesus into abandoning God's plan; three times Jesus put the devil in his place by quoting a verse of Scripture (Matthew 4:1–11). Because Satan had nothing powerful enough to withstand God's Word, he had to give up.

The Bible was much more than a "devil repellent," as far as Jesus was concerned, though. His feelings about Scripture are best summed up in His quote of Deuteronomy 8:3: "'Man does not live on bread alone, but on every word that comes from the mouth of God' (Matthew 4:4)."

The Word of God is what Jesus used to sustain Him throughout His life. When He was a young boy, He amazed the elders in the temple with His knowledge of God's Word (Luke 2:46–47). He spent much of His earthly ministry discussing Scripture and explaining it—particularly His role in it—to His followers (Luke 24:13–27). As He hung dying on the cross, He quoted the book of Psalms (Matthew 27:46). In short, God's Word was never far from His mind.

Jesus' desire is for His followers to approach Scripture with the same zeal, the same burning passion, that He had. Everything that we need to sustain us in our Christian walk—everything that we need to know about being like Christ—is found in God's Word. Jesus knew that, and He wants us to know it, too.

### *4. Love*

During His time on earth, Jesus demonstrated the purest form of love ever seen. It wasn't a love based on emotions. It wasn't a love based on merit. It wasn't a love based on mutual feelings. It was a selfless love, a sacrificial love—a perfect love.

Jesus loved us so much that He gave His life to save us—despite the fact that we, as a human race, rejected, despised, and ultimately killed Him. In the process, He gave us a model for loving others—family members, friends, acquaintances, strangers, and enemies alike—that, when properly followed, can changes lives forever.

The kind of love that Jesus modeled—the kind He expects from us—isn't easy to give. We humans prefer to *feel* our emotions before we demonstrate them. But that's not what Jesus expects from us. He didn't say, "Work on developing feelings of love for your neighbors," or "Open up your heart to your enemies." He said, "Show love to your neighbors," and "Demonstrate loving actions to your enemies."

There's nothing mushy or touchy-feely about the kind of love Jesus is talking about. It's all action, no talk—100 percent concrete, 0 percent theoretical. It involves working to meet a person's needs, regardless of what pride, prejudices, or prior experiences say we should do. It involves sacrificing our time, energy, and comfort for the sake of others. It involves giving all we have, just like Jesus did.

### *5. Servanthood*

Of all the things we know about Jesus, perhaps the most mind-blowing is that He, the King of Kings and Lord of Lords, came to earth as a humble servant. The life model that He chose to demonstrate to His followers was one of personal denial for the good of others.

### On a Personal Note

Make a list of three obstacles that are preventing you from fully committing yourself to Christ. These obstacles may include anything from inexperience (not knowing exactly what to do) to friends, family members, or even a spouse. When your list is complete, make an appointment with your accountability partner or someone discipling you to talk and pray about your obstacles. If you're in a Bible study or prayer group, pray about your obstacles there, too.

The most striking example of Jesus' commitment to service occurred on the night of the Last Supper. John 13:1–17 tells us that before the meal, Jesus removed His outer clothing, grabbed a towel, poured a bowl of water, and washed the feet of His disciples. Keep in mind that in the first century A.D., the primary mode of transportation was walking. The roads of the day were little more than dirt paths, and the shoes of choice were sandals. Are you starting to get the picture? Washing the feet of others was one of the dirtiest jobs imaginable. That's why it was usually assigned to the lowliest servants.

But Jesus wanted to show His disciples just how far He was willing to go in order to serve them. He said, "Now that I, your Lord and Teacher, have washed your feet, you also should wash one another's feet" (John 13:14).

Jesus expects a spirit of humility and service from His followers. And why shouldn't He? If the Son of God didn't consider Himself above becoming a servant, if He was content to lower Himself in order to accommodate other people's needs, what possible reason can we offer for not doing the same?

## Not Done Yet

We've covered a lot of material in this chapter but have yet to even scratch the surface of who Jesus is and what He means to us. As the apostle John wrote at the end of his Gospel, his biography of Jesus: "Jesus did many other things as well. If every one of them were written down, I suppose that even the whole world would not have room for the books that would be written" (John 21:25).

Therein lies the beauty—and the challenge—of following Christ. No matter how long or intensely we study His life, there will always be something new to learn about Him, something that will surprise us and broaden our understanding and appreciation of Him.

## Know What You Believe

How much do you know about Jesus? Here's a quiz to test your knowledge.

1. Which of the following claims did Jesus not make about Himself?
   a. "I am the way and the truth and the life."
   b. "I who speak to you am he [the Messiah]."
   c. "I and the Father are one."
   d. "I will be whoever you need Me to be."

2. Which of the following prophecies was not fulfilled in Jesus' life?
   a. The Messiah would be born of a virgin.
   b. The Messiah would be born in Bethlehem.
   c. The Messiah would always wear white.
   d. The Messiah would be rejected by the people.

3. What do we know for sure about Jesus' early years?
   a. As a nine year old, He learned how to eat insects from His cousin John.
   b. As a twelve year old, He amazed religious leaders with His knowledge of God's Word.
   c. As an eighteen year old, He helped tear down the original temple in Jerusalem and build a new one in three days.
   d. As a twenty year old, He warned His friend Lazarus that his poor eating habits could lead to an early death.

4. Which of the following is most likely true of Jesus' physical appearance?
   a. He had the features of a Middle Eastern Jew.
   b. He was pale and sickly most of the time.
   c. He weighed well over 300 pounds.
   d. He had six fingers on one hand.

5. Which of the following qualities did Jesus not model for His followers?
   a. Commitment
   b. Servanthood
   c. Dependence on God's Word
   d. Impatience with fools

*Answers: (1) d, (2) c, (3) b, (4) a, (5) d*

CHAPTER 4

# Holy Spirit!

## SNAPSHOT

Pastor Steve dragged his stool to the front of the room. "All right, let's get down to business," he said as he took his seat. "I can't write off those Krispy Kremes as a business expense unless we do something official as an evangelism class. So let's talk about how you're doing with the personal goals we set last week. Arlen, let's start with you. You said you were going to try to bring up spiritual topics in your carpool. How did that go?"

"It started out great," Arlen reported. "Monday and Tuesday we had some really good discussions about whether God exists and what it means to be a Christian."

"What about Wednesday?" Pastor Steve asked.

Arlen rolled his eyes. "One of the guys I ride with must have done his homework, because as soon as he got in the car on Wednesday, he started asking

## SNEAK PREVIEW

1. The Holy Spirit is God, just as God the Father is God, and Jesus is God; together they make up the Trinity–one God who makes Himself known in three persons.
2. All Christians are indwelled and sealed by the Holy Spirit the moment we repent and believe in Christ; the Holy Spirit's presence then remains with us constantly until we get to heaven.
3. Among His other responsibilities, the Holy Spirit convicts believers of sin in our lives, reveals God's truth to us, assists us in prayer, and gives us the spiritual gifts we need.

me about the Trinity."

Luke and Vince, who were sitting next to Arlen, shook their heads in sympathy. "Oooh, the Trinity, " Luke said. "That's a tough one."

"Tell me about it," Arlen replied. "I think the guy just wanted to make me look bad in front of the others. I can talk about God and Jesus all day. I can even talk about the Holy Spirit a little bit. But when it comes to explaining how all three of them fit together, I get real 'ummy.'"

"Ummy?" Pastor Steve asked.

"Yeah, I start saying, 'Um, um, um' a lot," Arlen explained.

"All right, let's talk about that," Pastor Steve said. "Does anyone else have a problem explaining the Holy Spirit or the Trinity?"

"I always tell people that the Holy Spirit is like Larry in the Three Stooges," Vince offered. "He doesn't really do much, but the other two wouldn't be the same without Him."

"I see," Pastor Steve replied with mock seriousness. He stopped and gave Vince a playful scowl. "We'll talk later about why Vince should never be left alone with an unbeliever. But, for now, does anyone have anything *helpful* to say about explaining the Holy Spirit or the Trinity?"

"I've never *had* to explain those things," Luke admitted. "But if someone ever asked me about them, I'd probably plead the Fifth Amendment."

"You'd refuse to answer on the grounds that it might *incriminate* you?" Pastor Steve asked.

"Or make me look stupid," Luke added.

"Anybody else have a suggestion?" Pastor Steve asked.

Max raised his hand in the back row. "Maybe we should just say that Christians don't have to *understand* that kind of stuff; we just have to *believe* it. You know, we could say it's one of those faith things."

"How about if we just say God works in mysterious ways, and leave it at that?" Leon suggested.

Pastor Steve looked at his notebook and pretended to jot down a message. "Memo to self," he murmured loud enough for everyone to hear. "Next time don't be so quick to volunteer for evangelism class. Explore nursery and children's church options first."

* * * * * * * * * * * * * * * *

For many Christians, the Holy Spirit is like the "key grip" or the "head gaffer" or the "best boy" in movie credits. We know He's important, but we're not exactly sure what He does.

Compared to the high profile of God and Jesus in the Bible and in our culture, the Holy Spirit is a relative unknown. If you're new to the church, you may have heard His name checked at baptisms and dedications ("In the name of the Father and of the Son and of the Holy Spirit . . ."), but chances are you probably haven't heard much about what He's like or what He does for us.

Don't let the lack of publicity fool you, though. The Holy Spirit is every bit as vital to our spiritual well-being as God the Father and Jesus Christ are. To dismiss Him as a minor biblical character or to take His work for granted is a slap in the face, as far as God is concerned.

The fact is, there is no element of the Christian life that doesn't require the Holy Spirit's assistance. He is intimately involved in everything from giving us the right words to say in prayer to helping us recognize golden opportunities to share our faith. He assists us in everything from discovering our God-given abilities to understanding God's will for our lives.

With that kind of résumé, the Holy Spirit deserves to be known. That's what this chapter is all about—discovering who He is and what He's all about.

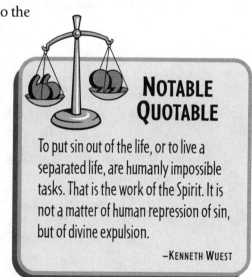

### NOTABLE QUOTABLE

To put sin out of the life, or to live a separated life, are humanly impossible tasks. That is the work of the Spirit. It is not a matter of human repression of sin, but of divine expulsion.

—KENNETH WUEST

## One Plus One Plus One Equals One

The Holy Spirit is *God*. Let's get that straight from the start.

When we refer to the Holy Spirit—or Holy Ghost, as He's sometimes called—we're not talking about an angel of the Lord or some general spirit of goodness and love that exists among all Christians. We're talking about a specific *person*—a specific person who is *deity*. We're talking about God the Holy Spirit.

God the Father is God. Jesus Christ, the Son, is God. The Holy Spirit is God. Add them up, and you get . . . one God.

If that equation doesn't make sense to you, you're not alone. The concept of the Trinity has been causing headaches for Christians for centuries. Let's see if we can sort out the basic facts of God's triune nature with a minimum of cranial discomfort. (Our first step will be to stop using phrases like "triune nature.")

We'll start with this absolute truth: God is one. Bible verses such as Deuteronomy 6:4 make that point perfectly clear. Grammatically speaking, there is no plural form for true deity. There's just the singular *God*. Within God's "oneness," though, He makes Himself known in three different persons: God the Father, God the Son, and God the Holy Spirit.

Each person of the Trinity has unique responsibilities. It's been said that God the Father originates, God the Son (Jesus) reveals, and God the Holy Spirit executes. We've already looked at the work of God and Jesus in the previous two chapters, and we'll take a closer look at what the Spirit "executes" later in this chapter. For now, though, what's important to understand is that, despite their different responsibilities, no person of the Trinity ever acts independently of the others. In other words, there is never any conflict or opposition among God, Jesus, and the Holy Spirit. God is perfect in His every attribute. That includes His unity and oneness.

Speaking of attributes, every perfection of God that we listed in chapter 2 applies to the Holy Spirit as well. The Holy Spirit is eternal, holy, immanent, just, loving, omnipotent, omniscient, sovereign, transcendent, and unchanging.

All three persons of the Trinity are equal, despite what we might assume based on their names and their relative fame. For example, God the Father does not hold seniority over God the Son. The Holy Spirit is not an executive vice president to God's CEO. Biblical phrases such as "God . . . gave His . . . Son" (John 3:16) may give the impression that God is the "boss" of the Trinity, issuing orders for the other two to follow. Remember, though, all three persons of the Trinity are *always* in complete agreement and unity concerning their work.

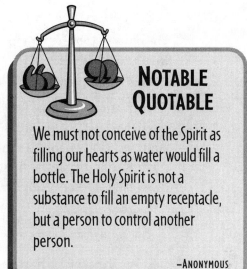

**NOTABLE QUOTABLE**

We must not conceive of the Spirit as filling our hearts as water would fill a bottle. The Holy Spirit is not a substance to fill an empty receptacle, but a person to control another person.

—Anonymous

Perhaps the best analogy for communicating the principle of the Trinity is water. Water exists in a solid form, ice; in a liquid form, water; and in a gaseous form, steam. Yet all three forms are still officially water. Ice, water, and steam are all $H_2O$; God, Jesus, and the Holy Spirit are all God.

Of course, like most analogies, this one breaks down if you try to push it too far. (For example, God does not change His form to become Jesus or the Holy Spirit like water changes its form to become ice or steam.) Even with its limitations, though, this analogy can be helpful in providing us a handle with which to grasp the basic truths of the Trinity.

Now that we've established the Holy Spirit's place in the Trinity and His relationship with God and Jesus, let's take a look at His role in history, starting in the Old Testament.

## That Old Testament Spirit

You won't find the Holy Spirit mentioned by name in the famous first verse of the Bible. You will, however, find Him in the second verse. Genesis 1:2 says, "The Spirit of God was hovering over the waters." While the universe was being spoken into existence, the Holy Spirit was right there, making it happen. His was the creative power that brought order out of chaos at creation.

The book of Job reveals a more personal aspect of the Holy Spirit's creative work. In Job 33:4, Elihu says, "The Spirit of God has made me; the breath of the Almighty gives me life." One breath from the Holy Spirit gave life to the entire human race.

After creation, the Holy Spirit involved Himself in the lives of His creatures, often in remarkable ways. The book of Judges makes it clear that the Holy Spirit equipped God's people to fulfill specific responsibilities that the Lord had given them. The Spirit gave ordinary people the power, courage, skill, and confidence to do extraordinary things. Here are a few examples:

- "The Spirit of the LORD came upon [Othniel], so that he became Israel's judge and went to war" (Judges 3:10a).
- "Then the Spirit of the LORD came upon Gideon, and he blew a trumpet, summoning the Abiezrites to follow him" (Judges 6:34).
- "The Spirit of the LORD came upon [Samson] in power so that he tore the lion apart with his bare hands as he might have torn a young goat" (Judges 14:6).

Othniel ended up rescuing the Israelites from the hands of the evil king Cushan-Rishathaim (Judges 3:10b). Gideon, who was a nondescript Israelite from a tiny clan in the tribe of Manasseh (Judges 6:15), led the entire nation of Israel in military victory against the Midianites. Samson wreaked havoc on the hated Philistines throughout his life using his extraordinary physical strength.

All of these men hold a special place in the history of God's people. What's important to recognize, though, is that when the time came for them to fulfill the Lord's plan, the Holy Spirit was right there to make sure that they were ready for what lay ahead. Their power came from Him, and their success was due to Him.

In Psalm 51:11, David identified another important work of the Holy Spirit: making it possible for humans to live God-honoring lives. David wrote this passage after having committed a series of horrific sins. (You'll find the details of them in 2 Samuel 11:1–12:25.) David felt distant from the Lord, and he begged God not to remove the Holy Spirit from his life. David knew that without the Holy Spirit's guidance, he had no chance of knowing, much less following, God's will for his life.

Verses such as Ezekiel 2:2 ("the Spirit came into me . . . and I heard him speaking to me") indicate that it was the Holy Spirit who revealed God's truth to the Old Testament prophets and prompted them to write down what they heard for future generations. The apostle Paul confirmed this in the New Testament when he wrote, "The Holy Spirit spoke the truth to your forefathers when he said through Isaiah the prophet . . ." (Acts 28:25).

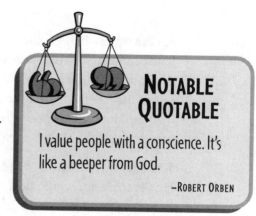

> **NOTABLE QUOTABLE**
>
> I value people with a conscience. It's like a beeper from God.
>
> –ROBERT ORBEN

So, because of the Holy Spirit:

- The world exists.
- The human race has life.
- The heroes of the Old Testament were able to demonstrate God's awesome power and perfect plan.
- Humans are able to understand and obey God's will.
- We have all the information we need to identify the Savior, not to mention God's future plans for His people.

And those are just the highlights of one Testament's worth of work. As far as we're concerned, the Holy Spirit was just getting warmed up!

## New Testament, Same Spirit

The New Testament begins with the account of Jesus' life on earth. That life began with the work of the Holy Spirit. Luke 1:35 tells us that it was the Holy Spirit who caused Mary, the mother of Jesus, to conceive her child. (Remember, Mary was a virgin.)

From the time of Jesus' birth until the time of His death and resurrection, the Holy Spirit provided strength, comfort, encouragement, support, and companionship to the Messiah. Jesus drew the kind of sustenance and strength from His relationship with the Holy Spirit that His human friends could not provide.

For example, when the time came for Jesus to begin His earthly ministry, the Holy Spirit appeared at His baptism to equip Him for the work that was to come. You might want to take a look at the account in Matthew 3:13–17, because it marks one of the rare recorded instances in which God the Father, God the Son, and God the Holy Spirit appear together. (The voice of the Father commends Jesus' baptism, and the Holy Spirit descends on Jesus like a dove.)

You can find references to the Holy Spirit scattered throughout Jesus' teachings. However, the most significant reference is found in John 14–16. In this passage, Jesus is calming His disciples' fears about what would happen to them after He left the earth. In essence, Jesus said to His followers, "You will not be alone when I leave, because My Father is going to send another helper—one who will be with you forever. You may be sad now, but when this new One comes, you're going to be glad you have Him."

Obviously, the Holy Spirit is the "parting gift" Jesus promised to His followers. The disciples didn't have to wait long for Him to arrive, either. A month or so after Jesus had returned to heaven, about 120 of His followers were meeting together for prayer in Jerusalem during the Feast of Passover.

In the middle of their meeting, a huge gust of wind blew through the room. Acts 2 describes a scene in which tongues of fire appeared briefly over the heads of everyone in the room. Verse 4 gives us this detail: "All of them were filled with the Holy Spirit and began to speak in other tongues as the Spirit enabled them." The commotion drew the attention of other Jews who had come to Jerusalem from near and far for the Feast of Pentecost. Imagine their surprise when they heard this group of uneducated fishermen and blue-collar followers of Jesus talking about the Lord in languages they could not possibly have known!

With that audacious entrance, the Holy Spirit began His personal work in the lives of all believers.

The disciples discovered very quickly that the Holy Spirit's authority was equal to that of God's. When Ananias "lied to the Holy Spirit" (Acts 5:3) about funds that were supposed to be directed to the church, his punishment was swift and final. Acts 5:5 says, "When Ananias heard this, he fell down dead." Ananias discovered too late that to sin against the Holy Spirit is to sin against God.

The apostle Peter tells us that the Holy Spirit oversaw the revealing and recording of God's Word, the Bible (2 Peter 1:20–21). The authors didn't decide what they wanted to write; the Holy Spirit decided for them, and they wrote as they were guided by Him.

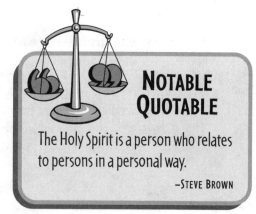

**NOTABLE QUOTABLE**

The Holy Spirit is a person who relates to persons in a personal way.

—Steve Brown

We could fill this chapter with details of the Holy Spirit's work throughout history. The Holy Spirit has been intimately involved in human activities since Day 1—literally. The good news for us is that He's still working as hard as He ever did on our behalf. Let's shift our focus from the past to the present and take a look at what the Holy Spirit does in the lives of believers today.

## The Holy Occupant and Sealant

One of the first things that happens when we repent and believe in Jesus is that we receive the gift of the Holy Spirit—the same gift that Jesus' disciples received 2,000 years ago. You'll find quite a few "gift announcements" in the New Testament confirming this fact:

- "I will ask the Father, and he will give you another Counselor to be with you forever—the Spirit of truth. The world cannot accept him, because it neither sees him nor knows him. But you know him, for he lives with you and will be in you" (John 14:16–17).
- "And hope does not disappoint us, because God has poured out his love into our hearts by the Holy Spirit, whom he has given us" (Romans 5:5).
- "Now it is God who has made us for this very purpose and has given us the Spirit as a deposit, guaranteeing what is to come" (2 Corinthians 5:5).

As gifts go, this one is unique. The Holy Spirit isn't a present that we appreciate for a while and then put away until the next time we want to use Him. Instead, as John 14:17 makes clear, the gift of the Holy Spirit involves a permanent residence in our lives. The official term for it is *indwelling*, meaning that when we become Christians, the Holy Spirit begins living *in* us. Think about that. The same Holy

Spirit who created the heavens and the earth takes up residence inside us.

The gift of the Holy Spirit is also unique in the fact that we have no choice in accepting it. If we claim the salvation that Jesus offers—if we make the decision to be His disciples—we have the Holy Spirit in our lives. That's the litmus test for Christians. If you have the Holy Spirit in your life, you belong to Christ and are guaranteed His salvation. If you don't have the Holy Spirit in your life, you do not belong to Christ. Those are the stipulations set down in Romans 8:9.

> **NOTABLE QUOTABLE**
>
> Even when there is no law, there is conscience.
>
> –PUBLILIUS SYRUS

The Holy Spirit doesn't sign yearly leases, either. When He moves in, it's forever—or at least until we get to heaven. He doesn't take off to go stay with friends when we sin and then wait for us to get our act together before moving back in. He stays with us through the good and the bad. No matter what we do or where we go, the Holy Spirit's presence remains with us. (That's unlike David's day, when the Holy Spirit, given a different ministry, could depart.)

Second Corinthians 1:22 says that God "set his seal of ownership on us [believers], and put his Spirit in our hearts." God's seal cannot be broken by anyone. Once the Holy Spirit is placed in our hearts, He's sealed there. What that means for us is security—and the peace of mind that comes from knowing that our salvation is signed, sealed, and guaranteed for eternity.

## The Holy Convictor

The Holy Spirit acts as our spiritual conscience, letting us know when we sin against God and urging us to repent (John 16:8). Anytime we feel pangs of guilt or regret—anytime we feel the need to ask God for forgiveness—we know that the Holy Spirit is at work.

Without His insistent prompting, we would be in a world of trouble. The fact is, our moral compasses are faulty. Our ability to rationalize, justify, and downplay our wrongdoings makes us incapable of gauging our spiritual condition. We can walk around blissfully unaware of the damage that our sin is doing to ourselves, others, and especially our relationship with God.

Remember how panicked David got at the thought of having the Holy Spirit removed from his life (Psalm 51:11)? David knew that without the Spirit giving him constant readings on his position with God, he was in trouble.

The result of the Holy Spirit's convicting work is a closer relationship with the Lord for us. Remember, sin interferes with our relationship with God. By keeping us informed of our sin and prompting us to confess it, the Holy Spirit works to ensure that we never drift away from God and His plan for our lives.

**NOTABLE QUOTABLE**

Trust that man in nothing who has not a conscience in everything.

—LAURENCE STERNE

## The Holy Counselor

In John 14:26 Jesus refers to the Holy Spirit as a "Counselor" who will be with us forever. The word *Counselor* can also be translated "Helper," which suggests that the Holy Spirit is someone we can call on whenever we're in trouble.

Having the Holy Spirit in our lives is like living with the world's smartest, most helpful, and best-connected roommate. He knows the solution to every problem. He knows the motives and hidden agendas of the people we deal with. He knows what the future holds and where every potential "land mine" between here and there is located. Most importantly, He knows what God has planned for our lives and how we can accomplish His will.

We don't have to invite this invaluable helper into our lives, because He's already here. All we have to do is turn the controls over to Him.

## The Holy Amplifier

The Holy Spirit makes prayer—life-transforming, God-honoring, world-changing prayer—possible. He does that by transforming our mere human utterances into the language of adoration, confession, thanksgiving, and supplication that pleases God and draws His blessing. (We'll look more closely at the various elements of effective prayer in chapter 9.)

Romans 8:26–27 doesn't offer a lot of details about how the Holy Spirit "amplifies" our prayers to God—and God's answers to us. However, we do know that the Holy Spirit "fills in" our prayers, taking needs before the Lord that we aren't able to express—or that we may not even be aware of.

**JUST WONDERING**

**When does the Holy Spirit give Christians their spiritual gifts?**
Most likely, the Holy Spirit bestows our spiritual gifts on us the moment we repent and believe in Jesus. That's not to say that we become aware of our gifts at that moment. In fact, there are some spiritual gifts that we may not recognize in ourselves until the end of our lives, when we look back and see what God accomplished through us.

## The Holy Gift-Giver

One of the most intriguing roles of the Holy Spirit is that of spiritual gift-giver. The Bible tells us that there are, or have been, eighteen to twenty spiritual gifts (depending on how they're divided or classified), necessary for the health and growth of the body of Christ. These gifts—that is, personal attributes, qualities, and talents—are like pieces in a jigsaw puzzle. When they're all put together, we can see the big picture of how God intends His church to operate. (We should point out that some gifts fulfilled specific, unique needs of the first-century church and are no longer necessary.)

To get you acquainted with how these gifts work, we've divided them into fifteen categories and provided a brief explanation of each one. (We'll explain these gifts in greater detail in chapter 13.) This master list was compiled from three different lists of spiritual gifts found in Romans 12, 1 Corinthians 12, and Ephesians 4.

1. ***Apostleship.*** This gift applied specifically to Jesus' handpicked disciples and perhaps a couple of other followers, such as Paul and Barnabas, who were instrumental in founding the church. Those who received the gift of apostleship were sent out by the Lord to complete His work. We include this gift on the list only for the sake of completeness. It's been retired and is no longer given out.

*2. Prophecy.* The gift of prophecy involved proclaiming the message of God and, in some instances, predicting the future. After the book of Revelation, which reveals what God wants us to know about the future, was written, there was no further need for the gift of prophecy. Like apostleship, it is no longer an active spiritual gift.

*3. Miracles and healing.* This gift involved performing special signs and supernatural works to prove the power of God. This gift was necessary in New Testament times because it authenticated the Gospel message. Today we have the Bible to do that.

*4. Tongues and interpretation of tongues.* The gift of tongues involves communicating in a language that the speaker has never learned. The gift of interpreting tongues is the ability to communicate the foreign message in a language hearers will understand.

*5. Evangelism.* This is the ability to proclaim the Gospel message in such a way that people understand and respond to it. The gift of evangelism can be exercised as effectively in one-on-one settings as it can from the pulpit.

*6. Pastoring.* This gift involves shepherding, caring for, and protecting God's people—usually in a leadership position. This gift is often tied in with teaching.

*7. Serving.* This gift involves meeting people's physical and emotional needs in a hands-on way, by getting personally involved in their lives and doing the menial tasks that other people may be unwilling

### Just Wondering

**Does the Holy Spirit still give the gifts of tongues and interpreting tongues today?**
Some Christian denominations, particularly Pentecostal churches, believe that the gifts of tongues and interpreting tongues are still vital to the body of Christ. They teach that these gifts are evidence of the Holy Spirit's presence in people's lives and are beneficial to worship. Other Christian denominations teach that the need for tongues no longer exists, so the Holy Spirit no longer hands out the gift. Regardless of your belief, it's important to understand that the gift of tongues must never be practiced without the gift of interpreting tongues (1 Corinthians 14:13–14). Uninterpreted tongues are of no use to anyone, since even the person doing the speaking doesn't know what's being said.

to do. Christians who have the gift of serving like to "get their hands dirty" when it comes to meeting other people's needs.

8. ***Teaching.*** This gift involves being able to explain God's truth to other people in ways that they understand and respond to. Sometimes this gift is given by itself and sometimes it's given as a package deal with pastoring. It's also closely related to the gift of wisdom and knowledge.

9. ***Faith.*** This is the ability to rely on God to have one's needs met. Obviously, all Christians have faith, but not all have the *gift* of faith. The difference between the two may be the depth of faith and the way it is expressed to others. Those with the gift of faith may serve as examples to their fellow believers of what faith can accomplish.

10. ***Encouraging.*** This gift involves providing encouragement and comfort to people, and spurring them on to achieve what God intends for them.

11. ***Distinguishing of spirits.*** This gift involves being able to tell the difference between true and false teaching. It was especially important in New Testament times, before the Bible had been completed. During that era, many teachers claimed to have received supernatural messages from God. Those people with the gift of distinguishing spirits were responsible for helping identify frauds.

12. ***Mercy.*** Those with this gift have a special ministry of kindness and assistance to the needy, particularly those who are sick or suffering.

13. ***Giving.*** Those with this gift demonstrate great generosity with what they have, no matter how much or how little that may be. There's also humility involved, since it requires no thought of repayment or acclaim.

14. ***Administration.*** This gift involves overseeing the day-to-day operations of the church.

15. ***Wisdom and knowledge.*** This isn't necessarily about being the smartest person in the room but being able to understand and communicate God's truth to other people.

The Holy Spirit distributes spiritual gifts according to His determination

(1 Corinthians 12:11). We don't get to pick our gifts or trade with others. The Holy Spirit distributes gifts according to His will because He knows best what's needed by the body of Christ, or the church, and what best fits each believer for service.

Together, all believers make up the body of Christ. If every person in the body had the same spiritual gift, the church would be a one-dimensional place. But with all believers contributing our Spirit-given gifts, we make the body of Christ complete. We complement each other. One person uses his or her strengths to make up for another person's weaknesses.

Every Christian receives at least one gift (1 Peter 4:10). Some people receive more than one. However, no one receives every spiritual gift. Anyone who possessed all of the gifts the Holy Spirit gives would never need anyone else—and that's certainly not the model the Lord intended for His followers.

We should point out that as Christians, we have a responsibility to practice acts such as faith, giving, and evangelism, regardless of whether or not we've been given those specific gifts. In other words, we can't sit back and say, "I don't have that gift, so I don't have to do that."

**On a Personal Note**

Spend some time going over the list of spiritual gifts in Romans 12, 1 Corinthians 12, and Ephesians 4. Ask the Holy Spirit to help you identify the gifts that you possess. Once you've narrowed the list down to a few specific gifts, start thinking about how you can put those gifts to use in your everyday life. For example, if the Holy Spirit makes it clear that you have the gift of evangelism, you might think of some creative and effective ways you could communicate the Gospel to your friends, family, and acquaintances.

Some gifts have a higher profile than others, but no gift is more important than another. The purpose of the gifts is not personal glory for us but the benefit of the body of Christ as a whole.

## The Holy Revealer

First Corinthians 2:10–11 indicates that the Holy Spirit assists us in understanding the deep things of God. Without Him, we would have no hope of comprehending the way God works. Finite minds are insufficient tools when it comes to grasping infinite concepts. The Holy Spirit knows the thoughts of God, because He is God. He reveals those thoughts to us because He loves us and wants what's best for us.

The Holy Spirit also reveals Scripture to us. But He does it in conjunction with our study. He doesn't just download the wisdom of the ages into our brains the moment we become Christians. If that were the case, we should be able to open to any passage in the entire Bible and be able to explain what's going on and what significance it has to our lives. Obviously, none of us has that ability.

What it comes down to is this: The Holy Spirit rewards our efforts to understand God's Word. The more effort we put into it, the bigger our reward will be.

## In Response

What should we do in response to the Holy Spirit's work in our lives? Keep in mind that service is a two-way street; the Holy Spirit serves us, and we serve Him. Here are four suggestions to help you give the Holy Spirit His due recognition, praise, and service in your life.

**NOTABLE QUOTABLE**

The Holy Spirit longs to reveal to you the deeper things of God. He longs to love through you. He longs to work through you. Through the blessed Holy Spirit you may have: strength for every duty, wisdom for every problem, comfort in every sorrow, joy in His overflowing service.

—T. J. Bach

***1. Look for evidence of the Spirit's work.*** If you're feeling ambitious, start a journal in which you keep track of the things the Holy Spirit accomplishes in and through you. For example, if you know what your spiritual gifts are, spend some time thinking about how those gifts have benefited other people or the body of Christ as a whole.

Be specific in the accomplishments you list. For example, if one of your gifts is mercy, write down some of the reactions and responses you've received from the people you've visited, cared for, and assisted. If one of your gifts is teaching, write down evidence of spiritual growth that you've seen in your "students."

Beyond your spiritual gifts, think of specific prayer requests that the Holy Spirit facilitated for you—situations in which you didn't even know what to pray for, yet still received an answer from God. Think of Bible passages that He's helped you understand and develop an appreciation for. Think of situations in which His counseling and help have made a real difference in your life.

Develop a habit of incorporating your list of the Holy Spirit's accomplishments into your prayer life, giving Him thanks and praise for what He does for you.

### *2. Live as though you're aware of who is dwelling in you.*

The Bible makes it clear that when we accept Christ, we are sealed with the Holy Spirit. What's more, the Holy Spirit is sealed in us. That means:

- Where we go, He goes.
- What we say, He hears.
- What we do, He sees.

**ON A PERSONAL NOTE**

To bring a broader element of praise to the Holy Spirit, come up with a list of specific situations in the past in which people used their spiritual gifts to help you. These situations might include anything from being led to Christ to being ministered to in the hospital. Once you've compiled a list, give the Spirit thanks for allowing you to benefit from His gifts to other believers.

That reality should make us think carefully about the things we put the Holy Spirit through. Ephesians 4:30 warns, "Do not grieve the Holy Spirit of God." If we're serious about heeding that warning, we have a responsibility to examine every area of our lives, including (1) the places we hang out, (2) the things we talk and joke about, (3) the way we spend our time, and (4) the attitude we demonstrate to other people. It even means looking at the things we put in our bodies. We are to make sure that all these areas conform with God's will for us.

The apostle Paul wrote, "Do you not know that your body is a temple of the Holy Spirit, who is in you, whom you have received from God? You are not your own; you were bought at a price. Therefore honor God with your body" (1 Corinthians 6:19–20). The bottom line is that we have a responsibility to create a home suitable for the Holy Spirit to live in.

### *3. Put your spiritual gifts to use.*

We'll explore the specifics of how you can use your spiritual gifts in ministry in chapter 13. For now, we need to point out that spiritual gifts are not given to us for our own personal enjoyment or satisfaction. The purpose of spiritual gifts is to benefit the entire body of Christ. If we don't use our gifts, we're not just hurting ourselves; we're hurting the entire body.

> **NOTABLE QUOTABLE**
>
> Abilities are like tax deductions–we use them or we lose them.
>
> –SAM JENNINGS

In order to put our spiritual gifts to use, we must pay attention to the Spirit's prompting and leading. For example, if you suspect that you have the gift of, say, evangelism, you need to be diligent in looking for opportunities—provided by the Holy Spirit—to share your faith with the people around you. Speak when you sense the Holy Spirit telling you to speak, and keep your mouth shut when you sense Him giving you a "Stop" sign. Either way, though, you need to be ready to follow His lead.

In other words, you need to make sure that when the Spirit is willing, your body is not weak.

### *4. Bear fruit.*

The Scriptures tell us that the Holy Spirit's work in our lives produces "fruit," just as seeds planted in soil produce plants. The "fruit of the Spirit" includes love, joy, peace, patience, kindness, goodness, faithfulness, gentleness, and self-control (Galatians 5:22–23).

The way to achieve these qualities in our lives is to familiarize ourselves with God's truth, meaning lots of quality time in God's Word, and learning to follow the Holy Spirit's leadings.

If we develop a pattern of obedience in our lives, we won't have to worry about how to show love, joy, peace, patience, kindness, goodness, faithfulness, gentleness, and self-control. Those qualities—or fruits—will grow naturally in our lives and become apparent to everyone around us.

# One More Thing

God has gone to tremendous lengths to make Himself known to us—as God the Father, God the Son, and God the Holy Spirit. If we choose to focus only on the "popular" aspects of His nature—the works of God the Father and Jesus—we are choosing to ignore one-third of who He is. And nothing good can come from that.

The Holy Spirit is Christ's personal gift to us. Why not make the most of it and discover just how life-changing His present can be?

# Know What You Believe

How much do you know about the Holy Spirit? Here's a quiz to test your knowledge.

1. Which of the following statements regarding the Trinity is accurate?
   a. God is one.
   b. When there is conflict between two or more persons of the Trinity, the majority rules.
   c. The Holy Spirit should be considered no more than an honorary member of the Trinity.
   d. The three persons of the Trinity are never mentioned together in the same verse anywhere in the Bible.

2. Which of the following is not true of the Holy Spirit's work in Scripture?
   a. He helped Jesus by distracting Satan during his temptation of Jesus.
   b. He equipped God's people to fulfill specific responsibilities that the Lord had given them.
   c. He gave life to the entire human race.
   d. He made it possible for people like David to live God-honoring lives.

3. Which of the following is not a responsibility of the Holy Spirit?
   a. Distributing spiritual gifts
   b. Amplifying our prayers to God

c. Providing wisdom and guidance in our lives
d. Downplaying our sins to God

4. Which of the following is not true of the Holy Spirit's work as a revealer?
   a. He will bless our efforts to learn more about God's Word by revealing God's truth to us.
   b. To the people who get really close to Him, He reveals things like winning lottery numbers and the details of future illnesses.
   c. Without Him, we have no hope of understanding the deeper things of God.
   d. He knows God's mind because He is God.

5. Which of the following is not a recommended response to the Holy Spirit's work in your life?
   a. Looking for evidence of His work to praise Him for
   b. Bearing the fruit of the Spirit
   c. Asking Him to reconsider His choice of spiritual gifts for you
   d. Living as though you're aware of who is dwelling in you

*Answers: (1) a, (2) a, (3) d, (4) b, (5) c*

CHAPTER 5

# What's the Good Word?

## SNAPSHOT

Becky glanced at the TV. The clock in Times Square read 11:22. "How many of last year's resolutions can you finish in thirty-eight minutes?" she asked.

Eddie turned around and scanned the bookshelf behind him. He grabbed a Bible, opened it up, mouthed a few words as though he were reading, and then set the book down on a coffee table. "There's one," he said with a grin. "Last year I made a resolution to read the Bible more."

"That was really your resolution?" Becky asked.

"Yeah, I was on a spiritual kick at the time, and I figured it might help me out," Eddie explained.

"So what happened?"

"I don't know," Eddie said. "I think I bought the wrong Bible."

"Why do you say that?" Becky asked.

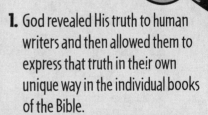

### SNEAK PREVIEW

1. God revealed His truth to human writers and then allowed them to express that truth in their own unique way in the individual books of the Bible.
2. God guided not only the creation of the Bible but the copying and translation of it as well, to ensure that nothing is added to it or subtracted from it.
3. As believers, our best response to the Bible is to read it, live it, and share it with others.

"Because it intimidates me," Eddie explained.

"I beg your pardon?"

"It intimidates me," Eddie repeated. "It's like the size of a cinder block. Plus, it's got the deluxe leather cover that makes it real impressive and important looking."

"What's the problem with that?" Becky asked.

Eddie shrugged. "I look at it and think, 'Who am I kidding? The last book I actually read and understood had the Hardy Boys in it. There's no way I can make it through something like that.'"

"Have you ever *tried* to read it?" Becky asked.

"No, and I'll tell you why," Eddie said. "I put the Bible in the same category as my great-aunt Rona."

"Huh?"

"Every year at our family reunion, I think about sitting down and having a conversation with my great-aunt Rona," Eddie explained. "She's in her late nineties, and I know that she has some interesting stories to tell and that I can probably learn a lot from her. But I never do it."

"Why not?" Becky asked.

"Well, for one thing, I'm afraid that I won't have a clue what she's talking about," Eddie admitted. "Plus, there are just too many other things that I'd rather do."

"Yeah, I guess that does put her in the same category as the Bible," Becky agreed.

"Of course, there's always the new year," Eddie reminded her.

"Are you going to make the same resolution again?" Becky asked.

"Sure, why not?" Eddie said, patting the Bible in front of him. "It worked for me this year."

* * * * * * * * * * * * * * * * *

Unbelievers can banish the Bible to the outskirts of their lives. They can pretend it has nothing relevant to say to them. They can treat it as they would any other literary masterpiece—as something best left to the experts. They can even ignore it completely, if they choose to.

None of those options is available to believers. If you're a Christian who's committed to honoring God and growing in your faith, the Bible is going to play a major role in your life . . . whether you like it or not.

The purpose of this chapter is to make that concept seem a little less unsettling and to make the Bible seem a little less intimidating. Obviously, we can't go into a lot of detail; otherwise, this would be a forty-volume series. Instead, we'll simply concentrate on the basics:

- what the Bible is
- how we got it
- what's in it
- what we should do with it

Ready? Take a deep breath and let's begin.

# What Is the Bible?

Let's start with the obvious. The Bible is the Word of God. Maybe you've noticed that throughout this book we use the terms *Bible, Scripture, Word of God,* and *God's Word* interchangeably. That's because when we talk about the Bible, we're talking about the Word of God. When we quote Scripture, we're quoting God's Word.

In fact, the only question regarding the Bible's status as God's Word is . . . *What in the world does it* mean *that the Bible is the Word of God?*

**NOTABLE QUOTABLE**

The Bible is worth all other books which have ever been printed.

—PATRICK HENRY

If you look at the individual books of the Bible, you'll find the names of human authors attached to them. Some of the prophets and Gospel writers even had their books named after them (Ezekiel, Obadiah, Mark, and John, to name a few). How can that be, if it's *God's* Word?

The answer can be found in 2 Peter 1:20–21: "Above all, you must understand that no prophecy of Scripture came about by the prophet's own interpretation. For prophecy never had its origin in the will of man, but men spoke from God as they were carried along by the Holy Spirit."

If that's not clear enough for you, try 2 Timothy 3:16: "All Scripture is God-breathed."

God originated Scripture. Every story, command, prophecy, parable, and promise in the Bible is there because God wants it to be. He has a purpose for all of it. In His perfect wisdom, and as part of His perfect plan, God has revealed Himself to us. He has given us a finite batch of information and said, "If you want to know about Me, My work, and My plans for you, read this. If you want to know more about Me, My work, and My plans for you . . . read it again."

When the time came to physically put His information into manuscript form, God chose to work through human authors. He could have done that by controlling every stroke of the writers' pens to make sure that every word appeared exactly as He intended, but He didn't. He could have dictated the words to the writers while they recorded them verbatim, like glorified stenographers, but He didn't.

Instead, God revealed His truth to human authors and inspired them to write down what they saw, heard, and experienced. What's more, God allowed the authors to use their own writing styles and personality traits to communicate His truths. The more time you spend in Scripture, the more its different styles and emphases become obvious.

That's not to say God ever gave up control of the project. He carefully monitored every word the human authors wrote, making sure that it conformed to His standards and communicated His exact truth. Nothing slipped by Him in the editing process. Every word received God's stamp of approval before it was made public. The fact that God is all-knowing means that we can rest assured that nothing in the Bible misrepresents God or His work. If it's there, it's because God intends for it to be there.

That's why Christians can say with assurance that the Bible *is* the Word of God.

If you've got a pencil handy, go back and circle the word *is* in the previous paragraph. Those are two letters you'll want to keep in mind when you discuss God's Word.

Some people would rephrase that statement to say that the Bible *contains* the Word of God. And while that may seem like a subtle difference at first glance, its implications are enormous.

If the Bible merely *contains* the Word of God, the dilemma is obvious: How do we know which parts of it are His Word and which parts aren't? More specifically, how do we know if the parts we put our faith in—those dealing with God's salvation, protection, guidance, forgiveness, and eternal life—are His Word or not?

If the Bible merely contained God's Word, it would be of little use to us. Every belief we chose to cling to would be a 50-50 proposition at best. *Maybe it comes from God; maybe it doesn't.* We could never know for sure.

The fact that the Bible *is* the Word of God solves those dilemmas for believers. It also presents us with implications that can't be ignored. The fact that the Bible is God's Word means that it is . . .

- our moral compass,
- our source of spiritual wisdom,
- our best glimpse at God and His work, and
- the ultimate proof and support of our faith.

Needless to say, the Bible deserves and demands serious exploration on the part of every believer.

## How Did We Get It?

Part of what makes the Bible awe-inspiring is the story of how it came to be. You already know that the Lord used human authors to write His Word. Now let's take a look at some of the facts that tell the larger story.

The Old Testament was written over a period of 1,100 years, from about 1500 B.C. to about 400 B.C., by dozens of authors scattered throughout the Middle East. Over time, the various texts were collected by Jewish scholars and divided into three categories: the Law, the Prophets, and the Writings.

The books were originally written in Hebrew. However, by about 250 B.C., many Jewish people were speaking Greek. In an effort to make Scripture accessible to the masses, a group of seventy-two Jewish scholars translated the Hebrew Old Testament into a Greek version known as the *Septuagint*. In the process, the scholars also rearranged the order of the books according to their subject matter. That same order is followed in our Bibles today.

**NOTABLE QUOTABLE**

I have spent seventy years of my life studying that Book to satisfy my heart; it is the Word of God. The Bible is stamped with a Speciality of Origin, and an immeasurable distance separates it from all competitors. I bank my life on the statement that I believe this Book to be that solid rock of Holy Scriptures.

—WILLIAM GLADSTONE

By the time Jesus came on the scene, the Old Testament was set. People generally regarded the entire collection as Scripture.

Compared to the Old Testament, the New Testament was practically a rush job. All twenty-seven of its books were written within one hundred years of Jesus' birth. Most of the books were written as personal letters from the author to a church or an individual. They were intended as tools of teaching and encouragement, a way of spreading eyewitness accounts of Jesus' earthly ministry, and instructions as to what His ministry should mean to the early Christians.

After the New Testament books (or letters) were completed, they circulated from church to church. Their teachings were used to define the beliefs of those who called themselves Christians.

During the third century, the books began to be collected and grouped into "gospels" and "epistles." Not all churches received copies of all of the books in circulation, so the collections differed from church to church. Each church's "mini-Bible" provided authoritative guidance for its members' faith and worship practices.

The problem with that system became apparent pretty quickly. Since different churches used different sets of books as their authority, Christian beliefs differed from place to place—sometimes radically so. Some churches included in their mini-Bibles books that were decidedly non-Christian. The different teachings caused rifts among various congregations.

So the question arose: Which books were actually inspired by God? Which ones were to be treated as Scripture?

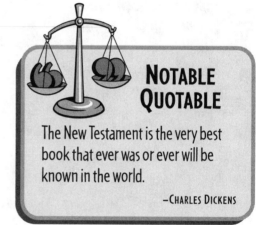

**NOTABLE QUOTABLE**

The New Testament is the very best book that ever was or ever will be known in the world.

—CHARLES DICKENS

The Christian leaders of the day decided that they needed one authoritative collection of books that could be used by all churches. So they met together periodically to discuss which books should be included in the "Canon"—that is, the completed collection of works to be recognized as Scripture.

The leaders used three criteria for determining whether a book should be included in the Canon:

1. Was it written by an apostle or an associate of an apostle?
2. Was it recognized as Scripture and used as such by churches?
3. Was it accurate factually and theologically?

Based on those criteria, the church leaders selected the twenty-seven books that now make up our New Testament. By as early as A.D. 367, the list of sixty-six books that make up our Bible was set.

As missionaries spread Christianity to the farthest reaches of the globe, the need for Bible translations grew. People wanted to understand Scripture in their own language. Sometime around 400, the Bible was translated from Greek to Latin in a version called the Vulgate, which was accepted as the authorized Scripture of the Catholic Church.

The Vulgate version eventually made its way to England. In the fourteenth century, scholars such as John Wycliffe began translating the Bible from Latin into English. Various English translations followed until 1611, when King James commissioned the most educated Bible scholars in his kingdom to create a definitive version of Scripture for the ages. The result was the King James Version of the Bible, which is still widely used today.

Since then, even more translations have followed—the New American Standard Bible (NASB), the New International Version (NIV), and the New King James Version (NKJV), to name a few.

Maybe this mini-history lesson is interesting to you; maybe it isn't. However, there's a truth we need to recognize among all of these dates and translations. God oversaw and guided not only the writing of His Word but the translation of it as well. That means we can open our modern translations of God's Word without having to wonder whether the things we're accepting as truth are actually mistakes or poor interpretations on the part of the people who have handled God's Word throughout the centuries.

**JUST WONDERING**

**What is the Apocrypha?**
The Apocrypha is a group of twelve to fifteen books (or parts of books) found in early Christian versions of the Old Testament that were not included in the Jewish Canon. Though the books of the Apocrypha provide a wealth of information about Jewish customs and history, they are not considered divinely inspired by most Protestants. The Roman Catholic Church, on the other hand, includes the Apocrypha in most of the Bibles it sponsors.

In other words, we can rest assured that our Bible is still the Word of God.

## What's in the Old Testament?

As we mentioned earlier in this chapter, the Bible is a collection of sixty-six books, divided into two Testaments, the Old and the New. The Old Testament covers the events starting with the creation of the universe and ending about four hundred years before Jesus' birth. The New Testament covers the events starting with the preparations for Jesus' birth and concluding with . . . well, the end of time itself.

The books of the Bible are written in widely diverse styles, reflecting the different backgrounds and personalities of the human authors. Obviously, we can't explore the books in detail in this chapter. However, we can give you a brief overview of each one, in order to acquaint you with its content.

Let's start with the thirty-nine books of the Old Testament.

*Genesis.* This book, attributed to Moses, covers everything from Creation to the Flood to the beginning of the Jewish nation. It includes the central theme of the Old Testament—God's work on behalf of His chosen people, the Israelites. Among the famous names you'll find in Genesis are Adam and Eve, Cain and Abel, Noah, Abraham, Isaac, Jacob, and Joseph.

*Exodus.* If you've seen the movie *The Ten Commandments,* you know what happens in this second book of Moses. You've got the story of Moses, the Israelites' slavery in Egypt, the ten plagues that resulted in their freedom, the crossing of the Red Sea, the beginning of the Israelites' forty-year wandering in the desert, and the presentation of the Ten Commandments.

*Leviticus.* This third book of Moses describes in great detail the laws, sacrifices, offerings, and regulations that the Israelites were expected to observe.

*Numbers.* The fourth book attributed to Moses details the final leg of the Israelites' wilderness journey and their arrival at the threshold of their destination, the "Promised Land."

*Deuteronomy.* This fifth book of Moses serves as Moses' farewell address to the people of Israel, who would be going to the Promised Land without him. If the Old Testament were a TV series, Deuteronomy would be a "flashback" episode. Moses reminds the

**NOTABLE QUOTABLE**

I am profitably engaged in reading the Bible. Take all of this book that you can by reason and the balance by faith, and you will live and die a better man. I believe the Bible is the best gift God has ever given to man. All the good from the Savior of the world is communicated to us though this book; but for this book we could not know right from wrong. All things desirable to man are contained in the Bible.

—Abraham Lincoln

people of all that God had done for them during their forty years in the wilderness and urges them to honor their covenant with the Lord. The Book of Deuteronomy ends with the death of Moses.

***Joshua.*** This book, written by Joshua, picks up where Deuteronomy leaves off, describing the Israelites' entrance into the Promised Land, their battles with the people occupying the land, and their eventual distribution of the land among themselves. The book concludes with Joshua's death.

***Judges.*** Generally credited to Samuel, this book describes the period in Israel's history between the death of Joshua and the appointment of the first king. Settled in the Promised Land, the Israelites faced constant attacks from their enemies. Every time an enemy challenged, God would appoint a judge to lead the Israelites in defeating their foe. Among the noteworthy names in the book are Samson, Gideon, and Deborah, the first female judge of Israel.

**NOTABLE QUOTABLE**

B.I.B.L.E. = Basic Instructions Before Leaving Earth.

—Unknown

***Ruth.*** The Book of Ruth tells the story of a Moabite woman (Ruth) who, after losing her husband, shows remarkable loyalty to her mother-in-law, even in the midst of a deadly famine. Eventually, Ruth meets and marries Boaz and becomes a direct ancestor of David—and of Jesus. The author of the book is unknown.

***1 Samuel.*** First Samuel records the events that led God to name Saul the first king of Israel, the details of Saul's failure as king, and the circumstances that brought David to the throne. The book includes the triumphant story of David's victory over the giant Goliath, but it concludes with the tragic story of Saul's suicide. The author of 1 and 2 Samuel is unknown.

***2 Samuel.*** Second Samuel details David's reign as the second king of Israel, beginning with his early military triumphs over the Philistines and continuing through his horrific series of sins involving Bathsheba and her husband, as well as the toll those sins eventually took on David's family and kingdom.

***1 Kings.*** This book, probably written by Jeremiah, begins with David's anointing of his son Solomon to succeed him as king. The book traces the highs of Solomon's reign, including his construction of the temple, as well as the lows, including his marriages to hundreds of pagan wives. After Solomon's death, the book details the split of the kingdom into two nations, Israel and Judah, and then traces the ups and downs of each nation as good and bad kings ascend to the thrones. The prophets Elijah and Elisha and the evil monarchs Ahab and Jezebel are among the other notable characters in the book.

*2 Kings.* The book records Elijah's unusual departure from earth, follows Elisha's ministry, and then settles into a pattern of introducing and briefly describing the succeeding kings of Israel and Judah, until both nations are eventually conquered and their people taken captive.

*1 Chronicles.* The two books of Chronicles, which are commonly credited to Ezra, are like a greatest-hits compilation of Israel's historical events. The first book traces Israel's history from Adam to David, highlighting such events as Saul's suicide, the ark of the covenant's arrival in Jerusalem, and David's ill-considered census.

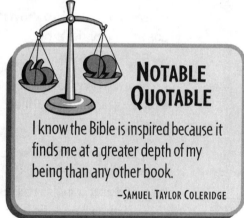

**NOTABLE QUOTABLE**

I know the Bible is inspired because it finds me at a greater depth of my being than any other book.

–Samuel Taylor Coleridge

*2 Chronicles.* Second Chronicles picks up the account of Israel's history with Solomon's request for wisdom. Among the other events spotlighted in the book are the construction of the temple; the rebellion against Rehoboam, Solomon's son; and the purification of the temple, after years of neglect and wickedness in Israel.

*Ezra.* The Book of Ezra, which bears the name of the man who wrote it, describes the return of the Israelites to their homeland after their captivity in Persia and the rebuilding of the temple in Jerusalem.

*Nehemiah.* The Book of Nehemiah, a companion piece to the Book of Ezra also written by Ezra, details the rebuilding of the protective wall around Jerusalem and the spiritual revival that resulted from Ezra's preaching.

*Esther.* The Book of Esther offers the exciting story of God's protection of His people from genocide, thanks to the efforts of a well-placed queen of Persia. Curiously, this is the only book of the Bible in which God is not mentioned. The author of the book is unknown.

*Job.* The Book of Job presents the story of a man (Job) whose faithfulness to God is tested by Satan in unimaginable ways. The majority of the book, whose author is unknown, is constructed as an extended conversation between Job and a few of his friends, who are attempting to "comfort" him in the midst of his sorrow. The author of the book is unknown.

*Psalms.* The Book of Psalms is a collection of 150 songs and prayers to God. The emotions expressed in individual psalms run the gamut from fear to joy, from doubt to unshakable confidence. Authors include David, Moses, and Solomon.

*Proverbs.* The Book of Proverbs is a collection of pithy statements, courtesy of Solomon (for the most part), that express truths about human behavior. The tone of the book is exceedingly practical.

*Ecclesiastes.* The Book of Ecclesiastes chronicles King Solomon's despair over his fruitless search for happiness and fulfillment in the midst of his wealth and power.

*Song of Songs.* Sometimes known as Song of Solomon, this book was also written by David's son, the third king of Israel. The book celebrates the love between a man and a woman, as well as between God and His people, using some pretty startling romantic imagery.

**NOTABLE QUOTABLE**

The Bible is no mere book, but a living creature, with a power that conquers all who oppose it.

—Napoleon Bonaparte

*Isaiah.* This book of prophecy, written by Isaiah, outlines the Lord's plan to judge Israel for its sin, as well as His plan to send a Messiah to save the world. Of all the prophetic books of the Old Testament, this is the one most often quoted in the New Testament.

*Jeremiah.* This book of prophecy, written by Jeremiah, warns the nation of Judah of God's impending judgment and describes the ultimate fall of Jerusalem.

***Lamentations.*** This book of poetry, attributed to Jeremiah, records five different laments over the fall of Jerusalem and the misery that resulted among the Jewish people.

***Ezekiel.*** This book of prophecy, written by Ezekiel, begins with a series of warnings regarding God's judgment of Jerusalem and the Jewish people. After the fall of Jerusalem, the prophet offers words of consolation and encouragement to the people, informing them that one day they will experience the perfect kingdom of God in the world.

***Daniel.*** The Book of Daniel, written by the prophet himself, contains two of the best-known examples of faithfulness in the entire Old Testament: (1) Daniel's refusal to alter his prayer habits, even though it meant being thrown into a pit of lions, and (2) Shadrach, Meshach, and Abednego's refusal to bow down to an idol, even though it meant being thrown into a flaming furnace. The book also contains Daniel's visions regarding the future of several nations, including Israel.

***Hosea.*** This book of prophecy, written by Hosea, uses family imagery to portray the unfaithfulness of Israel to God, her faithful "husband."

***Joel.*** The Book of Joel, written by the prophet himself, offers a warning to the people of Judah of a coming devastation—the "Day of the Lord."

***Amos.*** This book of prophecy, written by Amos himself, warns of God's impending judgment on several nations—most significantly, the materialistic, unjust, and unrepentant people of Israel.

***Obadiah.*** This brief prophetic book, written by Odadiah, warns the nation of Edom of God's coming judgment as a result of Edom's participation in Israel's downfall.

***Jonah.*** This book, which may or may not have been written by the prophet Jonah himself, chronicles the prophet's refusal to minister to the city of Nineveh, as the Lord commanded, and his subsequent period of reflection on his refusal . . . in the stomach of a large fish.

*Micah.* The book of Micah, written by the prophet himself, contains messages of both judgment and hope for the people of Israel and Judah.

*Nahum.* This prophetic book, written by Nahum, focuses specifically on God's judgment of the city of Nineveh for its wickedness, cruelty, and idol worship.

*Habakkuk.* The Book of Habakkuk, written by the prophet himself, is a dialogue between Habakkuk and God about wickedness and God's response to it.

*Zephaniah.* This prophetic book, written by Zephaniah, offers warnings of God's impending judgment against several nations, including Judah.

*Haggai.* The Book of Haggai, written by the prophet himself, describes the consequences of obedience and disobedience to God.

*Zechariah.* In the book that bears his name, the prophet Zechariah encourages the people of Judah to rebuild God's temple, and then makes some specific predictions regarding the two comings of the Messiah.

*Malachi.* The Book of Malachi, written by the prophet himself, offers hope to people who are discouraged by God's seeming inactivity by giving them a glimpse of the Lord's coming.

### Just Wondering

**How much of the Bible is still applicable today?**

All of it. Remember, God is not confined by our concept of time, and neither is His Word. Instructions that were given 3,000 years ago are still in effect today. Stories of ancient judgments can deepen our knowledge of who God is and what He's like. Descriptions of ancient worship procedures can give us a renewed appreciation for God's work of salvation. If you bring the right spirit and attitude toward your study, you can find useful, applicable information in any Bible passage.

## What's in the New Testament?

The New Testament is made up of twenty-seven books. Here's a quick summary of each one.

*Matthew.* The first of the four Gospels (that is, the biographical accounts of Jesus' time on earth) was written by Matthew, one of Jesus' twelve disciples. The primary purpose of Matthew's Gospel was to convince the original Jewish readers that

Jesus was their Messiah. That's why Matthew went to great lengths to show that Jesus is the fulfillment of Old Testament prophecies. One of the other notable elements of this book is its extensive coverage of Jesus' Sermon on the Mount.

*Mark.* The second Gospel was written by Mark, an associate of the apostle Peter. Mark's book focuses more on Jesus' actions than on His words. Mark also emphasizes the need for discipleship in light of Jesus' teachings.

*Luke.* The third Gospel was written by Luke, a medical doctor, and one of the apostle Paul's closest friends. Luke's Gospel emphasizes the works and teachings of Jesus that help us understand salvation. The book of Luke is where the Christmas story—at least, the most famous version of it—is found.

**ON A PERSONAL NOTE**

Make a list of some of the most famous Bible verses you can think of ("For God so loved the world"; "The LORD is my shepherd"; "The wages of sin is death"). Locate and mark the references for each verse (John 3:16; Psalm 23:1; Romans 6:23) so that you can find it in a hurry when you introduce the Bible to your unbelieving friends.

*John.* The fourth Gospel was written by the apostle John, who included several events in his book that aren't mentioned in the other three Gospels. John's purpose in writing his Gospel was to convince his readers to believe in Jesus—to the point of accepting Him as Savior.

*Acts.* The book of Acts chronicles the arrival of the Holy Spirit at Pentecost, the beginning of God's church, and some of the earliest Christian missionary trips. Among the major figures who play a role in Acts are Paul, Peter, Barnabas, Silas, and Stephen, the first Christian martyr. The author of the book is Luke (of Gospel fame).

*Romans.* The apostle Paul's letter to the Christians in Rome offers perhaps the clearest and most complete explanation of God's plan of salvation, and our need for it, in the entire Bible. Among the other topics covered in the book are sin, grace, faith, and holiness.

*1 Corinthians.* Paul's first letter to the Christians in Corinth offers warnings against spiritual pride and a divisive spirit among Christians. Paul also emphasized the need for sexual morality, worship, and church discipline. The famous "Love Chapter" is found in this book—specifically, chapter 13.

*2 Corinthians.* In Paul's second letter to the Corinthians, the apostle responded to efforts to undermine his ministry, shared his attitude toward painful circumstances, and offered God-honoring advice for financial giving.

*Galatians.* Paul's letter to the Galatians emphasizes that God is not interested in our empty works, but in the obedience that comes from an active faith in Christ. The book also recounts a confrontation between the two primary figures of the early church, Paul and Peter.

*Ephesians.* Paul's letter to the Christians in Ephesus is intended to help readers understand the scope of God's purpose, power, and grace—in the lives of individual believers and in the church. The book also offers specific instructions designed to enhance family relationships.

*Philippians.* In his letter to the Christians in Philippi, Paul called for Christlike humility, single-minded determination, and a joyful spirit among believers.

*Colossians.* Paul wrote this letter to the Christians living in Colosse to warn against false teachers and explain how believers can live holy lives.

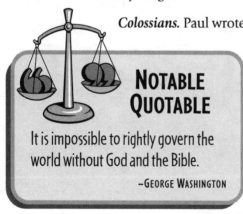

**NOTABLE QUOTABLE**

It is impossible to rightly govern the world without God and the Bible.

—GEORGE WASHINGTON

*1 Thessalonians.* Paul's first letter to the Christians in Thessalonica offers encouragement for new believers and a rather dramatic description of what will happen when Christ returns.

*2 Thessalonians.* Paul's second letter to the Thessalonians continues his in-depth description of Christ's return, followed by an emphatic instruction for believers to stand firm in our faith.

*1 Timothy.* Paul's first letter to Timothy, a young pastor, offers instructions for dealing with false teachings, handling church-related responsibilities, and appointing church officials.

*2 Timothy.* Paul's second letter to Timothy encourages boldness among believers and offers a sobering warning about life in the last days.

*Titus.* Paul's letter to Titus, another young church leader, focuses on teaching specific truths to different categories of believers. The book also offers some tips for living a godly life.

*Philemon.* Paul's brief letter to Philemon is a plea to the slave owner to forgive and set free a runaway slave named Onesimus.

*Hebrews.* The book of Hebrews demonstrates how Jesus is superior to angels, Moses, and Old Testament priests. The author, who is unknown, emphasized the importance of faith by spotlighting the most faithful people of the Old Testament.

*James.* The book of James, most likely written by the brother of Jesus, emphasizes a vital approach to the Christian life and offers some thought-provoking advice for controlling the tongue.

*1 Peter.* The apostle Peter's first letter offers instructions on how to be holy, how to submit to authority, how to respond to verbal attacks, and how to live for God.

*2 Peter.* Peter's second letter offers instructions on how to deal with false teachers, as well as a stark description of the Lord's return.

*1 John.* The apostle John's first letter urges believers to love one another and to carefully consider teachings before accepting them as fact.

*2 John.* John's second letter warns believers not to have anything to do with false teachers.

*3 John.* John's third letter instructs believers to show support, encouragement, and hospitality to our fellow Christian workers.

*Jude.* This letter, written by Jude (who may have been a brother of Jesus), warns believers against trying to take advantage of God's grace and forgiveness by sinning at random.

*Revelation.* The book of Revelation records the apostle John's visions regarding the last days of planet earth and God's final judgment of every person, living and dead. In this final book of the Bible, Christ returns to earth as King, Satan is defeated for good, the righteous receive eternal life, and the unrighteous are sentenced to eternity in the lake of fire.

Consider yourself officially introduced to the sixty-six books of the Bible. May you develop a long and meaningful relationship with each and every one of them.

## What Should We Do with It?

God has given us His Word—everything we need to know about Him, His work, His plan for our lives, and His plan for the world.

Now the ball's in our court. We have to decide how we're going to respond to God's Word; what we're going to do with it. Here are three suggestions to consider.

### *1. Read it.*

As we mentioned earlier, the Bible is an intimidating book—until you become familiar with it. Obviously, the best way to become familiar with it is to read it. The more time you spend in God's Word—getting used to its rhythm, its language, its setting, and its characters—the more accessible it will become.

**ON A PERSONAL NOTE**

Choose your favorite book of the Bible and come up with at least three reasons why it's your favorite. The next time someone mentions a book they've read recently, recommend your favorite to them and explain why you think they might enjoy it.

We're not talking about casual read-throughs here, about simply flipping through the pages of Scripture whenever you have a spare moment. We're talking about studying God's Word in a purposeful way. We're talking about working past the difficult text to find the truth that lies inside.

To put it simply, we're talking about forcing yourself to focus on the words you read until you understand them.

### *2. Live it.*

As believers, our responsibility to the Bible doesn't stop with studying its truths. James 1:22–25 makes that perfectly clear:

> Do not merely listen to the word, and so deceive yourselves. Do what it says. Anyone who listens to the word but does not do what it says is like a man who looks at his face in a mirror and, after looking at himself, goes away and immediately forgets what he looks like. But the man who looks intently into the perfect law that gives freedom, and continues to do this, not forgetting what he has heard, but doing it—he will be blessed in what he does.

We can't sit back like detached scholars and say, "Jesus' command in this passage would have been especially relevant to blah, blah, blah, given the political climate in Jerusalem among the yada, yada, yada"—and then leave it at that.

We have to recognize that the truths God communicates to us in His Word can and should be applied to our daily existence. For example, in Matthew 5:27–28, Jesus says, "You have heard that it was said, 'Do not commit adultery.' But I tell you that anyone who looks at a woman lustfully has already committed adultery with her in his heart."

Clearly, Jesus was saying that lustful ogling is sin—a kind of mental adultery—and that we have a responsibility to eliminate it from our lives. Reading that passage should inspire us to think about the way we look at people and perhaps change some of our "viewing habits."

Second Timothy 3:16 tells us that God's Word is "useful for teaching, rebuking, correcting and training in righteousness, so that the man of God may be thoroughly equipped for every good work." The Word of God tells us what we need to do and how we need to live in order to accomplish the things God has in store for us. It only makes sense for us to follow His instructions.

### *3. Share it.*

Keep in mind that other people are intimidated by the Bible, too. Figuratively speaking, they're standing on the shore, waiting for someone in the water (that is, people who are familiar with the Bible) to reassure them that it's okay to come in—or, better yet, someone to take them by the hand and lead them into the water one step at a time.

You can be that leader. You can introduce your friends and family members to the Bible simply by quoting a verse every once in a while or by sharing some of your favorite Bible stories in conversation. If you pique people's curiosity or share something relevant to their lives, you may inspire them to check out the Bible for themselves.

Remember, the word *gospel* means "good news." And, like all good news, the Word of God—the story of His work in the world and especially His gift of salvation—is meant to be shared. We'll talk more about how to share your faith in chapter 12. For now, we'll simply suggest that as you read Scripture and apply it to your life, you also think about who would benefit from hearing the things you're learning and how you might explain those things to them.

## One to Grow On

No matter how big of a challenge the Bible may seem like to you, don't lose sight of one very important fact: You know the Author personally.

You don't have to wonder what certain phrases in His Word mean or how He intends for you to respond to a particular instruction. You can ask Him yourself in prayer. Remember, if you're a Christian, the Holy Spirit dwells in you. He is always ready, willing, and able to reveal God's truth to you.

## Know What You Believe

How much do you know about the Word of God? Here's a quiz to test your knowledge.

1. Which of the following best describes the process by which the Bible was written?
   a. God used the Bible writers as "human keyboards," tapping out in their brains the exact words He wanted written.
   b. God used the Bible writers as stenographers, instructing them to quote Him verbatim while He talked.
   c. God organized a writing competition of sorts; the top sixty-six submissions were chosen for inclusion in the Bible, based on the quality and uniqueness of the writing.

d. God gave the Bible writers the information He wanted to include in His Word and allowed them to communicate that truth in their own style.

2. Which of the following is not true of the Old Testament?
   a. Completed in less than one hundred years
   b. Contains prophecies about Jesus
   c. Includes books written by men with names like Habakkuk and Haggai.
   d. Made up of thirty-nine books

3. Which of the following is not true of the New Testament?
   a. Not completed until about A.D. 400
   b. Most of it was written by Jewish men
   c. Contains at least a dozen books written by the apostle Paul
   d. Made up of twenty-seven books

4. Which of the following characters has a book of the Bible named after him?
   a. Moses
   b. Amos
   c. Hezekiah
   d. Noah

5. Which of the following is not a God-honoring response to the Bible?
   a. Sharing it
   b. Living it
   c. Changing it
   d. Reading it

*Answers: (1) d, (2) a, (3) a, (4) b, (5) c*

CHAPTER 6

# All About Evil

## SNAPSHOT

"Everybody ready to see the final scores for all three games?" Matt asked as he pressed the "Enter" key on the computer scoring panel.

"Oh, man," Eric said when the scores flashed on the overhead screen. "I don't mean to offend anyone, but we stink at bowling."

"Hey, speak for yourself, Gutter Boy!" Brady objected. "This is the first time I've bowled in ten years. At least *I've* got an excuse."

"And, don't forget, I was on pace to break 200 in the second game, before I got this blister on my thumb," Matt added.

"Well, then, I was just bowling to the level of my competition," Eric decided.

"What about you, Mr. 7-10 Split?" Matt called. "What's your excuse?"

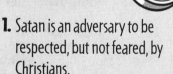

### SNEAK PREVIEW

1. Satan is an adversary to be respected, but not feared, by Christians.
2. Satan's purpose is to thwart the work of God in and through the lives of Christians.
3. Hell is the eternal fate of everyone who rejects God's gift of salvation, which came in the form of His Son, Jesus Christ.

Alex looked up from tying his shoes. "I didn't have my concentration," he replied. "I was thinking about something I heard this morning."

"What did you hear this morning?" Eric asked.

"My son singing, 'Hell ain't no bad place to be,'" Alex replied.

Brady nodded his head slowly. "AC/DC, circa 1980," he said.

"You know that song?" Alex asked with a hint of accusation in his voice.

Brady shrugged. "What can I say?" he replied. "I was into heavy metal when I was a kid. That was one of the albums I got rid of when I became a Christian."

"I don't want to make too big a deal of it," Alex said. "But I can't have my son going around singing stuff like that."

"It's all part of the partying mind-set," Brady explained. "Kids think hell is the place to be because that's where all the fun people are going. They figure they can party with their friends there forever without having to worry about anyone spoiling their good times."

"They'd rather laugh with the sinners than cry with the saints," Eric said.

"Billy Joel, circa 1978," Brady said.

"Stop doing that!" Alex barked.

"Hey, do you guys ever imagine what hell is really like?" Matt asked.

Eric thought for a moment. "I picture it as an enormous drivers' license branch," he said. "Just a bunch of people waiting in an endless line, without even knowing what they're waiting for. Then, maybe every million years or so, just when you start to see the front of the line, someone comes along and tells you you're in the wrong place. So you have to start all over again."

"That's pretty good," Matt acknowledged, "but I've got a better one. I picture hell as one giant room with big-screen TVs all over the walls. But, the thing is, you don't have the remote control for any of them."

"Oh, that's just cruel," Alex groaned.

"Right," Matt said, "so every time you start to get interested in a good ball game or something, someone flips over to a gardening show or the Teletubbies."

"I've got one," Alex offered. "Life in hell is like one giant leg cramp—you know, the kind that wakes you up in the middle of the night and feels like it's never going to go away. Well, in hell, it *won't* go away."

* * * * * * * * * * * * * * * * *

Learning everything you can about an opponent is a wise strategy, whether you're talking about baseball, military warfare, or Christianity.

A good scouting report, advance word of how your opponent functions, can help you understand his strengths, weaknesses, and tendencies. More importantly, it can help you plan your strategies for avoiding those strengths, taking advantage of the weaknesses, and preparing for what's likely to come.

**NOTABLE QUOTABLE**

There ain't no fans, nor no rest and, brother, there ain't no Cokes in hell.

—UNKNOWN

As Christians, our opponent is Satan, and our scouting report is God's Word. Our "scout" is God Himself, who's been battling Satan since before time began. God knows Satan's every trick, so there's nothing the devil can do to surprise the heavenly Father—or those who have studied His scouting report.

Think of this chapter as an overview of that scouting report, a starting point in understanding Satan, his demons, his future abode, and the final destination for all who follow him—hell, a *real* place.

## Nine Things You Need to Know About Satan

You can call him Lucifer, Beelzebub, Belial, the devil, the Evil One, the Tempter, the Father of Lies, the Serpent, the Dragon, the accuser, the Enemy, or just plain old Satan.

Just don't call him fictional. Satan is not . . .

- a name given to the impersonal force of evil in the world,
- a mythical creature dreamed up by some ancient storyteller in order to explain the bad things that happen in the world, or
- a pretend bogeyman Christians use to scare each other into obeying God.

Satan exists as surely as we do. What's more, if you call yourself a Christian, he has his sights set on you. Pretending that he's not real or that he's not something to be concerned about does not rob him of his power. In fact, it actually makes his job easier.

**JUST WONDERING**

**Why is Satan called by so many different names in the Bible?** Each name reflects a different aspect of his nature. For example, *Satan* (Matthew 4:10) means "adversary." *Devil* (Matthew 4:1) means "slanderer." *Beelzebub* (Luke 11:15) refers to his position as head of the demons. *Belial* (2 Corinthians 6:15) refers to his worthlessness and wickedness. Put his names together, and you get a pretty good idea of what our opponent is like.

A better solution is to learn what the Bible has to say about him. We'll get you started by highlighting nine important facts about the Evil One, some that you may have heard before and some that may surprise you.

### *1. Satan is a creature.*

Satan is a creature. We're not talking about a *creature* in the animal sense. We're referring to the fact that Satan was created by God. The Bible doesn't tell us *when* he was created, but apparently it was some time before the creation of man, since Satan seems to have been waiting in the Garden of Eden for Adam and Eve (Genesis 3:1).

The fact that Satan is a creature means he is not a god. A created being cannot be deity. Satan doesn't possess the perfections of deity that we looked at in chapter 2. Obviously, he is neither holy nor just. He's not omnipotent (all-powerful), either, though he does have superhuman power. He's not omniscient (all-knowing), though he does have superhuman intelligence.

Satan is an angel—a cherub, to be specific (Ezekiel 28:14). But not just *any* angel. Ezekiel 28:12 indicates that Satan (represented as the "king of Tyre" in this passage) was the crowning achievement of God's angelic creation, the cream of the cherubic crop.

Despite his lofty position, he is still a created being, which means he ultimately answers to God. Remember, no creature can ever be greater than the One who created him.

### *2. Satan is the original sinner.*

We know how and when sin started in the human race. Adam and Eve gave in to Satan's temptation in the Garden of Eden and disobeyed God's command (Genesis 3:1). But where did Satan's sinful nature come from? Obviously, he was already wicked before his encounter with Adam and Eve.

The Bible doesn't give us a lot of information about Satan's younger days, but it's logical to assume that he was created with free will, just as humans were. First Timothy 3:6 sheds some light on the circumstances that caused Satan to abuse his free will and oppose God. Apparently, Satan believed that he was too good to be a mere creature, and that he should have been receiving some of the attention that God was getting. Satan thought he was entitled to a piece of the glory pie, and he set his sights on getting it, one way or another.

Isaiah 14:13–14 lays out Satan's plan in five steps:

- "I will ascend to heaven."
- "I will raise my throne above the stars of God."
- "I will sit enthroned on the mount of assembly."
- "I will ascend above the tops of the clouds."
- "I will make myself like the Most High."

Talk about wanting it all! Satan made it clear that he wasn't prepared to settle for anything less than equality with God.

You can imagine how God felt about Satan's challenge. Quicker than you can say, "Beelzebub," God booted Satan from his position of glory. And so began the ultimate battle between good and evil.

### *3. Satan doesn't look like you imagine.*

News flash: The devil doesn't have horns on his head. He's not red all over. He doesn't clomp around on cloven hooves. He doesn't sport a tail. And he doesn't carry a pitchfork.

Though the Bible doesn't offer us any candid snapshots of the Evil One, we can get a sense of what his appearance is like from descriptions of other angels in Scripture. For example, take a look at the account in Luke 2:8–20 of the visit of the "heavenly host" to the shepherds on the night of Jesus' birth. Phrases such as "the glory of the Lord shone around about them" convey a sense of beauty and wonder in regard to the angels' appearance.

In Revelation 19:9–10, John became so overwhelmed by his face-to-face encounter with an angel that he literally began to worship the creature, who quickly corrected John's mistake. Apparently, there's an awe-inspiring quality to God's crew of heavenly messengers.

**NOTABLE QUOTABLE**

One is always wrong to open a conversation with the devil, for, however he goes about it, he always insists upon having the last word.

–ANDRÉ GIDE

As the chief angel of God's creation, Satan likely shares the angelic qualities described in these passages. In other words, in contrast to the ugliness of his work, Satan himself is likely a visually stunning creature.

### *4. Satan doesn't live where you imagine.*

One popular notion of the devil has him constantly devising and perfecting new tortures in hell to torment unbelievers. Many people, Christians and non-Christians alike, picture Satan as a brimstone-loving demon who feels completely at ease in the fiery depths of hades, cackling maniacally at the misery all around him.

The truth can be found approximately 180 degrees away from that assumption. This may come as a surprise to you, but the devil is no more eager to live in hell than anyone else is. The place of eternal torment isn't his handiwork. It's not built to suit his personality. In fact, he wants nothing to do with the joint.

Satan does not live in hell. In fact, nowhere does Scripture suggest that Satan's *ever* been to hell. Satan is a wandering spirit. He generally splits his time between the earth and God's throne (Job 1:6–12).

Don't misunderstand, though; Satan's ultimate destination is hell—or, more specifically, the lake of burning sulfur. And when he gets there, it won't feel like home to him. He won't be inflicting the torture; he'll be *enduring* it, along with everyone else sentenced to eternal damnation. Revelation 20:10 guarantees that the devil "will be tormented day and night for ever and ever."

### *5. Satan has more authority than you imagine.*

Quick, who is "the god of this age" (2 Corinthians 4:4)? And who is "the prince of the kingdom of the air" (Ephesians 2:2)?

If you answered "God the Father" and "Jesus Christ," in that order, you'd probably get several affirming nods from other believers. But you'd be wrong.

The correct answers are Satan and . . . Satan.

That's right, Satan is the ruler of this world. He has supreme authority over the cosmos. We are living in his dominion. We should point out, though, that Satan enjoys world dominance only because God allows him to as part of His (God's) sovereign plan. It's not like Satan overpowered God or wrested control of the world from Him when He wasn't looking. Satan wields supreme authority over the cosmos only because God gives him permission to.

> **NOTABLE QUOTABLE**
>
> The devil is merely a fallen angel, and when God lost Satan he lost one of his best lieutenants.
>
> –WALTER LIPPMANN

We should also point out that Satan is a lame-duck ruler—that is, he has no future. The world will be ripped from his grasp when Christ returns to defeat him and his forces. The clock is ticking on Satan's reign, but, for the time being, he maintains his control.

### *6. Satan is a world-class multitasker.*

In addition to ruling over this world, Satan devotes his time and energy to three other significant endeavors. First, *Satan accuses believers before God* (Revelation 12:10). The image here is of a prosecuting attorney, leveling charges of sin against us before the throne of God the Judge.

We certainly give him enough evidence to go on, don't we? It's not hard to picture him waving a file folder six inches thick, full of details of our various sins, arguing, "These sins demand punishment!"

Fortunately for us, we have a defense counselor who makes O.J.'s Dream Team look like a bunch of first-year law students. Jesus counters Satan's every accusation with a simple declaration: "That person's sins are covered under My blood. They have been forgiven." (For more details on this heavenly courtroom battle, check out 1 John 2:1–2.)

A defense like that doesn't leave much room for rebuttal, especially when the Judge is the Defense Attorney's Father. With those words from Jesus, God declares, "Case closed." And then Satan starts over again with his next prosecution.

Second, *Satan acts as a tempter,* something he's been doing since the earliest days of the human race. As we mentioned earlier in the chapter, it was Satan, in the form of a serpent, who talked Eve into taking a bite from the forbidden fruit in the Garden of Eden. Verses such as 1 Corinthians 7:5 make it clear that Satan still has God's people in his temptation crosshairs.

We should point out that even with his most persuasive temptations, Satan has no chance of "stealing" us from God. Romans 8:38–39 assures us that no one and nothing can ever separate us from God's love. Satan can, however, create "static" in our personal connection with God. He can disrupt our closeness and make us

### Just Wondering

**Why did Satan tempt Jesus? Did he really think he could persuade Jesus to sin?**

Matthew 4:1–11 indicates that Satan must have thought it was worth a try. If he could have persuaded Jesus to deviate from God's plan even slightly, Satan could have claimed victory over God. Satan's goal was to get Jesus to accept the glory that was due Him without the suffering of the Cross. One fact that often gets overlooked in discussions of Jesus' temptation is that the things Satan promised to Jesus were actually Satan's to give. Remember, he is the ruler of this world.

susceptible to outside influences.

He can also negatively affect the impact we have on others. If he can get us to give in to temptation under the right circumstances, he can do serious damage to our reputation and make us look like hypocrites to the people who are watching us.

Third, *Satan acts as a confuser*—that is, he blinds unbelievers to the truth of the gospel. There are countless ways he does this. For example, he often . . .

- convinces unbelievers that all Christians are hypocrites,
- loads unbelievers up with so many questions and doubts that they have no idea what's right and what's wrong, and
- persuades unbelievers that all religious beliefs are equally valid and that there are many paths to God.

Only someone who's good at what he does could operate so effectively on so many different fronts. Needless to say, the devil is good at what he does.

### *7. Satan is more versatile than you might imagine.*

The problem for us is that the devil has a multivolume playbook. It's impossible to anticipate what he's going to do next because there are so many different things he *can* do. If all we had to prepare for were, say, temptation, we'd be set. We could know that anytime we faced a tempting situation, we were being attacked.

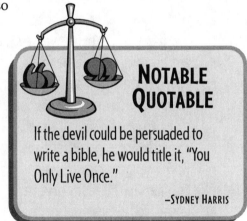

**NOTABLE QUOTABLE**

If the devil could be persuaded to write a bible, he would title it, "You Only Live Once."

—Sydney Harris

But temptation is just the tip of the iceberg. If that doesn't work, Satan can gear his attacks to take advantage of our vanity, pride, or insecurity. He can appeal to our doubts, fears, or prejudices. Whatever area appears most vulnerable to him is where he will attack. And, most of the time, we won't even see him coming. In fact, much of the time, we won't even know he's been at work until the damage has been done.

Keep in mind that Satan's goal isn't something dramatic, like getting us to bow down and worship him. That's not what he's going for. His purpose is simply to spoil God's plan in any way he can. In our lives, that means making sure that we are as ineffectual as possible, that we won't do anything to further God's kingdom or spread the good news of Christ.

> **JUST WONDERING**
>
> **What are demons?**
> Contrary to countless Hollywood portrayals, demons aren't ghosts or the spiritual remains of wicked dead people. They are fallen angels who joined Satan in his rebellion against God. For the most part, they're invisible to us, just as God's angels are. However, it is possible to experience demonic presence and witness demonic work. Like Satan, demons oppose God and His will. Their purpose is to thwart God's work whenever and wherever possible. That makes them sworn enemies of all committed believers.

Satan's primary mode of operation is to convince us that our own pursuits, interests, preferences, and priorities are as valid as God's plan for us. If the devil can get us focusing on what we think is best for us, his work is done.

The problem with facing an opponent who does most of his work in secret and who is content to make slow but gradual progress in our lives is that we tend to underestimate him. If Satan looked and acted the way he's portrayed in horror movies or TV shows—as, say, a twenty-foot-tall demon-dragon who hurls fireballs and drags innocent victims kicking and screaming to hell—he'd have our full attention. Bible sales would be through the roof as people scrambled to find ways to combat the evil monster.

In his present form, though, Satan is often viewed as nothing more than a minor annoyance or a bothersome pest—like that friend in high school who always got you in trouble, someone to be avoided, but not necessarily someone to be afraid of or even given much respect.

And that's a problem.

### *8. Satan is not an opponent to be taken lightly.*

The New Testament book of Jude refers to an obscure, but telling, incident between Michael, the powerful archangel mentioned throughout Scripture, and Satan. Apparently, there was a dispute between the two over the body of Moses.

The details of the story aren't important. What's important is Michael's obvious respect for Satan's power. The archangel refused to go one-on-one with the devil. Verse 9 says that Michael, "did not dare to bring a slanderous accusation against" Satan. Instead, Michael called for the Lord to rebuke him.

You know you're dealing with someone to be reckoned with when an archangel has to call for backup in order to confront him.

First Peter 5:8 offers this warning: "Your enemy the devil prowls around like a roaring lion looking for someone to devour." That sounds like considerably more than a minor annoyance or a bothersome pest.

If you're still inclined to underestimate Satan, check out Ephesians 6:10–18, which gives us a list of the equipment—the "full armor of God"—that we need in order to do battle with him. Our regulation gear for any encounter with the devil must include the following:

- "the belt of truth" (verse 14)—that is, a knowledge of God's truth to combat Satan's lies
- "the breastplate of righteousness" (verse 14)—that is, the kind of character that honors God
- "the shield of faith" (verse 16)—that is, the confidence in God and His faithfulness that protects us from the doubts and fears that Satan fires our way
- "the helmet of salvation" (verse 17)—that is, the assurance that Satan can do nothing to change our eternal fate
- "the sword of the Spirit" (verse 17)—that is, the Word of God, which is powerful enough to drive Satan away under any circumstances

James 4:7 offers a short and sweet battle plan: "Submit yourselves, then, to God. Resist the devil, and he will flee from you." We're not talking about a one-time preparation, where you submit yourself to God once and for all and receive all-time immunity from Satan's attacks. We're talking about a daily habit here. We're talking about consciously and purposefully . . .

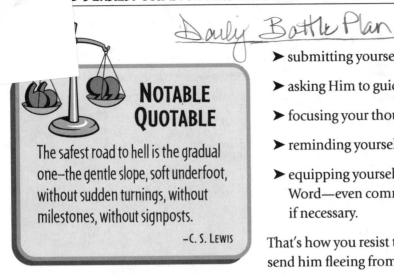

Daily Battle Plan

- submitting yourself to God every morning,
- asking Him to guide your thoughts and actions,
- focusing your thoughts on His truth,
- reminding yourself of His faithfulness, and
- equipping yourself with ammunition from His Word—even committing passages to memory, if necessary.

That's how you resist the devil. That's how you send him fleeing from you.

**NOTABLE QUOTABLE**

The safest road to hell is the gradual one–the gentle slope, soft underfoot, without sudden turnings, without milestones, without signposts.

–C. S. LEWIS

### *9. Satan has lost the war.*

Jesus' life, death, and resurrection defeated Satan for good and sealed his ultimate fate. Whatever slim chance Satan might have thought he had of overthrowing God vanished the moment Jesus emerged from His tomb. Sin and death, Satan's two closest allies, had been defeated for good at that point.

The only reason Satan wasn't shipped off to hell right then and there is that God still has work to do in the world. Specifically, He wants to make sure that as many people as possible have a chance to hear about and accept His gift of salvation. So while that work is being done, Satan remains in power. But he knows the end is coming.

Revelation 19:11–21 reveals that Jesus will return to earth for one final battle against Satan. Actually, it will be more of a rout than a battle. Christ is going to mop the floor with the devil and his forces. After his defeat, Satan will be thrown into the lake of fire, where he "will be tormented day and night for ever and ever" (Revelation 20:10). That's how Satan's story ends—and Satan knows it.

That makes him especially dangerous to us. With his time running out, Satan is looking to do as much damage as he can to God's work. He is relentless in his attacks against believers, knowing that if he can silence, discourage, or tempt us, he can impact the entire body of Christ.

In short, Satan is guaranteed to fall, but he's not going down without a fight.

# Three Things You Need to Know About Hell

Satan's fate is sealed. He will be spending eternity in torment in the lake of fire. And he won't be alone. Revelation 20:11–15 describes the final judgment of everyone human who's ever died. Verse 15 says, "If anyone's name was not found written in the book of life, he was thrown into the lake of fire."

The only way to get one's name in the Book of Life is to repent and believe in Jesus. Those who refuse to do that will suffer the eternal consequences of their decision.

Eternity in hell is a difficult concept to accept, especially if you have non-Christian friends and family members. There are, however, a few things that you need to understand about God's judgment of the unrighteous.

### *1. Hell is not God's choice for any of His creatures.*

Let's take care of the inevitable question right away: How can a loving God send people to hell? Perhaps the best way to answer it is with a question of our own: How much more could our loving God have done to make sure that no one goes to hell?

Let's take care of the ridiculous expectations first. As we explained in chapter 2, God is perfectly holy, perfectly just, and absolutely unchanging. His holiness means He can have nothing to do with sin. His justice demands that sin be punished by death. His unchanging nature means that nothing can be done to "lessen" His holiness or His justice.

God, by definition, cannot change to accommodate our sinful nature. Furthermore, it's the height of arrogance to believe that He should.

**JUST WONDERING**

**Should Christians fear demons?**
No, but we should respect their power. The New Testament records a handful of encounters between Jesus and demonic spirits. In those encounters, the demons recognized not only who Jesus was, but also that they had no power against Him. In one case, a group of demons had to ask Jesus' permission before they could enter a herd of pigs (Mark 5:1-13). As followers of Christ, we have access to power much greater than that of demons. However, that doesn't change the fact that demons are powerful spirits and are not to be "played with."

Now let's review the facts:

- God gave us (the human race) paradise in the Garden of Eden. He met all our needs, including food, companionship, work, and fellowship with Him. But we wanted more.
- God gave us one rule to follow: "Don't eat the fruit from the tree of the knowledge of good and evil." That's it. What could have been simpler or clearer? Unfortunately, that proved to be one too many commands for us to follow.
- God created us with the freedom of choice, instead of compelling us to worship and obey Him. We used that freedom to disobey Him.
- God could have dropped us like a hot potato after our disobedience and left us to suffer in our sinfulness for eternity. We could hardly blame Him if He had. After all, He gave us a chance, and we blew it.
- God loved us so much that He offered an almost unthinkable sacrifice. He sent His only Son to earth to take the punishment for our sins. He allowed Jesus to be mocked, ridiculed, beaten, tortured, and executed, because there was no other way for us to have eternal life with Him.
- God said all we have to do in order to receive eternal life is repent of our sins and believe in His Son. That's it—a simple two-step process that anyone can do anytime.
- God gave us the Bible, which explains everything we need to know about becoming a Christian and living a Christian life. He also instructed His followers to spread the news of Jesus' sacrifice and what it means to us to the entire world.

### On a Personal Note

How would you explain hell to an unbelieving friend or family member? It's a question worth considering. You can't "scare" people into giving their lives to Christ, but you can make them aware of the consequences of their decision not to follow Him. Investigate the Bible references in this chapter, as well as any others you find, and come up with an accurate description of what eternity apart from God will be like –one that you can use when you share your faith.

God reaches out to us with the gift of His salvation. He's done all the work, even to the point of initiating the giving process. With outstretched hands, He says, "Here's My gift to you. If you take it, you'll have eternal life with Me and you'll never have to worry about going to hell." All we have to do—wait, let's turn up the volume for this—ALL WE HAVE TO DO IS ACCEPT HIS GIFT OF SALVATION.

Only those who refuse God's gift will face eternity in hell. So, if that's the case, who's sending who to hell?

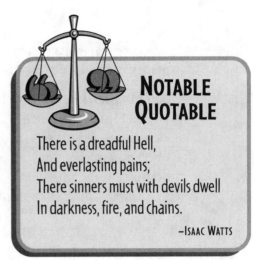

**NOTABLE QUOTABLE**

There is a dreadful Hell,
And everlasting pains;
There sinners must with devils dwell
In darkness, fire, and chains.

—Isaac Watts

### *2. Hell is a fate to be avoided at all costs.*

Contrary to the sentiments of countless rock 'n' roll odes, hell is not a place where proud sinners will party with their unrepentant friends throughout eternity. Anyone who had the slightest inkling of what hell is really like would do everything in his or her power to escape it.

Hell is a place of unimaginable and unending torment. In addition to the flames that will burn forever, Luke 16:24 suggests that the condemned in hell will suffer from agonizing thirst that will never be quenched. If you've ever been dehydrated after a game or after spending time in the summer sun, you know how powerful the need for water can be. Imagine having that kind of thirst and *never* being able to quench it. (Almost makes you want to drink a glass of water right now, doesn't it?)

Perhaps the most startling warning about hell comes from Jesus Himself in Mark 9:43–48:

> If your hand causes you to sin, cut it off. It is better for you to enter life maimed than with two hands to go into hell, where the fire never goes out. And if your foot causes you to sin, cut it off. It is better for you to enter life crippled than to have two feet and be thrown into hell. And if your eye causes you to sin, pluck it out. It is better for you to enter the kingdom of God with one eye than to have two eyes and be thrown into hell, where "their worm does not die, and the fire is not quenched."

Anyplace that is less preferable than physically removing one's body parts is a place to be avoided at all costs.

### *3. There will be no reprieve.*

The Bible makes it clear that the punishment for refusing God's gift of salvation is eternal—as in, forever. "He will punish those who do not know God and do not obey the gospel of our Lord Jesus. They will be punished with everlasting destruction and shut out from the presence of the Lord and from the majesty of his power" (2 Thessalonians 1:8–9).

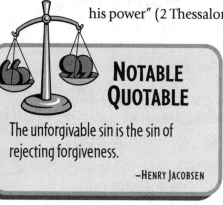

**NOTABLE QUOTABLE**

The unforgivable sin is the sin of rejecting forgiveness.

—HENRY JACOBSEN

Jesus said that those who do not repent and believe in Him "will go away to eternal punishment, but the righteous to eternal life" (Matthew 25:46). You'll notice that the same word is used to describe both eternal fates. If eternal life is guaranteed, so is eternal punishment.

God will not have a change of heart a couple million years or so into eternity and decide that the people in the lake of fire have suffered enough. When He removes His presence from them, it is forever. And that means their suffering is forever.

## Is That Your Final Response?

What's all this to us? As Christians, we don't have to worry about going to hell when we die. How, then, should we respond to this information about Satan, demons, hell, and eternal damnation? Actually, there are three logical responses we should consider.

### *1. Praise*

Considering topics such as Satan and eternal suffering should inspire us to redouble our efforts to show our thankfulness to God. First, there's the fact that because we're protected by God, we don't have to fear Satan or his demons. The apostle John put it this way: "You, dear children, are from God and have overcome them, because the one who is in you is greater than the one who is in the world" (1 John 4:4).

Second, there's the recognition that we, all of us, deserve eternal punishment in hell for our sin. Only God's grace and the sacrificial gift of His Son saves us.

### *2. Determination*

Knowing what awaits people who refuse God's gift of salvation should light a fire under us to make sure that everyone in our circle of influence is aware of that salvation. God has given believers a vital role in spreading the good news of His Son. What we need to understand, though, is that we're literally facing a matter of life and death—eternal life and death, that is. And the stakes don't get any higher than that.

**ON A PERSONAL NOTE**

Make a list of the people you know who, based on what you know of their spiritual condition, would be condemned to hell if they were to die today. The purpose of this exercise is not to depress you but to motivate you. You see, you have the information your friends and loved ones need to escape their eternal fate.

### *3. Vigilance*

One of the most dangerous things you can do is assume that you know all you need to know about Satan, that you've completely figured out his mode of operation, and that you've completely safeguarded yourself against his attacks. The fact is, nothing is predictable or even recognizable about Satan's attacks.

As soon as you let down your guard, Satan will be on you like paparazzi on British royalty, convincing you to give in to temptation, anger, doubt, or fear; disrupting your relationship with God; and reducing your effectiveness as a witness to unbelievers.

The problem is, the moment you congratulate yourself on winning one battle, you're halfway to losing the next one. There is no cease-fire where Satan is concerned. He wants to thwart God's purposes and will work tirelessly to do so.

That's why it's vital for you to keep your guard up. Continue to study God's scouting report of our opponent. And, above all else, make sure that your protective armor is firmly attached.

## Know What You Believe

How much do you know about Satan and his dominion? Here's a quiz to test your knowledge.

1. Which of the following is true of Satan?
   a. He is the ruler of hell.
   b. He is a deity, but not part of the Trinity.
   c. He was created wicked by God.
   d. He spends time in heaven.

2. Which of the following is most likely part of Satan's appearance?
   a. An angelic glow
   b. A red tint
   c. Clawlike fingernails
   d. A muscular physique

3. Which of the following is not one of Satan's primary endeavors?
   a. Confusing unbelievers about the nature of God's forgiveness
   b. Accusing Christians of sin before God's throne
   c. Tempting believers into failure
   d. Creating new demons to combat the increasing number of new Christians

4. Which of the following items is not part of the armor of God described in Ephesians 6:10–18?
   a. The belt of truth
   b. The helmet of salvation
   c. The face mask of denial
   d. The shield of faith

5. Which of the following is not true of hell?
   a. It is something to be avoided at all costs.
   b. It has its good points and its bad points, just like any other place.
   c. It is never-ending.
   d. It's not God's choice for any of His creatures.

*Answers: (1) d, (2) a, (3) d, (4) c, (5) b*

CHAPTER 7

# Living in Paradise

## SNAPSHOT

"Okay, like I was saying, the name of the game is 'Heaven,'" Kris explained to the group. "You get five seconds. If you can't come up with something, you're out. I'll start, and then we'll go clockwise around the table. Ready? Here goes. In heaven . . . no one works overtime."

"In heaven . . . everyone has a Tennessee drawl," June said.

"In heaven . . . all dogs are black labs," Kim added.

"In heaven . . . all changing rooms in women's clothing stores have lights with dimmer switches on them," Sue said.

"In heaven . . . no one calls anyone else 'Dude,'" Greta added.

"In heaven . . . golfers are not considered athletes," Kris continued.

### SNEAK PREVIEW

1. Heaven is the eternal destination of everyone who accepts God's gift of salvation, which came in the form of His Son, Jesus Christ.
2. Ultimately, the specific details of heaven are beyond our comprehension.
3. Angels are simply God's messengers, serving Him and Christ's church on earth; to think of them as anything more than that is a mistake.

"In heaven . . . um, they—" June stammered.

"Time's up!" Greta announced. "You're out!" June shook her head and pulled her chair back from the table.

"Okay, my turn," Kim said. "In heaven . . . babies have a self-cleaning feature, like ovens do."

"In heaven . . . all changing rooms in women's clothing stores have lights with dimmer switches on them," Sue said.

"You just said that!" Kris pointed out.

Sue smiled as she pulled her chair back from the table. "I know," she said, "but I thought it was too good to use just once."

"Okay, here we go again," Greta said. "In heaven . . . the phone hookup guy has to wait for *you*."

"In heaven . . . teachers get paid more than professional athletes," Kris added.

"In heaven . . . they have those—oh, what do you call those little things?" Kim said as she gestured frantically.

"Time's up!" Kris announced. "Kindly remove your chair from the table."

"And then there were three," Sue said.

"Okay, last round," Greta said. "In heaven . . . no one uses their astrological sign as an excuse for their personality flaws."

"In heaven . . . no one in your family ever asks when you're going to get married or whether you're dating anyone," Kris added.

"Oh, that's a good one," Greta acknowledged. "I mean, in heaven—"

"You're out!" Sue called from the side. "Game over!"

"In heaven . . . they know how to do *real* party games," Greta muttered.

* * * * * * * * * * * * * * * *

What *is* heaven like? *After Life,* a 2000 Japanese film, offered a unique view of the world beyond this one. In the film, characters were given a chance to select one memory from their earthly lives to take with them into eternity. Heaven, then, became that moment for them. For example, if someone were to choose, say, the moment he first tasted filet mignon, his heaven would be an eternal experience of that first taste of steak.

**NOTABLE QUOTABLE**

It is strange how, when we imagine heaven, we think of it as somehow shadowy. We color it with the tints of moonlight, sleep, and the faces of the dead. But there are no shades there; there is the substance of joy, and the vitality of action. When we are there, and look back on earthly life, we shall not see it as a vigorous battlefield from which we have gracefully retired; we shall view it as an insubstantial dream, from which we have happily awoken.

—AUSTIN FARBER

Obviously, the film is the product of the screenwriter's imagination. Most people who believe in heaven would agree that it's not a glorified rerun. But what if it were? What if you had to choose one memory from your earthly existence to hold onto for eternity? What would it be? Do you think it would be enough to sustain you forever and ever? More importantly, if you knew that's what heaven was all about, would you want to go there?

Although most of us have earthly memories we wouldn't mind reliving again and again, to view that as "heaven" would be to seriously underestimate what God actually has in store for believers.

So, if heaven isn't a continuous loop of our all-time favorite moments on earth, what is it? What has God come up with as a reward for those of us who accept His gift of salvation? What is this goal that we're all working toward?

Think of this chapter as a primer for eternity, a brief tour of the heavenly realm—or, at least, what we know of it—and an introduction to some of its residents, namely, the angels.

## Eight Things You Need to Know About Heaven

If you're an aficionado of the Game Show Network—or just game shows—you know that there's always a moment in every game when the host turns to the announcer and says, "Tell our contestants what they're playing for!" Sometimes it turns out to be a new car; sometimes it turns out to be a year's supply of Sue-Bee honey. (Either way, the studio audience will "ooh" and "aah" as though they've just discovered the Hope Diamond. But we digress.)

In the Christian life, our grand prize is heaven. It's only fitting, then, that we show you what you're "playing" for.

In the pages that follow, you'll find eight facts about heaven, some of which may seem familiar to you and some of which may come as a surprise.

### *1. Heaven is the eternal reward of all believers.*

God doesn't call any of His followers to a nice, comfortable earthly existence. His will for our lives rarely coincides with our own. What's more, the work He requires of us quite often . . .

- involves more than a little personal sacrifice,
- brings us into contact with people we otherwise probably wouldn't associate with,
- puts us at odds with our friends and family members, and
- makes us vulnerable to the attacks of others.

And, though we may suppress it for as long as we can, sooner or later the question is bound to pop up: *What's in it for us?*

The answer, of course, is heaven—the privilege of spending eternity with God.

When Jesus said, "For God so loved the world that he gave his one and only Son, that whoever believes in him shall not perish but have eternal life" (John 3:16), He was talking about eternal life in *heaven*. When Jesus said to the repentant thief on the cross next to His, "I tell you the truth, today you will be with me in paradise" (Luke 23:43), He was setting up a rendezvous in *heaven*.

Getting a handle on what heaven *is*, however, can be tricky. The Bible doesn't exactly give us a color brochure of the place. In the pages that follow, we will try to acquaint you with what God's Word does say about our eternal dwelling place.

For now, though, we'll simply point out that God considered heaven worth the life of His only Son.

### *2. Heaven is God's dwelling place.*

If you remember only one fact about heaven, this is the one: God is there. We could pare the list down to this single point and still say everything we need to say about the Christian afterlife. You see, *heaven is God's presence.* Just as fire produces heat, God's presence produces heaven.

To extend that analogy a little further, we'll point out that the closer you get to fire, the warmer you feel, because fire is the source of heat. God, on the other hand, is the source of all joy, contentment, wisdom, and fulfillment.

Therefore, the closer we get to Him . . .

- the happier and more joyful we'll feel,
- the more content we'll be simply to enjoy His goodness,
- the more complete our understanding of Him and His work will be, and
- the more fulfilled we'll be.

Those are tantalizing prospects, especially when you consider that heaven offers us the opportunity to be this close to God—forever.

Revelation 22:5 suggests that the light of God's presence fills every nook and cranny of our eternal home. Think of it as sunshine on steroids. God's presence will permeate completely. No place and no one in heaven will be untouched by His glory.

**JUST WONDERING**

**Should I feel guilty about not being excited about heaven?**
Not necessarily. Like the rest of us, your attitude toward enjoyment and "fun" is tainted by your sin nature. You can't appreciate the perfection of heaven because you have no clue what perfection is really like. Therefore, descriptions of heaven—especially the ones that feature endless praise and worship—tend to inspire boredom and dread, instead of excitement and anticipation. If you're not excited about the prospect of eternity in heaven, ask the Holy Spirit to clear up your thinking, rearrange your priorities, and give you a sense of what perfect joy, contentment, and fulfillment will be like.

### *3. The architectural design of heaven is unprecedented.*

Most of what we know about the physical layout of heaven comes from the apostle John's description in the last two chapters of the Bible, Revelation 21 and 22. Here are some of the highlights:

- Officially, our eternal dwelling place will be known as the "new Jerusalem"—that is, the Holy City (Revelation 21:2).
- The city's overall appearance will be crystalline and golden (Revelation 21:11, 18).
- The city will be constructed as an enormous equilateral cube, with each side measuring in at about 1,400 miles—or 12,000 stadia, if you prefer (Revelation 21:16).
- The city's foundation will be made up of twelve layers of stones inlaid with jewels (Revelation 21:19–20).
- The walls of the city will be made of jasper, a kind of quartz (Revelation 21:18).

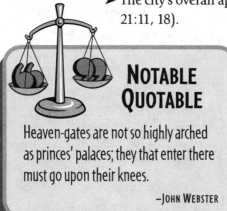

**NOTABLE QUOTABLE**

Heaven-gates are not so highly arched as princes' palaces; they that enter there must go upon their knees.

—John Webster

- The walls of the city will be approximately 200 feet thick—or 144 cubits, if you prefer (Revelation 21:17).
- The walls of the city will have the names of the apostles engraved on their foundation layers (Revelation 21:14).
- Each of the city's walls will contain three solid pearl gates (Revelation 21:12–13, 21).
- Each of the twelve gates (three on each of the four walls) will be named for one of the tribes of Israel (Revelation 21:12).
- New Jerusalem will feature plenty of waterfront property; the "river of the water of life" will flow from God's throne right through the middle of the city (Revelation 22:1–2).

- The Tree of Life, which you may remember from the Garden of Eden story in Genesis 2, will be centrally located in the Holy City (Revelation 2:7).
- The main thoroughfare of New Jerusalem will be made of transparent gold (Revelation 21:21).
- The main attraction of the city will be God's throne, which will be situated before an immense sea of glass, surrounded by a rainbow—and made all the more intimidating by the thunder and lightning roaring from it (Revelation 4:1–6).

If these descriptions inspire more "Huh?" than "Wow!" in you, don't fret. Understanding what heaven looks like isn't a prerequisite for getting in. You may or may not be able to picture a city constructed as a cube or streets paved with clear gold or solid pearl gates. What's ultimately important is that you understand that *everything* about heaven will inspire a deep sense of awe, appreciation, and excitement in us.

You don't have to be a gemologist to recognize that sapphires, emeralds, topaz, amethysts, and the rest of the precious stones mentioned in Revelation 21—not to mention the pure gold everywhere—will make a pretty impressive sight. Likewise, you don't have to be a student of apocalyptic literature to recognize that the heaven John saw in his vision will exceed even our loftiest expectations.

**ON A PERSONAL NOTE**

Make a list of the people you've known who, based on everything you know about their lives and their commitment to Christ, are likely in heaven right now. Your list may include family members, friends, classmates, coworkers, and casual acquaintances. Try to imagine how each of them might describe heaven to you, based on their firsthand observations.

### 4. *Every believer will have a permanent residence in heaven.*

In 2 Corinthians 5:1, the apostle Paul described our earthly body as a "tent," a temporary dwelling. He then contrasted that with what awaits us in heaven—"an eternal house . . . not built by human hands." Imagine having a place to call home forever and ever!

Now imagine having a home designed and built by the Lord Himself. Before Jesus left His disciples, He made them this promise: "In my Father's house are many rooms; if it were not so, I would have told you. I am going there to prepare a place for you" (John 14:2). When it comes to house construction, you can't ask for anyone better qualified than Jesus. Not only does He have extensive carpentry skills, He can point to the entire universe as a showcase for His creativity and design.

**NOTABLE QUOTABLE**

Modern man, if he dared to be articulate about his concept of heaven, would describe a vision which would look like the biggest department store in the world, showing new things and gadgets, and himself having plenty of money with which to buy them.

—ERICH FROMM

By the way, if the idea of having a "room" in heaven seems anticlimactic to you, consider this: The New King James Version translates the word in John 14:2 as "mansions."

Regardless of its size, though, we can rest assured that our permanent dwelling in heaven will exceed our every expectation. If you're unsure about that, take a look at the universe that surrounds you and consider that it was a *six-day* job for the Lord.

Imagine what He's done in the 2,000-plus years He's been working on our heavenly homes!

### *5. Heaven will be a place of unimaginable happiness.*

Revelation 21:3–4 offers one of the most striking descriptions of heaven in all of Scripture: "Now the dwelling of God is with men, and he will live with them and be their God. He will wipe every tear from their eyes. There will be no more death or mourning or crying or pain, for the old order of things has passed away."

Among the things that will pass away are our earthly bodies, along with all of our disabilities, sickness, and pain. No longer will we be hindered by imperfect bodies. Our new models will be perfect—and built to last forever.

Likewise, all of our emotional frailties will be rendered obsolete. None of us will ever have to deal with depression, sadness, or loss in eternity. Can you imagine what that will be like?

### *6. Heaven will be "Worship Central."*

If you had to sum up life in heaven in one word, your best bet would probably be *worship*. The image of heaven presented in the book of Revelation is one big worship-fest. Take a look at some of these passages:

> And the twenty-four elders, who were seated on their thrones before God, fell on their faces and worshiped God, saying: "We give thanks to you, Lord God Almighty, the One who is and who was, because you have taken your great power and have begun to reign." (11:16–17)
>
> After this I heard what sounded like the roar of a great multitude in heaven shouting: "Hallelujah! Salvation and glory and power belong to our God, for true and just are his judgments." (19:1–2)
>
> Then I heard what sounded like a great multitude, like the roar of rushing waters and like loud peals of thunder shouting: "Hallelujah! For our Lord God Almighty reigns." (Revelation 19:6)

If the prospect of worshiping for eternity seems less than thrilling, it's because our perception of worship is imperfect, to say the least. For many Christians, worship is an obligation, a Sunday responsibility, a way of "paying God back."

Worship in heaven, on the other hand, will be less of a responsibility and more of a natural reaction. Worship in heaven won't be a matter of having to put in a couple of hours in front of God's throne every day before we're allowed to go off and do the heavenly things we enjoy. Instead, it will likely be an automatic response to the glory of God all around us.

#### JUST WONDERING

**How will I be able to enjoy heaven if I know that some of my friends and family members are suffering in hell?**
From a biblical perspective, we can theorize that the new bodies we receive in heaven will include new memory banks, meaning that our time on earth, and the relationships we formed here, will be forgotten. Another possibility is that God will give us His perspective on eternity, and that will be enough to "wipe away" our grief and mourning. From a practical standpoint, though, we can render the entire question moot by doing everything we can to make sure that everyone we care about–that is, everyone we come into contact with–joins us in heaven!

Remember, in heaven—at Worship Central—we'll be able to see God up close and personal. And what we see will amaze, delight, and awe us—and will continue to amaze, delight, and awe us forever. Just as a great play in a baseball game makes fans stand up and cheer, a glimpse of God's glory will make the citizens of heaven worship. And the fact that God's glory will be *everywhere* in heaven means that our worship will always be fresh, exciting, and vibrant.

### *7. Heaven is only the beginning of our rewards.*

Rewards await many of us in heaven. The apostle Paul wrote: "For we must all appear before the judgment seat of Christ, that each one may receive what is due him for the things done while in the body, whether good or bad" (2 Corinthians 5:10). This isn't a judgment to determine whether a person goes to heaven or hell. This judgment is strictly for believers.

We can't "earn" our way into heaven with our good works; salvation is a gift from God. However, the way we live our lives *after* we receive God's gift of salvation—specifically, the priorities we set for ourselves and the work we accomplish according to God's will—will determine whether we receive additional rewards or not.

The Bible indicates that these additional rewards will be presented in the form of crowns. Second Timothy 4:8 refers to the "crown of righteousness." James 1:12 mentions the "crown of life." First Peter 5:4 talks about the "crown of glory." What's more, 1 Thessalonians 2:19 suggests that people who come to know Christ as a result of our witness will become our crown of rejoicing.

What will we do with those crowns? Revelation 4:10–11 presents the image of God's creatures throwing their crowns before His throne, as the ultimate gesture of worship and praise. Giving our crowns to God is a way of acknowledging that He alone is worthy of worship and praise. The Bible doesn't specify how many crowns are available to us, but it does make it clear that the privilege and honor of offering crowns to God is much more significant than our earthly minds might imagine.

### *8. Ultimately, heaven is beyond our wildest imagination.*

We can never fully understand the wonders awaiting believers. First Corinthians 2:9 makes this point quite clearly: "No eye has seen, no ear has heard, no mind has conceived what God has prepared for those who love him." We can catch glimpses of our eternal home in a few select passages of Scripture, but the complete concept of heaven is unfathomable to us—at least, for now.

The problem is that heaven is perfect. Having spent all of our time in an imperfect world, we're easily overwhelmed by the idea of perfection in any sense. The fact is, we can't begin to imagine what it's like to live in a place with no . . .

- family tensions
- insecurity
- jealousy
- ulterior motives
- concerns about keeping up appearances
- financial pressures
- self-loathing
- greed
- betrayal
- snobbery

We can *dream* about such a place, and we can *anticipate* it, but we can't truly comprehend it until we see it for ourselves.

### Just Wondering

**Why does Revelation 21:1 refer to a "a new heaven and a new earth"?**

The apostle Peter indicated that on the "day of the Lord"–that is, Christ's return–"the heavens will disappear with a roar; the elements will be destroyed by fire, and the earth and everything in it will be laid bare" (2 Peter 3:10). In their place, God will create a new heaven and a new earth. After that, the place Jesus has prepared for us–the New Jerusalem–will descend from the sky until it touches down on the brand-new earth. And that's where eternity for us will take place.

## Three Things You Need to Know About Angels

No discussion of the heavenly realm would be complete without a look at certain celestial beings that have gained a curious prominence in our society. You can find angels on TV, in the movies, on videos, in commercials, on product labels, on clothes, on bumper stickers, on Christmas trees—not to mention on thousands of knickknack shelves.

But who are they and what do they do? Here are three things you should be aware of when it comes to angels.

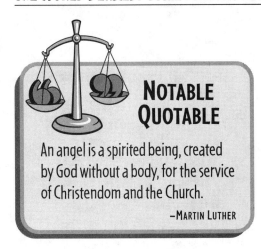

**NOTABLE QUOTABLE**

An angel is a spirited being, created by God without a body, for the service of Christendom and the Church.

—MARTIN LUTHER

### *1. Angels are creatures.*

Angels were created by God, just as we were. The Bible doesn't give us a date for the creation of angels, but it's logical to assume that they were part of the "heavens and the earth" mentioned in Genesis 1:1.

The fact that angels were created means they're *not* deity. (A created being cannot be God.) Angels don't possess the perfections of God that we looked at in chapter 2. They're powerful (Psalm 103:20), but they're not all-powerful. They have a more complete view and understanding of God, His will, and His work than we do—after all, they dwell in His presence—but they're not all-knowing. They will never die (Luke 20:36), but they have not existed forever.

Like all created beings, angels answer to God. They act at His command. They go only where He tells them to go, do only what He tells them to do, and say only what He tells them to say. Contrary to most Hollywood portrayals, they don't "freelance" by getting involved in the lives of unsuspecting people, teaching them valuable life lessons, before returning to heaven bathed in a glowing light.

The fact that Satan and his demonic followers were once angels suggests that angels were created with free will—that is, the ability to *choose* to serve and obey God or not. Angels, however, do not qualify for God's gift of salvation. Hebrews 1:14 makes a distinction between "those who will inherit salvation" and "angels."

### *2. Angels have played a role in some of the key moments of Bible history.*

A good rule of thumb for Bible study is that angels signify important events. If an angel appears in a story you're reading, it's a good bet that something remarkable or significant is about to happen. Check out this illustrious sampling of angelic appearances:

- In Genesis 18, angels announced that Abraham and Sarah, both of whom were well past retirement age at the time, would have their first child, thus beginning the Jewish nation.

- In 1 Kings 19, an angel brought food and comfort to the prophet Elijah during his time of need.
- In Daniel 6, an angel held the mouths of hungry lions closed in order to protect the prophet Daniel, who had been sentenced to death in the lion's den.
- In Luke 2, an angel announced the birth of Jesus to a group of nearby shepherds, thereby giving them a chance to worship the newborn king and inspire a slew of Christmas carols.
- In Acts 5 and 12, an angel released the apostle Peter from prison—twice.
- In Acts 8, an angel directed a Christian named Philip to the chariot of an Ethiopian traveler who was having problems understanding Scripture. Philip was able to answer the man's questions and lead him to Christ.

Don't get the wrong impression here. Sure, angels were present for quite a few Kodak moments in history. But they were in no way calling the shots in any of them. Psalm 103:21 makes it quite clear that angels are "servants who do [God's] will." Period.

### JUST WONDERING

**Do people become angels when they die?**

No. Contrary to popular belief, people aren't given wings, a halo, a white robe, and their own cloud when they depart this planet. They don't become "guardian angels" who are charged with protecting their loved ones, either. Angels and humans are two distinctly different creatures. Humans never become angels, and angels never become human.

***3. Angels are working-class heavenly beings.*** Because of the spectacular nature of some angelic appearances in Scripture—not to mention the influence of mythology—we may be tempted to give angels more credit than they deserve. It's a problem that's been around for a while. In fact, angel *worship* was a fairly common practice in biblical times.

The author of the New Testament book of Hebrews kicks off his letter with an in-depth comparison of Christ and angels, in an effort to prove Christ's superiority. The capping argument is the fact that the heavenly Father says of His Son: "Let all

**NOTABLE QUOTABLE**

It is not known precisely where angels dwell—whether in the air, the void, or the planets. It has not been God's pleasure that we should be informed of their abode.

—VOLTAIRE

God's angels worship him" (Hebrews 1:6). In review, angels are the worship*ers*; Christ is the worship*ee*.

The apostle John learned that lesson during the vision that resulted in the book of Revelation. As John was being shown glimpses of the heavenly realm, he encountered an angel who told him to write what the angel called "the true words of God" (Revelation 19:9). John was so overwhelmed by the angel's appearance that he fell at the angel's feet to worship him. You can almost hear the embarrassment in the angel's voice in Revelation 19:10 when he told John to knock it off: "Do not do it! I am a fellow servant with you and with your brothers who hold to the testimony of Jesus. Worship God!" In other words, don't confuse the worshiper with the worshipee.

Psalm 8:5 tells us that humans were created "a little lower than the heavenly beings"—that is, just below the angels. However, 1 Corinthians 6:3 suggests that in eternity, our positions will change. In that verse, the apostle Paul asks the Corinthian believers, "Do you not know that we will judge angels?"

Let's make this as clear as possible. Angels are God's messengers, His servants—nothing more, nothing less. They serve a valuable role in accomplishing God's work in the world, but they are *not* the originators of that work. They don't protect us; God protects us. They don't watch over us; God watches over us. They don't guide us; God guides us. The fact that angels may be involved in those efforts should not divert our eyes from the One who is ultimately responsible for our well-being.

In short, there's nothing about angels that justifies our worship, praise, or even much of our attention. Any emphasis we place on the work of angels rightfully belongs to God.

# In Response . . .

We know what heaven will mean to us *after* we die. But what about now, while we're still living? How should we react to the knowledge that such a perfect future awaits us? Here are three logical responses to consider.

### 1. *Joy*

A response of joy should be a no-brainer. Who wouldn't be stoked beyond measure, knowing that eternal happiness is guaranteed? What we need to consider, though, is how to make our joy *known* — not only to God, who's responsible for it, but to unbelievers, who can benefit from it.

**NOTABLE QUOTABLE**

Though Christians believe in heaven, sometimes they act as though going there were a calamity.

—HENRY JACOBSEN

Where God is concerned, we can make our joy known through praise, adoration, and thankfulness. Every time we pray, every time we worship, we should have thoughts of eternity plastered on our frontal lobes. In fact, we can even set aside certain times to worship God *specifically* for the gift of eternal life.

We can also memorize such verses as Revelation 21:4 ("There will be no more death or mourning or crying or pain, for the old order of things has passed away") and 2 Corinthians 5:1 ("Now we know that if the earthly tent we live in is destroyed, we have a building from God, an eternal house in heaven, not built by human hands"). Knowing such verses will not only fuel our worship, it will help us maintain our joy about heaven even when the circumstances of our everyday lives are . . . well, less than joyful.

Where unbelievers are concerned, we can make our joy known in the way we act and talk about our future. We can project the kind of confidence, assurance, and eagerness that will attract the attention of people less certain about their eternal destiny. Who knows? The Holy Spirit may use our joy to bring others to Christ.

### 2. *Anticipation*

Paul explained, "Our light and momentary troubles are achieving for us an eternal glory that far outweighs them all. So we fix our eyes not on what is seen, but on what is unseen. For what is seen is temporary, but what is unseen is eternal" (2 Corinthians 4:17–18).

Sure, as Christians, we have our hands full trying to . . .

- accomplish God's work in the world,
- discover His will for our lives,
- maintain a consistent Bible study,
- share our faith with unbelievers, and
- live in a God-honoring way.

Such duties, though, don't mean we can't look ahead from time to time. Come on; this is heaven we're talking about!

When the pressures of trying to live a Christian life in a non-Christian world get to be too much, it's nice to know that we can escape temporarily by dreaming of the place where "our type" are not only accepted but welcomed with open arms.

### 3. *Resolve*

Heaven is not what you'd call an acquired taste. It's not something that only "certain" people will enjoy or benefit from. Knowing what we know about eternal life in God's presence—not to mention the only alternative to it—should motivate us to make sure that every family member, friend, coworker, and casual acquaintance in our sphere of influence will be with us in heaven.

You can find tips for sharing your faith in chapter 12. For now, we'll simply emphasize the importance of assuming the role of human "signposts" who constantly point the way to God and His eternity.

**ON A PERSONAL NOTE**

How would you explain heaven to an unbelieving friend or family member? It's a question worth considering. After all, the apocalyptic language of Revelation may be a little too difficult to understand or appreciate for most non-Christians. How can you bridge that gap? How can you communicate what heaven is like in a way that does it justice, yet still makes sense to people who are uninterested in biblical imagery? Investigate the Bible references in this chapter, as well as any others you find, and come up with an accurate description of what eternity with God will be like–one that you can use when you share your faith.

Toward that end, the goal should be that no one gets "lost" on our watch, that everyone we encounter knows exactly how to get to the heavenly Father—that is, by confessing and believing in Jesus—and what awaits them after they die.

## Know What You Believe

How much do you know about heaven and angels? Here's a quiz to test your knowledge.

1. Which of the following is not true of heaven?
   a. It is never mentioned by name in the Bible.
   b. It is God's dwelling place.
   c. It is a place of constant worship.
   d. It is the eternal reward of all believers.

2. Which of the following is not a physical feature of the New Jerusalem, according to Revelation 21–22?
   a. Walls 200 feet thick
   b. Gates made of solid pearl
   c. Streets made of transparent gold
   d. Rivers flowing with pure chocolate

3. Which of the following will be present in heaven?
   a. Death
   b. Worship
   c. Sickness
   d. Unbelief

4. Which of the following is not true of angels?
   a. They were used by God to assist such Bible characters as Abraham, Elijah, and Peter.
   b. They were created before humans.
   c. Because they are spiritual beings, they are much weaker, physically speaking, than humans.
   d. They often serve as God's messengers.

5. Which of the following is not a logical response to heaven on the part of believers?
   a. Anticipation
   b. Resolve
   c. Joy
   d. Fear

*Answers: (1) a, (2) d, (3) b, (4) c, (5) d*

CHAPTER 8

# Will This Be on the Test?

## SNAPSHOT

"I would definitely say it's been a growing experience for me," Cliff said. He half expected to hear Carl or Kenny snicker behind him, but they just nodded their heads in agreement.

"I'm so glad to hear that," Pastor Singleton said with a broad smile. "I was afraid that people might get frustrated trying to keep up with the schedule. Three chapters a day can be a lot, especially in some of the . . . shall we say, less action-packed books of the Bible."

"But they're *all* interesting; that's what's amazing to me!" Carl chimed in.

"Amen to that!" Pastor Singleton said. "It does this old man good to hear you say that. I was afraid that my generation was the last one to truly appreciate Old Testament study."

### SNEAK PREVIEW

1. Studying God's Word is the lifelong responsibility of every Christian.
2. There are many resources available to assist us in understanding God's Word.
3. When we study a Scripture passage, we should consider what it meant to its original readers, what application it has to our lives, why it's included in God's Word, what connection it has to other Bible passages, and what we will take away from it.

"I can't wait to get to my Bible every morning," Kenny said. "It's exciting not knowing what you're going to learn next!"

"Oh, how I wish I could listen to your testimony all day," Pastor Singleton said as he glanced at his watch. "Unfortunately, I'm due at a board meeting in five minutes." He gave them each a warm smile and a wave and then walked out the door.

Cliff, Carl, and Kenny looked at each other, their smiles still frozen on their faces. "Is he gone yet?" Cliff asked through his teeth.

Kenny glanced out the church door and nodded. All three of them exhaled at the same time.

"Oh, man," Carl said, "what's the punishment for lying to the senior pastor?"

"What were we supposed to say?" Kenny asked. " 'Yeah, we're still on pace to make it through the Bible in a year, but we haven't remembered a word we've read since the middle of Genesis'?"

"Will somebody *please* explain the beginning of Numbers to me?" Cliff asked. "It's like someone dropped a couple pages from a census report right into the middle of the Bible without anyone noticing."

"You know what?" Carl said. "We're getting ready to have a Bible study in a couple minutes. Maybe we should start working on a positive attitude."

"Yeah, you're right," Kenny agreed. "I can say something positive about the Book of Numbers."

"What?" Cliff challenged.

"It's not Leviticus," Kenny said.

"Amen to that!" Carl and Cliff shouted in unison.

* * * * * * * * * * * * * * * *

In chapter 5, we looked at what the Bible *is*. We're going to kick off this chapter by taking the opposite approach and look at what the Bible *isn't*.

The Bible is not . . .

- an "elective" in the Christian life,
- a thoughtful gift from God for people who are into reading,
- a luxury item for people who have extra free time they can devote to it,
- something that's just nice to have around in case we need it, or
- a Sunday fashion accessory.

The Bible is, in fact, the lifeblood of the Christian faith.

The author of Hebrews 5:12–14 took his readers to task for their lackadaisical approach to the Bible. Look at his words: "In fact, though by this time you ought to be teachers, you need someone to teach you the elementary truths of God's word all over again. You need milk, not solid food! Anyone who lives on milk, being still an infant, is not acquainted with the teaching about righteousness. But solid food is for the mature, who by constant use have trained themselves to distinguish good from evil."

As far as the author was concerned, the idea of a Christian who needed to be taught the basic truths of God's Word was as unsettling and unnatural as an adult drinking mother's milk from a bottle.

With so much to be learned, so much to be gained, and so much to be experienced, the author was disgusted that the Hebrew Christians were content to remain relatively ignorant about God's Word. Apparently, the Hebrew Christians assumed that just being saved was enough for them. They were content to live on "baby food" their entire Christian lives instead of digging into the "meat" of God's Word. What they didn't realize is that they were missing out on much-needed spiritual nourishment.

If you want to think of it in more contemporary terms, the idea of someone being content with merely accepting God's gift of salvation and not exploring the truths of His Word is like someone receiving a free pass to Disney World and choosing to spend their entire stay next to the turnstiles at the front entrance because they figure the walk to the rides and attractions is too much work. So, to answer the question in the chapter's title, no, we don't study Scripture because it will be on a test. We study because we need it to grow and mature as Christians.

## So Many Approaches, So Little Time

If not studying God's Word isn't an option, we next have to decide how we're going to approach our story. Let's take a look at some of the different options.

### *The Storybook Approach*

The Bible works on one level as pure literature, a Book full of memorable stories. If you commit to reading it as a piece of literature, you will find stories that excite you (see Abraham's near sacrifice of Isaac in Genesis 22), as well as stretches of text that are about as exciting as a small-print legal disclaimer (see the entire Book of Leviticus).

You'll find stories that touch you (see the parable of the lost son in Luke 15) and stories that repulse you (see the brutal siege of Samaria in 2 Kings 6). You'll find square-jawed heroes (David, Daniel, Shadrach, Meshach, and Abednego) and hissable villains (King Herod, Queen Jezebel, Goliath). You'll find romance (Isaac and Rebekah, Jacob and Rachel, Boaz and Ruth), intrigue (Judas Iscariot betraying Jesus for money), and surprise endings (Jesus Christ's future return to earth to claim what's rightfully His).

If you like historical nonfiction, you can find definitive accounts of the beginning of the world, the earliest days of the Jewish nation, life in captivity, the earliest missionary journeys, the origin of the Christian church, and much more.

If you choose to approach the Bible from a literary perspective, you'll get a good overview of its diversity and scope. In the process, you'll also learn who the main characters are, what they did, and what happened to them as a result.

**JUST WONDERING**

**Does God punish people for not studying His Word?**
He doesn't take back His gift of salvation, if that's what you're asking. However, He does withhold the blessings and growth that come from regular, committed Bible study—blessings such as wisdom, discernment, peace of mind, spiritual maturity, and confidence.

The drawback of approaching the Bible as literature is that it makes you a spectator instead of a participant. Studying the Bible means involving yourself in the passages you read. The stories are not purely for our enjoyment. They are intended to reveal God and His work to us in ways that strengthen our knowledge of and faith in Him.

### *The Inspiration Book Approach*

The Bible contains some of the most comforting passages in all of literature:

- "Even though I walk through the valley of the shadow of death, I will fear no evil, for you are with me; your rod and your staff, they comfort me" (Psalm 23:4).
- "Because of the LORD'S great love we are not consumed, for his compassions never fail. They are new every morning; great is your faithfulness" (Lamentations 3:22–23).
- "And surely I am with you always, to the very end of the age" (Matthew 28:20b).

We can use Scripture as a pick-me-up whenever we're feeling down. For example, we can look for . . .

- words of encouragement when we break up with a boyfriend or girlfriend,
- words of comfort when we lose a loved one,
- words of calm when our world seems to be spinning out of control,
- words of assurance when we're frightened,
- words of motivation when we're lethargic, and
- words of clarity when we're confused.

And, if we look hard enough, we'll find the words we need. The Bible is full of comfort and inspiration. Reading certain passages can help us feel closer to the One who made us and who watches over us.

The drawback to focusing our attention on matters of inspiration is that it doesn't expose us to the complete work of God. Almighty God is not some grand greeting card designer in the sky, dispensing Christian clichés to make us feel better. He's the Sovereign Deity whose power should leave us in awe.

God doesn't exist to make us feel better. In fact, there are times when God chooses to make us quite uncomfortable, to pull us out of our comfort zones and stretch us in ways we've never experienced before. That's how we grow as Christians.

But if we confine our study time to the "Hallmark" passages of the Bible, we'll miss out on that stretching and growth.

### *The Rule Book Approach*

The Bible can also be studied as the ultimate arbiter of right and wrong. If you want to know what you can and can't do—what's acceptable and what's not, as far as God is concerned—the Bible is the place to go. In it, the dos are pretty clear and the don'ts are unmistakable. Study them long enough, and you can set some pretty clear standards and boundaries for yourself.

You can start with the Ten Commandments and figure out how they apply to your life. Take the command "Remember the Sabbath day by keeping it holy" (Exodus 20:8), for example. The Christian equivalent of the Sabbath is our day of worship, which is traditionally Sunday. Using the rule book approach to Scripture, you would first ask the question, "What, specifically, should I do to keep that day set apart from the rest of my week?" From there, you can develop guidelines as to what is and isn't acceptable for you to do on Sunday.

Beyond the Ten Commandments, you've got Jesus' commands in the Gospels, as well as the instructions that God gave us through Paul, Peter, John, and the rest of the New Testament authors. Here's just a sampling:

- "Do not judge, or you too will be judged," (Matthew 7:1)

**NOTABLE QUOTABLE**

I study my Bible as I gather apples. First, I shake the whole tree that the ripest may fall. Then I shake each limb, and when I have shaken each limb, I shake every branch and every twig. Then I look under every leaf.

—MARTIN LUTHER

- "Therefore go and make disciples of all nations, baptizing them in the name of the Father and of the Son and of the Holy Spirit, and teaching them to obey everything I have commanded you" (Matthew 28:19–20a).
- "Don't have anything to do with foolish and stupid arguments, because you know they produce quarrels" (2 Timothy 2:23).
- "Therefore, rid yourselves of all malice and all deceit, hypocrisy, envy, and slander of every kind" (1 Peter 2:1).
- "Do not love the world or anything in the world" (1 John 2:15a).

You can find instructions and guidelines in Scripture that can be applied to every situation you will ever face. But if looking for rules to live by is your entire focus in studying God's Word, you're going to miss out on a lot of important concepts, including grace, forgiveness, and worship.

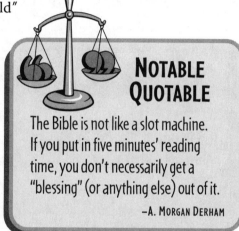

> **NOTABLE QUOTABLE**
>
> The Bible is not like a slot machine. If you put in five minutes' reading time, you don't necessarily get a "blessing" (or anything else) out of it.
>
> –A. MORGAN DERHAM

### *The Self-Help Book Approach*

The Bible can certainly be approached as the ultimate source for self-improvement tips. For one thing, God's Word is chock-full of role models for us to study and emulate. If we look carefully at their stories, try to understand why they did what they did, and break down their life changes into easily followed steps, we too can develop . . .

- the courage of Shadrach, Meshach, and Abednego,
- the encouraging spirit of Barnabas,
- the faithfulness of Daniel,
- the patience of Job, and
- the tough-love skills of Paul.

In addition to the biographical models, you've got entire passages of Scripture devoted to making us more loving (1 Corinthians 13), more serving, (John

13:1–17), more generous (Mark 12:41–44), and just generally more exemplary (1 Peter 2:11–21).

The problem with a self-help approach to Bible study is that it tends to ignore passages that aren't directly and immediately applicable—which, as it turns out, is a significant chunk of the Bible.

### *The Hebrews 4:12 Approach*

Hebrews 4:12 says, "For the word of God is living and active. Sharper than any double-edged sword, it penetrates even to dividing soul and spirit, joints and marrow; it judges the thoughts and attitudes of the heart."

> **NOTABLE QUOTABLE**
>
> No one ever graduates from Bible study until he meets its author face to face.
>
> —Everett Harris

*That* is the ideal attitude to take into Bible study.

To say that this approach combines the elements of the other four would be selling it short. The Hebrews 4:12 approach views the Bible as a living entity, capable of infiltrating every area of our lives and impacting us at our very core.

Yes, the Bible can entertain and challenge us. Yes, it can inspire us. Yes, it can guide us. Yes, it can improve us.

But it can also *define* us. It can dictate who we are. It can recalibrate our internal settings.

This is the way David approached Scripture (even though, technically, Hebrews 4:12 wasn't written until a millennium or so after David's death). Look at his words in Psalm 119:97–105:

> Oh, how I love your law! I meditate on it all day long. Your commands make me wiser than my enemies, for they are ever with me. I have more insight than all my teachers, for I meditate on your statutes. I have more understanding than the elders, for I obey your precepts. I have kept my feet from every evil path so that I might obey your word. I have not departed from your laws, for you yourself have taught me. How sweet are your words to my taste, sweeter than honey to my mouth! I gain understanding from

> your precepts; therefore I hate every wrong path. Your word is a lamp to my feet and a light for my path.

Do you think David was born with that kind of zeal for God's Word? Probably not. It's likely something that grew within him as he spent more and more time familiarizing himself with Scripture.

The same holds true for us. We may not have been born with a desire to be changed by God's Word. In fact, we may not even have had that desire when we gave our lives to Christ. But we can develop that desire, the same *need* for Scripture that David had. All it takes is . . .

- a commitment to spend time regularly studying God's Word and
- a willingness to reflect on what we read.

Any changes that occur in our lives will be initiated by God, so we'll leave the details of that to Him. What we can do is give you some tips for developing consistent, committed, and effective Bible study habits.

## The Four Ps of Bible Study

Our attitude toward Bible study will go a long way toward determining whether our study is ultimately successful or not. Specifically, there are four "P Attitudes" that we need to bring to our investigations of God's Word.

### *1. Priority*

The first hurdle to starting a personal Bible study is finding the time to spend in God's Word. We live in a world of ever-changing schedules and constant demands on our . . . blah, blah, blah.

Let's get this straight. We're not talking about scheduling another work meeting, social engagement, or personal pastime. We're talking about something *important.* In every schedule, there are "have-to's," "need-to's," and "like-to's." The "have-to's" are the things that are so important, we don't even think of them as priorities. For example, we *have* to sleep, eat, shower, and work or go to school. But those aren't things we schedule in our daily planners, because they're givens—they're "have-to's."

On the next level of priority are the "need-to's," the responsibilities we *need* to make time for in order to maintain a healthy, well-balanced life. Those might include things like working out, dating or spending time with our spouse, cleaning our house, and getting our car serviced.

Finally, there are the "like-to's," the things that we prefer to do when we get a spare moment. Those might include anything from going to a movie to playing recreational badminton.

The point we need to make is that studying God's Word should not be a "like to" priority for us. It's not something that we should consider as simply a great way to spend our free time. Think about how often we get around to other "like to" activities. Once a week? Twice a month? That's not acceptable where Bible study is concerned. God's Word deserves to be more of a priority.

Oh, and by the way, Bible study isn't a "need to" priority, either.

Studying God's Word is an absolute "have to," every bit the priority that working, showering, and sleeping are. (We'll explore how to give God's Word that kind of priority in your life in chapter 17.) If that seems like an overstatement, consider the fact that we can't grow as Christians without studying God's Word. And not growing as Christians simply isn't an option.

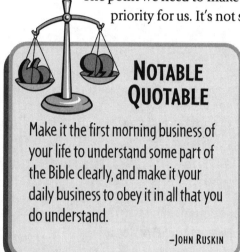

**NOTABLE QUOTABLE**

Make it the first morning business of your life to understand some part of the Bible clearly, and make it your daily business to obey it in all that you do understand.

—John Ruskin

Why? Because when we refuse to grow in our faith, we're not just hurting ourselves. Remember the body of Christ—the idea of all Christians working together as one unit to accomplish God's will in the world? If we don't grow, by refusing to make Bible study a top priority in our lives, we're creating a handicap for the entire body of Christ.

### 2. *Purposeful*

We can't expect to open a Bible to a random page, read a couple of verses, and receive the blessings and wisdom from it that God intended any more than we can expect to open a phone book, pick out a random name, and find our spouse for life.

Bible study requires a purposeful attitude. The good news is that that sounds a lot more complicated than it really is. For example, starting in Genesis and reading straight through to Revelation in order to find out what's in the Bible is a purposeful approach. Studying the life of Jesus in the first four books of the New Testament is a purposeful approach. Later in this chapter, we'll describe some more purposeful approaches to Bible study that you might consider.

The point we want to emphasize is that our approach to studying the Bible shouldn't be haphazard. Sure, there's truth to be discovered on every page. But until we see the "big picture"—how those different truths fit together—we can't fully appreciate God's Word.

### 3. *Prayerful*

Prayer is to Bible study what low expectations are to Chicago Cubs baseball fans: an absolute necessity. Remember, with Bible study, we're talking about attempting to understand the wisdom of God using our finite brains. We need all the help we can get.

Fortunately, we have access to all the help we need. The Holy Spirit is like the "lifeguard" of Bible study, always vigilant, always ready to save us whenever we get in over our heads.

If we want to stretch that analogy even further, we could say that some portions of the Bible—the Book of Genesis or the Gospels, for example—are like zero-depth pools. They're beginner-friendly. They allow us to ease our way in slowly, to get our feet wet before we continue on to deeper areas. Other portions—the books of Leviticus and Revelation, for example—are like riptides right off the shore: A couple of steps in, and suddenly we're struggling to stay afloat.

**JUST WONDERING**

**Should I feel guilty about neglecting my Bible study?**
Guilt really isn't something you can *choose* to feel. You can decide how you're going to deal with it, but you can't force yourself to experience it. If you do experience guilt feelings over your lack of time spent studying Scripture, it may be God trying to tell you something. Needless to say, it would probably be a good idea to respond constructively to those feelings.

**NOTABLE QUOTABLE**

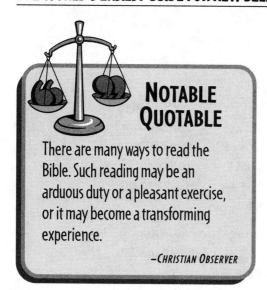

There are many ways to read the Bible. Such reading may be an arduous duty or a pleasant exercise, or it may become a transforming experience.

—*CHRISTIAN OBSERVER*

In both of those extremes, as well as everything in between, it's nice to know that there's always Someone on duty to help us when we start to feel a little uncertain about our "swimming" skills. So we come to Scripture with a prayerful attitude, asking for direction from the Holy Spirit.

If we want to get specific, there are three things we need to ask of the Holy Spirit every time we open God's Word:

1. a clear head, so that we can block out the events of the day and concentrate on what's before us;
2. an open heart, so that we can be receptive to the leading of Scripture; and
3. a special wisdom, so that we can understand truths far beyond the limits of our IQ.

Prayer is also appropriate *after* Bible study. If we learn something new about God or His work in the world, we should mention it to Him and give Him the praise He deserves.

**NOTABLE QUOTABLE**

If a man's Bible is coming apart, it is an indication that he himself is fairly well put together.

—JAMES JENNINGS

### *4. Permanent*

With so many things vying for our attention every day, there's a very real chance that whatever we learn in our Bible study today will be a distant memory by the time tomorrow rolls around. That's why it's vital that we keep a written record of our studies.

The technical name for it is journaling. (We'll explore how it can be used in prayer in chapter 9.) Journaling reflects an attitude that insights into God's Word are worth recording and recalling. Think of a journal as a Bible study "diary." As you study a passage, you can write down the following:

- any emotional reactions you have to it—that is, if it makes you feel thankful, guilty, secure, or anything else

- any connections to other Bible passages that pop into your head—that is, if it reminds you of another incident or principle in Scripture
- any questions you have about it—why it's in the Bible, what it's supposed to mean, whether you can learn anything from it, and so on
- any motivation that it gives you—that is, if it inspires you to share your faith with a coworker, restore your relationship with a former friend, or investigate a specific area of your Christian faith

Over time, you can begin to incorporate your journal into your Bible study. With a little knowledge and experience in God's Word under your belt, you can go back through your journal and investigate some of the questions you had about earlier studies.

You can also use your journal as a spirit booster when you start to doubt your Christian growth. When you go back and look at some of your earliest questions and comments about Scripture, you'll be able to see just how far you've come and how much you've grown.

## Tool Time

All right, we've got the project laid out in front of us. Now let's talk about the tools we need in order to build a sturdy Bible study habit.

As far as expenses go, Bible study ranks somewhere between rubberband collecting and golf. The good news about purchasing Bible study tools, though, is that any investment in making God's Word clearer or more personal to us immediately pays for itself in the eternal scheme of things.

### Just Wondering

**What should my Bible study journal look like?**

Obviously, most of it will depend on your personal preferences. But here are three suggestions you might want to consider: (1) Devote one full page to each day's study. You don't necessarily have to fill each page, but you should get in the habit of writing more than a couple of sentences about each study.
(2) Write the Bible reference at the top corner of the page for easy reference when you're flipping through your journal. (3) Write in complete sentences, instead of using fragments and shorthand. It will make for easier interpretation when you go back over what you've written. Otherwise, you may not have any clue about what you were trying to communicate.

Let's take a look at some of the different Bible study resources you might want to check out.

### *1. Bible(s)*

Shopping for a Bible in a well-stocked Christian bookstore is like trying to choose a cereal in the breakfast food aisle of a supermarket. There are just too many tasty options to consider.

First of all, you have to choose a translation. But which one? The NIV? The KJV? The NKJV? The NASB? The NLT? The NCAA? The ASAP? The MSRP? (Okay, those last three aren't really Bible translations—yet.) As you probably gathered from the word *translation*, the differences among the various Bibles involve language. In short, some translations are easier to understand than others. Likewise, some translations are considered "truer" to the original texts than others.

If you're a novice when it comes to Bible study, you might want to concentrate on comprehension first. Find a Bible that you can understand. Nearly all of the Bible passages quoted in this book come from the New International Version (NIV). If you've been able to understand them, that might be a good place to start your search. Compare and contrast different versions to see which one works best for you. Ask your pastor, Sunday school teacher, or trusted Christian friends for their opinions. In other words, put some thought into your selection of a Bible.

Whatever translation you decide on, make sure that it comes in a study Bible format. (Most of the major Bible translations do.) A study Bible is a must for new believers. Among the features study Bibles offer are:

- individual book introductions that explain when the book was written, who wrote it, who it was written to, what was happening while it was being written, what's in it, and how it's related to other books,
- notes at the bottom of each page that provide helpful information about individual verses, and
- cross-references to other verses that deal with the topic you're studying.

You might also want to consider gradually stocking your bookshelf with different Bible translations so that you have immediate access to different phrasings of the passage you're studying. You'd be surprised at the effect a simple word change here and there can have on your interpretation and understanding of a particular Bible passage. The result of a well-stocked bookshelf will be a broader understanding of the passages you study.

### *2. Journal*

You can find blank journals at most discount department stores. The size, shape, and model you choose will depend on how you plan to use your journal. Do you want something portable? Something whose outward appearance matches its inward importance? Something that will lie flat on a table for easy writing? It's up to you. As long as it can be written in, it can be a journal.

### *3. Bible dictionary*

You're going to run across some unfamiliar words in Scripture. A Bible dictionary will provide you not only with the definitions of those words, but some history and related facts to help you better understand the context of the passages you're reading.

### *4. Concordance*

There will be occasions in your Bible study when you'll want to find a particular verse or passage, or when you'll want to find additional passages on the topic you're studying. That's where a concordance comes in handy. A concordance contains an alphabetized list of important words and topics in the Bible. Each entry is followed by a list of passages that contain the word. Many study Bibles have mini-concordances in them.

If you have a study Bible, its concordance will probably be sufficient to get you started in your own personal Bible study. In time, though, you'll want to move up

**ON A PERSONAL NOTE**

Set aside some time to spend at your local Christian bookstore, "test-driving" Bibles in order to find one that's right for you. Begin each test-drive in the interior of the Book, carefully considering the translation, the information that's included, the layout, the readability–anything that will affect your study habits. Once you've settled on the interior you like, you can choose the style and model of the exterior. Depending on your store's selection, you may be able to choose anything from a standard softcover edition with the words "Holy Bible" as the only design element to a deluxe genuine leather hardcover edition with your name embossed in gold lettering right on the cover. Remember, though, as with most things, it's what's inside that really counts.

to a more comprehensive model, one that meets your growing Bible study needs. If you don't have a study Bible, you'll need to find a concordance you can use.

### *5. Atlas*

A Bible atlas is a collection of maps of the Middle East and surrounding areas at various points in Bible history. Not only does it give you a chance to see how the land changed over the years, it also gives you a sense of location for Bible events. For example, when you read that Jesus passed through Samaria on His way to Jerusalem, an atlas can give you an idea of how far the journey was. Good study Bibles contain most of the maps you'll need for your Bible study. If you don't have a study Bible, try to find an inexpensive Bible atlas that works for you.

### *6. Commentary*

A commentary is a resource written by a Bible expert that offers insight and analysis of what's being communicated in each verse. As was the case with your Bible, you'll need to find a commentary that you can understand. Unfortunately, most theologians and Bible commentators aren't known for their breezy writing style. You should be able to find one that works for you, but it may take some time. Ask someone at your local Christian bookstore for help.

### *7. Books written about the Bible*

Many great books have been written about God's Word. Such books can provide insight, illustrations, and perspective that you can't get from reference material. Keep in mind, though, that while these books can be used to *supplement* your Bible study, they should never replace it. In other words, don't let the time you spend reading *about* God's Word replace the time you spend reading God's Word.

We should emphasize that everything on this list except the Bible and the journal are optional. They're great tools to have around, but they're not absolutely necessary. In other words, it is certainly possible to have a life-changing Bible study without them.

## Study Hall of Famers

Earlier in the chapter we mentioned the importance of being purposeful in our approach to Bible study. Here are a few Bible study ideas that you might want to consider.

### *1. Through the Bible*

You start with Genesis 1 and work your way through the Bible at the rate of one chapter a day. That's a leisurely pace, to be sure. If you're extremely consistent in your study, it will take you about three years and three months to complete the entire book.

Along the way, you'll encounter some dry spots. Some books will seem to go on forever. However, when you're finished, you will have a sense of the big picture of Scripture. You'll know not only who the major characters are, but how they're related. You'll also have a working knowledge of how the books of the Bible are arranged.

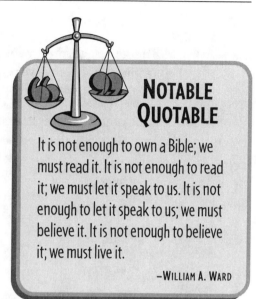

**NOTABLE QUOTABLE**

It is not enough to own a Bible; we must read it. It is not enough to read it; we must let it speak to us. It is not enough to let it speak to us; we must believe it. It is not enough to believe it; we must live it.

—WILLIAM A. WARD

### *2. Biography of Jesus*

You start with Matthew 1 and work your way through the Gospels (Matthew, Mark, Luke, and John), studying the life of Jesus from four different perspectives. At the rate of one chapter a day, you can finish all four books in about three months.

Not only are the Gospels easy to read and full of familiar stories (the Christmas story of Jesus' birth, the Easter story of Jesus' death and resurrection), they also contain a wealth of applicable information. Just about every word that Jesus spoke has an important lesson in it, if we look hard enough. (Most Bibles print the words of Jesus in red type for easy reference.)

### *3. Book study*

You focus your attention on one book of the Bible at a time, and not necessarily in order. Depending on the book you select, your study may take anywhere from five months (for the Book of Psalms) to, well, one day (the Books of Obadiah, 2 John, 3 John, and Jude). The upside of this type of study is that you can cut your teeth on books that hold your interest (such as Genesis or Acts) before you move on to more challenging books.

### *4. Topical study*

This one requires a concordance. You choose a topic and then study several different passages throughout Scripture that are related to that topic. For example, the topic of romantic love may take you from the Old Testament Song of Songs to the famous "Love Chapter" of the New Testament, 1 Corinthians 13.

Among other topics ripe for study are . . .

- forgiveness
- heaven
- God's will
- sexuality
- anger

A topical study is a great way to get a biblical perspective on a subject that you may be wrestling with. On the other hand, you need to make sure that you choose a wide variety of passages to study so that you get an accurate reading of what the Bible has to say on the subject.

**ON A PERSONAL NOTE**

Ask the person who led you to Christ or some other trusted Christian friend to recommend a favorite book of the Bible for you to study. As you learn more and more about the book, share your discoveries with your friend.

### *5. Character study*

Perhaps you'd prefer to study the life of a famous Bible character. Scripture offers a wealth of complex, imperfect characters whose lives can serve as both sterling examples and warnings to us. Studying their experiences and their interactions with the Lord can give us insight into our own lives and relationships with Him.

If you're curious about which characters are worth studying, check out Hebrews 11, which is known as the "Faith Hall of Fame." Each of the characters listed in the passage demonstrated faithfulness that earned God's stamp of approval. That's something worth investigating, wouldn't you say?

# Dissecting God's Word

All right, we've got the mind-set, we've got the strategy, we've got the tools, and we've got the material to be studied. Now let's get specific. How, exactly, do we study a passage in God's Word?

Obviously, everyone has unique study habits and patterns. There are, however, five questions that can be applied to any type of study, in any book of the Bible.

### *1. What did this passage mean to its original readers?*

The Old Testament was written for Jewish people. Jewish religious practices, beliefs, and history figure prominently in it. In order to fully understand what's going on, we have to familiarize ourselves, at least a little, with those practices, beliefs, and history. (The ever-helpful study Bible offers this kind of information at the beginning of each book and in the notes related to individual verses.)

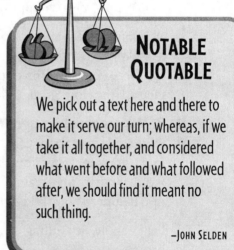

**NOTABLE QUOTABLE**

We pick out a text here and there to make it serve our turn; whereas, if we take it all together, and considered what went before and what followed after, we should find it meant no such thing.

—John Selden

Books in the New Testament were also written to specific audiences, which means each of them has a unique slant. For example, the gospel of Matthew was intended for Jewish people, while Luke's gospel was directed to Gentiles. As a result, though they're both telling the same story, each author emphasizes a different aspect of Jesus' life. Recognizing those different emphases can go a long way toward helping us understand more fully who Jesus is.

The books by Paul, Peter, John, and other New Testament writers were actually letters written to specific first-century churches (or groups of churches) who were facing specific problems and challenges in their congregations. In order to fully appreciate those books, we need to understand the underlying circumstances that caused them to be written in the first place.

### *2. Does this passage have any obvious application to my life?*

Some Bible passages, such as Matthew 5:44 ("Love your enemies and pray for those who persecute you"), are pure application. Other passages, such as Luke 13:15 ("You hypocrites! Doesn't each of you on the Sabbath untie his ox or donkey from the stall and lead it out to give it water?"), obviously have no bearing on your day-to-day life. Most passages fall somewhere between those two extremes.

You need to ask yourself whether the passage you're studying contains any of the following:

- commands for you to obey
- reminders of sin that you need to confess
- examples for you to follow or learn from
- words of comfort to help you through a painful situation
- principles for improving your interpersonal relationships

You don't want to stretch a passage's meaning to fit your personal situation or try to make connections where there are none. If you're not sure whether a passage applies to your situation or not, write down your questions in your journal and then ask the Holy Spirit to clarify things for you.

### *3. Why is this passage included in God's Word?*

Bible study isn't about you; it's about God. The fact that a passage can't be applied to your personal situation doesn't diminish its value. If a passage is in God's Word, it's there for a reason. That reason may not be obvious to us, but it's there. And it's our responsibility to find it and understand it.

For example, depending on the verses you're studying, you might ask, "Does this passage . . .

- illustrate God's ability to take care of His people in even the most extreme situations?"
- serve as a warning about God's response to sin?"
- make clear just how perfect God's plan is?"

- offer necessary background information to help us understand Jesus' work on earth more fully?"

If no answers jump out at you, take a look back at the circumstances of the book's writing. Knowing who the material was intended for originally may help you understand its purpose.

### *4. Does this passage have a connection to other Bible passages?*

Why did Jesus' disciples believe that the Old Testament prophet Elijah had to come again before the Messiah would show up (Matthew 17:10)? Why did Jesus quote Psalm 22:1 when He was on the cross (Matthew 27:46)? Is there any significance to the fact that Jesus was in the tomb for three days and Jonah was in the belly of the fish for three days?

Drawing lines between related Scripture passages will help us develop a big-picture view of God's Word. Your concordance will come in handy in answering these questions, but it won't be able to highlight all connections. You'll also have to rely on your memory and your journal. If something about a passage seems familiar, go back and review some of your earlier journal entries to see if you can make the connection.

As we warned earlier, though, don't try to force connections between passages or convince yourself that common ground exists where it doesn't.

### *5. What am I going to take away from this passage?*

The answer to this question is what you will include in your journal. You can base your answer on your responses to the previous four questions. Keep in mind, too, that you can study the same passage ten different times and come up with ten different answers to this question.

That's the beauty and the challenge of studying God's Word.

## A Sneak Preview

We've spent two chapters now talking about God's Word and how to study it (see also chapter 5). And we're still not done. In chapter 17, we get down to the nitty-gritty of developing a personal Bible study habit, including . . .

- how to choose the best time of day to study,
- how long you should spend in study, and
- how to decide whether group Bible study is right for you.

Check it out.

## Know What You Believe

How much do you know about Bible study? Here's a quiz to test your knowledge.

1. Which of the following is a true statement?
   a. Bible study is just icing on the cake, as far as God's concerned; all that really matters to Him is that we repent and believe in Christ.
   b. The only Bible passages that God expects us to study are the ones that directly affect our everyday lives.
   c. Effective Bible study requires supernatural assistance.
   d. Most people are born with a desire to read and understand God's Word.

2. Which of the following is not one of the four "P Attitudes" of Bible study?
   a. Purposeful
   b. Prayerful
   c. Permanent
   d. Phlegmatic

3. Which of the following is not necessarily a helpful tool for Bible study?
   a. Scanner
   b. Commentary
   c. Concordance
   d. Atlas

4. Which of the following is not a recommended Bible study option?
   a. Studying the life of Jesus in the Gospels
   b. Focusing on one Bible book at a time

c. Reading until you get bored
d. Working your way through the entire Bible

5. Which of the following is not a helpful question to ask when trying to understand a Bible passage?
a. Why is this passage included in God's Word?
b. What else could I be doing with my time right now?
c. What am I going to take away from this passage?
d. What did this passage mean to its original readers?

*Answers: (1) c, (2) d, (3) a, (4) c, (5) b*

CHAPTER 9

# Dear God

## SNAPSHOT

"Would you like some fresh ground pepper on your salad?" the waiter asked.

"No, thank you," Deb replied.

"And you, ma'am?"

Sharon kept her head bowed and eyes closed and said nothing.

"Sharon," Deb said with a nervous laugh, "he asked if you want pepper on your salad."

Sharon's lips moved slightly, but no sound came out.

Deb gave the waiter an apologetic smile. "She's, um, not feeling very well right now," she said. "I don't think she wants any pepper."

The waiter shrugged and walked away.

### SNEAK PREVIEW

1. As Christians, we pray not to influence or change God's plan, but to become part of it.
2. Our prayers–the way we speak to God and the things we pray for–should reflect the fact that God knows everything, including what's best for us.
3. Our prayers should include four elements: adoration, confession, thanksgiving, and supplication.

Deb gave Sharon an icy stare. "What are you *doing?*" she hissed.

Sharon looked up. "I'm praying; why?" she asked.

"You looked like you were nodding off," Deb said. "I thought you were going to go face-first right into your Thousand Island dressing. It was really embarrassing."

"There's nothing to be embarrassed about," Sharon said. "I pray before every meal."

"Well, aren't you a good little Christian," Deb said. "And what happens if you forget or if someone interrupts you right in the middle of your prayer? Does God zap your taste buds and make everything taste like cabbage?"

"No, sometimes He just seats really annoying people at my table," Sharon said with a smile.

"Go ahead and finish your prayer," Deb insisted.

"Thank you," Sharon replied.

Deb waited for Sharon to bow her head, then said, "Maybe later we can get everyone in the restaurant to hold hands and sing, 'Kumbaya' over dessert."

* * * * * * * * * * * * * * * *

Prayer has been called . . .

- the lifeblood of Christianity,
- the source of a believer's strength,
- one of the two most important weapons Christians have to defend themselves against Satan (the other being God's Word), and
- the most effective vehicle for changing the world.

Needless to say, serious topics call for serious preparation. In gathering the material for this chapter, we've picked the brains of some of the leading experts on prayer, pored over hundreds of the most famous prayers ever written, and delved deeply into the historical records of answered prayer.

After amassing an impressive body of information, and after rewriting, revising, and clarifying every paragraph and every sentence to ensure maximum comprehension and understanding, we are prepared to offer you a guarantee. If you will commit yourself wholeheartedly to . . .

- investigating the Bible passages we highlight in this chapter, along with any other relevant prayer passages you discover,
- talking to your pastor or other mature Christians about any prayer questions you may have, and
- applying every principle and every piece of advice in this chapter to your own prayer life,

we guarantee that you will . . . still not understand how prayer works.

Let's be clear here. The Lord says . . .

- "Ask and it will be given to you" (Matthew 7:7).
- "If you believe, you will receive whatever you ask for in prayer" (Matthew 21:22).
- "I will do whatever you ask in my name" (John 14:13).

But nowhere in the Bible does He say, "Let me show you what prayer's all about."

Job 11:7 asks, "Can you fathom the mysteries of God? Can you probe the limits of the Almighty?" The fact is, some things about God and His work are knowable; some things aren't. In this chapter, we're going to stick with the knowable. Instead of trying to solve the mystery of how prayer works, we're going to focus on the nuts and bolts of the process itself—namely, *why* we pray and *how* we pray.

# P-R-A-Why?

What's a good reason to pray? In answering that question, we may be tempted to fall back on platitudes and declare that *any* reason is a good reason to pray. But that's not true at all. For example, there's nothing "good" about praying for God to . . .

- give you enough money to hire Bill Gates as your personal secretary,
- break the leg of an opposing quarterback so that your team has a better chance of winning, or
- supernaturally lower your blood-alcohol level when a police officer pulls you over after a party.

Some people pray "just to be safe." They're not really convinced that prayer does much good, but they're worried that something might happen if they *don't* pray. So they throw up a few quick words of thanks, maybe speed through a recital of the Lord's Prayer, and then get on with their day.

For them, prayer is like a good-luck charm. Say a prayer, and you'll have a good day. Forget to pray, and watch out. With that kind of attitude, it doesn't take long for the *ritual* of prayer to become more important than the prayer itself. Praying becomes about as spiritually rewarding as brushing your teeth or taking your vitamins.

This "superstitious" attitude not only underestimates the power of prayer, it makes God look bad. You see, God isn't motivated by vengeance. He's not going to send a string of bad luck your way to get even with you for forgetting to pray. That's not how He works at all.

Don't forget; prayer is a privilege. If you choose not to take advantage of it, that's your loss. Missing out on an opportunity to talk personally with the Creator of the universe is punishment enough. God's not going to put a "hex" on you to rub salt in the wound.

That's not to say that you won't suffer the consequences of a faulty prayer focus. The fact is, the wrong approach to prayer can have a negative effect on your relationship with the Lord. Certain kinds of prayer requests promote a self-centeredness that can disrupt your Christian walk.

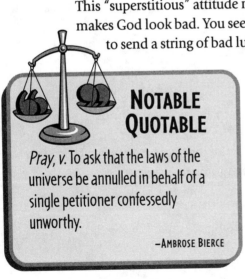

**NOTABLE QUOTABLE**

*Pray, v.* To ask that the laws of the universe be annulled in behalf of a single petitioner confessedly unworthy.

—Ambrose Bierce

Whether you're creating a brand-new prayer life for yourself or revamping some old prayer habits, the place to start is your attitude toward God. In the most famous prayer ever uttered, Jesus summed up in four words the perfect prayerful attitude toward His Father: "Your will be done" (Matthew 6:10).

Contrary to popular opinion, we don't pray to influence or change God's will or plan; we pray to become a part of God's will or plan.

Remember, God is loving and all-knowing. His plan for our lives is perfect. Not only does He want what's ultimately best for us, He knows exactly how to bring it about. Praying with the right attitude is simply a matter of recognizing God's perfections—a matter of deferring to His expertise and attaching ourselves to His perfect will.

## ACTS-ion!

If attitude were everything when it comes to prayer, we could end this chapter right here. But having the right attitude, knowing *why* we pray, is only the beginning of a healthy prayer life. The next step is understanding *how* to pray, knowing what to say when your head's bowed and your eyes are closed.

Fortunately for us, the Bible offers some excellent models to follow. First, there's the Lord's Prayer (Matthew 6:9–13), the *Citizen Kane* of prayers, from which we just quoted. This is the prayer Jesus used to teach His disciples to pray, and it's still recited by believers around the world today.

Second, there's the Book of Psalms, which is like a "greatest hits" compilation of Old Testament prayers. No matter how you're feeling or what your circumstances are, you can find a psalm that speaks to you—or, more accurately, you can find a psalm that speaks to *God* for you. Jesus Himself quoted psalms throughout His life, and even during His time on the cross (compare Matthew 27:46 with Psalm 22:1).

Third, there are the prayers of dozens of Bible characters scattered throughout Scripture. The heartfelt praise and requests of everyone from Moses (Exodus 15:1–18) to Deborah (Judges 5:1–31) to Daniel (Daniel 2:20–23) are recorded in God's Word.

By studying these biblical examples, we can pick up some valuable clues as to the kind of prayers that honor God—not to mention the kind of prayers that are, in turn, honored by Him.

One of the most basic and popular models of God-honoring prayer is called "ACTS," which is an acronym for the four elements that are necessary in any healthy prayer life:

- Adoration
- Confession
- Thanksgiving
- Supplication

Let's take a look at these elements to see how each one contributes to a healthy, well-rounded approach to prayer.

## A: Adoring God

The first element of prayer, the "A," is adoration. In simplest terms, prayer is a conversation between you and God. As is the case with all communication, the better you know the person you're talking to, the more effective, rewarding, and fulfilling your conversation will be. What's unique about God, though, is that the more you get to know Him—by studying His Word and by examining the things He's done in your life and in the lives of others—the more impressed you'll be. (Remember, He's perfect, so He has no flaws to temper your excitement about His awesome attributes.)

If you find yourself impressed by who God is, the last thing you want to do is keep your feelings to yourself. Prayer gives you an outlet for sharing your adoration and awe with God Himself. The fact is, every time you pray, you have a chance to praise God in a one-on-one setting. That's not an opportunity to take lightly. You see, without praise, prayer becomes a self-centered activity. Instead of focusing outward, on God, you start to focus inward, on your own situation and requests—and nothing good can come from that.

If you're serious about wanting to develop an effective prayer life, you've got to know how to give God effective adoration and praise—just like the psalmists did. In their prayers, the psalmists focused on three specific areas of praise that you can use as starting points for your own prayers. The psalmists praised God for . . .

- who He is
- what He's done
- what He's doing

Let's take a look at each of these areas to see if we can pick up some important tips.

### 1. *Praising God for who He is*

God wants to hear from us what it is about Him that amazes us, excites us, and makes us thankful. The more specific we are in our praise and adoration, the more effective our prayers will become.

David, the author of Psalm 103, understood this. Look at the way he described God's mercy: "He does not treat us as our sins deserve" (verse 10). Or consider the way he communicated the idea of God's sovereignty: "The LORD has established his throne in heaven, and his kingdom rules over all" (verse 19).

In the space of twenty-two verses in Psalm 103, David managed to squeeze in references to almost a dozen of God's attributes. In other psalms, David chose to single out one or two attributes and focus his entire prayer on them. (There are no minimum requirements of attributes per prayer when it comes to praising God.)

Keep in mind, though, that simply mentioning God's

**ON A PERSONAL NOTE**

Be careful not to praise God for the wrong reasons. You may be tempted to use adoration as a way of "buttering up" God before asking Him for things in prayer. It's the same method you've probably used on a boss or teacher some time ("Have you lost weight? You look really good. By the way, I need Friday off."). With God, it usually goes more like this: "O Lord, You are all-powerful and all-knowing, full of grace and love. And that's why I'm turning to You now, asking You to give us good weather for our golf tournament." The thing is, it's tough to fake sincerity when the One you're talking to can read your mind. God knows when you're being genuine and honest with Him and when you're "praising" just to get something you want. So if you're not going to approach God with sincere praise that comes from the bottom of your heart, you might as well not even bother praising Him at all.

attributes in prayer is *not* quality praise and adoration. Praising God involves making His attributes personal. If you say, "God, You are gracious," all you're doing is stating the obvious. What you need to do is ask . . .

- What does His grace mean to me?
- When have I experienced it in the past?
- What would my life be like if I hadn't experienced it?

These are the kind of questions you'll need to wrestle with as you search for ways to praise God for who He is.

### 2. *Praising God for what He's done*

The Bible is a record of God's work on behalf of His people. Some of the stories of His work are action packed; others are more subdued. Some are flat-out miraculous; others are ordinary. Yet all of them are amazing for one reason: They're evidence of God's concern and care for us.

If you're looking for actions to praise God for, head for the nearest Bible. Start with the first page and work your way through the Old Testament, looking for records of God's work. Then do the same with the New Testament. By the time you're finished, you should have enough raw material for praise to last you . . . oh, a millennium or so.

If you opt for this beginning-to-end search method, the first act of God you'll come to is Creation (Genesis 1:1). Check out how the author of Psalm 104 incorporated praise for God's creation into his prayer:

- "He makes springs pour water into the ravines" (verse 10).
- "The trees of the LORD are well watered" (verse 16).
- "There is the sea, vast and spacious, teeming with creatures beyond number" (verse 25).

You'll notice that the psalmist is doing more than saying, "Lord, You create pretty sunsets." He's connecting the dots between different areas of creation to show just how perfect the Lord's design of nature is. Springs provide water for animals and people alike. Trees provide a home for birds. The oceans provide a home for sea life and food for sea creatures and humans alike. In other words, a long look at God's creation reveals that everything was made for a purpose.

We should point out that these aren't the kind of observations that just occur to people out of the blue. The psalmist must have spent a good chunk of time studying the natural world around him and applying what he found to what he knew of God. The result was that he was able to bring specific, thought-out praise to God.

You can do the same thing—even if you're not the outdoors type. All it takes is an awareness of the world around you and a God-centered perspective. Put it this way: If you're constantly looking for new things to praise God for, you'll find them.

And creation is just the beginning (literally) of what God has done. Every book in the Bible contains stories of His work. Many books contain hundreds of stories. You can build an entire prayer's worth of praise around any of them.

Of everything God has done, though, there's one thing that deserves our praise 24/7. That's the sacrifice He made to give us eternal life. God sent His Son to earth as a human being, knowing that He would be mocked, laughed at, rejected, betrayed, beaten, tortured, and murdered. How horrible do you think it must have been for God to let Jesus go, knowing what was in store for Him? How excruciating do you think it was for Him to watch the people He was trying to save viciously kill His Son?

How can you praise God enough for making that kind of sacrifice for you?

### 3. *Praising God for what He's doing*

God didn't retire when His plan of salvation was finished. Every day, He continues to do more praiseworthy things than we could count in a lifetime. Lamentations 3:22–23 says, "Because of the LORD'S great love we are not consumed, for his compassions never fail. They are new every morning; great is your faithfulness."

"New every morning"—sounds like it belongs in a

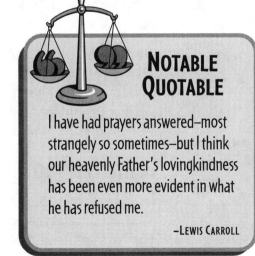

**NOTABLE QUOTABLE**

I have had prayers answered–most strangely so sometimes–but I think our heavenly Father's lovingkindness has been even more evident in what he has refused me.

–LEWIS CARROLL

commercial for milk or bread, doesn't it? *Guaranteed freshness.* Think of the Lamentations passage as a commercial for God. We never have to worry about a shortage of things to praise God for, because He ships in a whole new truckload every morning for us to discover and think about. Our supply is endless—if we're paying attention, that is.

David certainly paid attention to God's work in his life. As a result, he came up with one of the most famous examples of praise ever written in Psalm 23. In just six short verses, David managed to praise God for (1) providing for him: "I shall not be in want"; (2) helping him get his head together: "He leads me beside quiet waters"; (3) keeping him safe in dangerous situations: "I will fear no evil"; and (4) guaranteeing his future: "I will dwell in the house of the LORD forever."

Notice the way David added a personal touch to each of his praises. He didn't just say, "God, You are a great provider and protector"; he said, "[Because of You] I shall not be in want" and "I will fear no evil, for You are with me." David wasn't just praising God for things he'd read about; he was praising God for things he'd experienced firsthand.

That's the kind of adoration God prizes.

Don't misunderstand, though. God doesn't *need* your adoration. In fact, it's safe to say that praising God will do a lot more for you than it does for Him. God *knows* that He's perfect. He doesn't need compliments from us to feel good about Himself. He doesn't have self-image problems. He doesn't need an ego boost.

Praising God gives you a chance to show the Lord, yourself, and the people around you that you "get it." It's really simple. You either recognize and appreciate what God does in your life and in the world, or you don't. If you recognize it, you gain a whole new understanding of the world around you. You see things more clearly. The whys and hows of everyday life make more sense to you.

## C: Confessing Sin

The second element of prayer is *confession*. Nothing messes up our relationship with God like sin. Every time we give in to temptation, every time we let our emotions dictate our actions, every time we put our own needs ahead of others', every time we ignore the Bible's instructions, we drive a wedge between us and God.

Don't misunderstand—sin doesn't *end* our relationship with God. If we believe in Jesus, *nothing* can ever separate us from God (Romans 8:38–39). Sin *can*, however, create all kinds of problems in our relationship with our heavenly Father. And those problems will remain until we open up to Him about what we've done wrong and ask Him to forgive us.

David, the king of Israel, learned the hard way that nothing is lonelier than being separated from God by sin. You can find the story of David's sin, which involved adultery, an illicit pregnancy, and eventually murder, in 2 Samuel 11:1–12:23.

**NOTABLE QUOTABLE**

Do not pray for easy lives. Pray to be stronger men.

—JOHN F. KENNEDY

You can find David's *reaction* to his sin in Psalm 51. Look carefully, and you will also find some tips for praying for forgiveness. For example, consider David's statement to God in verse 4: "Against you, you only, have I sinned." David wasn't worried about his reputation or even his conscience. He was worried about the effect his sin had on his relationship with God. That's why he poured out his feelings in prayer. He had to know that everything was okay with that relationship before he did anything else.

We need to develop that same attitude toward sin in our own prayers for forgiveness. It's not enough to say to God, "Oops, my mistake," and leave it at that. Instead, we've got to step up and take full responsibility for the devastation our sin causes—not only in our own lives, but in the lives of other people and especially in our relationship with God.

It's also important to approach God with the same sense of wonder and unworthiness that David displayed in Psalm 51. Even though David had probably experienced God's forgiveness dozens of times before, he didn't take it for granted. He didn't come to God with an attitude of "I'm here; this is what I did; now where's my forgiveness?" It was more like "I can't believe You would forgive someone who sins like I do."

Notice too that David wasn't after a quick fix. He didn't treat prayer like a drive-thru car wash, a place to get a quick soul cleaning before heading off down the road. David seriously wanted to change the way he acted and the decisions he made. In verse 10, he even asked God for a new heart! That same desire for change should be at the center of our prayers for forgiveness.

## T: Thanksgiving Year-Round

The third element of prayer is thanksgiving. Do you have a place to live? A family that loves you? Friends who care about you? How about an education? Do you have access to water and food whenever you need them? Do you have your sight? Are you generally healthy? Do you live in a safe neighborhood? Can you worship God freely, without worrying about being arrested or killed? Do you have enough clothes to keep you warm? Do you have any talents, skills, or abilities? Do you have the mental ability to understand what you're reading? Have you ever noticed the beauty of the world around you? Do you have any leisure time? How about a job that allows you to support yourself or your family? Does your future look bright? Do you believe you'll go to heaven when you die?

If you answered yes to any of these questions, you have a lot to be thankful for. If you answered yes to *most* of them, you may not even realize just how blessed you really are. And that's a problem.

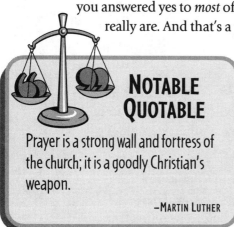

**NOTABLE QUOTABLE**

Prayer is a strong wall and fortress of the church; it is a goodly Christian's weapon.

—MARTIN LUTHER

You see, if you don't have a clue about what you've been given, you don't have much to talk to God about. You may think you do, but you don't. Remember, one-sided prayer really isn't prayer at all. If you're loading God up with new requests all the time and not giving Him His due when He comes through for you, you can't really claim to have a healthy relationship with Him.

Some people try to excuse their one-sided approach to prayer by citing God's omniscience, the fact that He knows everything. They say, "God already knows I'm thankful for everything He does for me. I don't need to tell Him." But that doesn't work. It's like saying, "My parents know I care about them; it's okay if I treat them a little shabby," or "My boyfriend already knows I love him; I don't need to spend any time with him." If nothing else, it's just plain rude.

Worse than that, though, it's also a sign of misplaced prayer priorities. If you look at giving thanks to God as a minor part of your communication with Him, or as something you can skip when time is running short, you need to rethink your prayer structure.

Being thankful isn't a matter of making God feel good. God's not going to throw a fit or start pouting because you forget to say thank you for something. Being thankful is about getting your head straight. You're either the type of person who recognizes and appreciates what God does for you, or you're the type who takes Him for granted.

The psalmists knew how to give God His due. When the Lord did something for them, they were all over it with gratitude and appreciation. And it wasn't just, "Thanks, God—that was a nice thing to do." No, the psalmists would go on for paragraphs about how God's actions had made a difference in their lives. They didn't just want to say, "Thanks"; they wanted to make God look good in the process.

Psalm 116 is a good example of how seriously the psalmists took thanksgiving. In the psalm, the author offers thanks to the Lord for answering an unspecified prayer. For some people, that would have been the end of the story. But not for the psalmist. He didn't end his prayer there. He still had one more thing to do: "I will fulfill my vows to the LORD" (verse 14).

Vows were serious business in ancient Israel. They were like unwritten contracts. If you made one, you were expected to keep it, no matter what. From the psalmist's point of view, giving thanks in prayer was like keeping a vow. If you didn't do it, you were breaking a legal agreement.

The psalmist's prayer of gratitude was not just a way of saying thank you but a way of paying tribute to the Lord. God had honored the psalmist by answering his prayer; the psalmist honored God by making a big deal of it.

When God answers your prayers, He's entitled to your gratitude. It's that simple. If you don't give Him your gratitude, you're sabotaging your prayer life. Halfhearted thanks have no place in our prayers.

So how do you develop a thankful spirit? Glad you asked. Here are a few suggestions:

### *1. Feel it before you say it.*

Expressing thanks isn't hard. You do it all the time. When a guy behind the counter at Burger King hands you a Whopper, you say, "Thanks." When someone says they like your shirt, you say, "Thanks." When someone stops to help you fix a flat tire, you say, "Thanks."

Maybe you're really thankful when you say it, or maybe you're just trying to be polite. Either way, no one's going to question your motives. No one except God, that is. When it comes to being thankful to God, either your feelings come from your heart or they don't. And if they don't, don't bother trying to fake it. God will know.

Earlier, we gave you a list of questions to get you thinking about what you have to be thankful for. If you're not sure that your thankfulness is coming from your heart, try asking, "What if?" For example, What if you'd been born in East Africa and had to worry about you and your family starving to death? What if you suddenly lost your home and had to live on the streets?

When you think about what *could be*, it tends to make you appreciate what *is*. And once you start to feel that appreciation, you can tell God all about it.

Being thankful is more than just saying thanks. It's also a way of admitting that you depend on God for the good things in your life. It's a way of recognizing that without God's help, life would be miserable.

### *2. Count your blessings—literally.*

You live in a busy world. Every day you have dozens of conversations, assignments, and requests to keep track of. Throw in the hundreds of messages you get daily from the TV, radio, and newspaper, and you've got a horde of information scrambling for a prime spot in your memory. The more people and images you encounter, the tougher it becomes to remember them all.

This information overload explains why, if you're not careful, you can lose track of what God has done in your life. The details of His work tend to get swept away when the next wave of information comes crashing in.

If you *are* careful, on the other hand, you'll find a way to anchor that information so that it doesn't get lost. That's where a prayer journal comes in handy. When you pray for something, make a habit of writing down the request and putting the date next to it. When God answers your prayer, do the same. That way, you'll not only have documented proof of God's work in your life (which may come in handy the next time you're feeling down or abandoned), you'll also have a cheat sheet for your prayers of thanksgiving. When it comes time to share your gratitude with God, you'll have mini "cue cards" to work from.

Keep in mind, though, that some of God's answers to prayer are more obvious than others. If you want a complete prayer journal, you're going to have to learn to recognize and appreciate even the small things that God does for you. It will take some work, at first. Until you discover the many different areas of your life where God's answers to prayer can be found, you may get discouraged in your search.

Don't give up, though. With a little practice, you'll get the hang of it. Once you get used to looking for answered prayers, you'll see them everywhere.

**JUST WONDERING**

**Why do people end their prayers with the words "in Jesus' name"?**

Jesus is the One who makes it possible for us to speak directly to God. Remember, our sin created a chasm between us and God, who is holy and separate from sin. Jesus' sacrifice on the cross bridged that chasm and restored the lines of communication between us and our heavenly Father. Concluding our prayers with the words "In Jesus' name" is a way of acknowledging our debt to and complete dependence on God's Son.

### 3. *Make sure your attitude matches your words.*

The psalmists didn't write down their prayers strictly for themselves. They were creating material for worship services. They knew their prayers would be read in front of a group. That meant anything they said about God would be broadcast throughout the area. Like good marketing people, the psalmists jumped on the opportunity to tell others about all that God had done for them.

It wasn't enough for them to say, "Thank You, God, for all You've done for me." No, they had to make a big deal of it. If you read between the lines of many psalms, one of the emotions you'll find is amazement. The attitude that comes across is "Can you believe the almighty Creator of the universe is doing personal favors for somebody like *me?*" And that's a great attitude to have, because it's something everyone can relate to. If you, a normal person, have the guts to start telling others what the almighty Creator is doing in your life—how He listens to and answers your prayers—you'll find that people respond in amazing ways. If you don't think you're the type of person God can use to change lives, think again.

There's one more thing to keep in mind as you're kicking around this idea of thankfulness. *Someone* has to get credit for the good things that happen in your life. Usually what happens is that if God doesn't get it, you do. When people who don't know you well see the blessings in your life, they may assume that you're something special or that you've done all right for yourself. If you don't do anything to change that impression, it's like taking credit for God's work.

Does that sound like something you want to do?

## S: Supplication

The final element of prayer, the "S," is supplication, the part where we take our requests to God. Generally, supplication comes in two flavors: *petition*, which is making requests for yourself, and *supplication*, which is making requests for others. Let's start with petition.

The Bible is full of godly petitions, prayers in which everyone from Moses to Jesus made personal requests of God. So obviously there's nothing greedy or selfish about trying to get your needs taken care of through prayer—as long as your attitude is right.

Earlier in this chapter we discussed the importance of focusing on God and His will when we pray. This is especially important when it comes to petition. If God's will is your number-one priority, your prayer requests for yourself will reflect that.

If you go to the Lord with a list of specific things that you want Him to do in your life, what you're really saying is, "Why don't You hop in the backseat for a while, God, and let me take the wheel. I know more about what's best for me than You do." No matter how self-assured you are, you've got to admit that that's a pretty dumb attitude to take with an all-knowing deity.

The all-star pray-ers who wrote the Book of Psalms knew that God's will for their lives was always better than any plan they could come up with on their own. That's why you'll find prayers like these scattered throughout the book:

- "You are my rock and my fortress. For the honor of your name, lead me out of this peril . . . I entrust my spirit into your hand. Rescue me, Lord, for you are a faithful God" (Psalm 31:3, 5 NLT).
- "Teach me to do your will, for you are my God. May your gracious Spirit lead me forward on a firm footing."(Psalm 143:10 NLT).

The psalmists' plan of action was to lay out their situation before God and ask, "What do *You* want to do about this, Lord?" After that, they asked, "How do You want to use *me* in this situation?" That's a great example to follow.

You may think you have a pretty good idea about what's best for you. You don't. You may be tempted to offer God some advice on what He should do in certain situations. You shouldn't. God isn't sitting around waiting for your suggestions. He has a plan in the works, whether you care to recognize it or not.

If you want to be part of God's will, an instrument in His plan, then pray for His guidance. Give up your own notions of what needs to happen, and go with God's flow.

That same principle applies to intercession. Bringing the needs of other people to the Lord's attention and praying for His will to be done in their lives is one of the most powerful expressions of love at your disposal. But if you're going to do it, do it right.

Here are a few tips to help you get the most out of your intercession.

### JUST WONDERING

**How do I know what God's will is?**

The more time you spend talking to God and reading about Him in His Word, the better you'll get at recognizing His will—what He wants and doesn't want for you. The better you get at recognizing His will, the more effective and streamlined your petitions will become. If you're a beginner when it comes to prayer and don't have any idea what God's will looks like, your best bet is simply to bring all of your requests to God and ask Him to help you recognize His will for each one.

### *1. Get the story.*

The more you know about people, the better you can pray for them. If you care enough about someone to get God involved in his or her life, it's only natural that you'd want to find out as much as possible for your prayers. Keep your ears open whenever you're around the people you're praying for. Learn to listen "between the lines" when they talk to find out how they're feeling and what they're facing in their lives. You might even want to keep a prayer journal handy so that when you get a minute or two to yourself, you can jot down any needs or requests that you stumble onto.

Even if you haven't got a clue about what's going on in someone's life, you can still pray for that person. There are times when it's okay to say, "Lord, I'm not sure what's going on with Homer today, but please help him."

pray for guidance & a sense of peace if not sure what to pray for

You could even get more specific, if you wanted. You could say, "Lord, please guide Homer in the decisions he has to make today," or "God, please give Homer a sense of peace about whatever's worrying him." Praying for guidance and a sense of peace is like giving cash for Christmas. It's always appreciated, and everyone can use it.

### *2. Give God room to work.*

When you pray for someone—especially for someone you really care about and know well—you may be tempted to believe that you know what's best for that person. The problem is, you don't know what the person really needs. And neither does the person you're praying for. Since only God knows what's going on inside and outside, only He can decide what someone *really* needs.

Remember; the way you look at a person's situation and the way God looks at it are completely different. For example, based on what you know, you might be okay with offering God prayer requests like these:

- "Please help Dad get the promotion to vice president that he deserves."
- "Please don't let Mario's grandmother die of cancer. You know how close Mario is to her. If she dies, he'll never get over it."
- "Please let Brian get accepted to Yale."

- "Help LaTonya see that she needs to get rid of the guy she's dating because he's a jerk."

What you may *not* know is that . . .

- the stress of being a vice president would make your dad's life miserable and cause him serious heart problems.
- Mario is already suffering every day because he sees his grandmother in such pain all the time. His grandmother has told him she's ready to die, and Mario is learning to accept it.
- the University of Minnesota has a program better suited for Brian's ultimate career choice—even though Brian doesn't even know what that choice is yet.
- the guy LaTonya is dating is just immature. He has the potential to become an ideal husband and father.

Ask God to show you His solution

Kind of helps to have the big picture, doesn't it? Until you do, you're just guessing at what's best for the people you pray for. That's why, instead of trying to come up with your own solutions, you're always better off asking God to show you His.

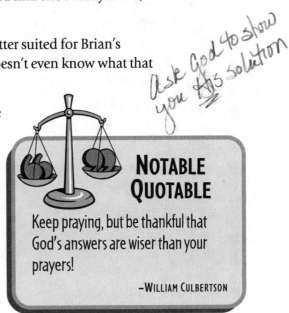

> **NOTABLE QUOTABLE**
>
> Keep praying, but be thankful that God's answers are wiser than your prayers!
>
> –WILLIAM CULBERTSON

### 3. *Get your hands dirty.*

Prayer is not a white-collar job; it's blue-collar work. If you're not willing to get involved in the lives of the people you pray for, all you're really doing is dumping work on God's desk. It's like saying, "Here, God; take care of this for me."

A better way to approach your role in prayer is to ask, "Hey, God, how do You want to use me in this situation?" or "What can I do to be part of Your will in this person's life?" It's the difference between trying to direct God and letting Him direct you.

## Doing It Right - Requires Practice

The great thing about prayer is that you don't have to have any special knowledge or skills to get started. You don't have to learn an ancient language. You don't have to memorize any secret codes. You don't have to enter any passwords to get "online." You just say the words, and God listens.

**ON A PERSONAL NOTE**

To avoid getting into a "prayer rut," try stepping outside your comfort zone and expanding your idea of what prayer is. For example, you might try a prayer session in which you don't say a word. Spend a half hour just listening to God. Or, instead of telling God how great He is, express your feelings in a drawing, painting, or song. Put your natural talents to work. Write an acrostic prayer, like the author of Psalm 119 did. Come up with an analogy that expresses your personal feelings, like the author of Psalm 102 did. Think of your own ideas to spice up your prayers.

Simple, right? Well, yes . . . and no.

Here's the thing. The bow-your-head-and-say-whatever-comes-to-mind method of prayer is okay for beginners. But your prayers, like every other area of your Christian walk, must mature over time. "Now I lay me down to sleep" works for a four year old, but not for an adult.

Prayer is a skill. To master it, you need to practice it. The more you practice, the better you get. As you practice, you'll need to keep four things in mind.

***1. Be creative.***

How seriously do you take your prayers? How much time do you spend in preparation before you actually start talking to God? If you're like a lot of Christians, you might have answered, "Very seriously," to the first question and "Huh?" to the second.

The idea of *preparing* to pray may not have crossed your mind. When it's time to pray, you just open your mouth and let it rip. After all, isn't prayer a spontaneous thing?

Not the way the psalmists looked at it. A quick stroll through the Book of Psalms will give you an idea of how important it was to the psalmists to get their prayers just right. Though some of the psalms are similar in style and wording, all of them have characteristics that set them apart.

The author of Psalm 117 said everything he needed to say in two verses. The author of Psalm 119 took 176 verses to communicate his thoughts and feelings to God. But that's not all. As an added challenge, he designed his prayer as an acrostic. For each of the twenty-two consonants in the Hebrew alphabet, there are eight verses that begin with that letter. How long do you think that took to write?

The psalmists seem to have done their best not to repeat themselves in prayer. In trying to keep their prayers fresh and interesting, they drew on the creativity and imagination that the Lord had blessed them with. Look at the images and language of Psalm 102: "My heart is stricken and withered like grass. . . . Because of the sound of my groaning my bones cling to my skin. I am like a pelican of the wilderness . . . an owl of the desert . . . a sparrow alone on the housetop" (vv. 4–7 NKJV).

By drawing on his knowledge of nature and choosing just the right words, the psalmist was able to create a "visual" prayer. You can actually "see" what he's saying and how he feels. (In case you're wondering, pelicans, owls, and sparrows all live in isolated, lonely places.)

The psalmist could have said, "God, I feel lonely." It would have had the same meaning. But it wouldn't have been the same prayer. The psalmist chose instead to go the extra mile and spice up his prayer with images that the Lord would appreciate. He wanted to bring something creative and different to his conversation with God.

Along those same lines, get a load of these descriptions of the Almighty in Psalm 97: "Clouds and thick darkness surround him. . . . Fire goes before him and consumes his foes on every side. The mountains melt like wax before the LORD" (v. 2–3, 5).

Melting mountains? Now that's a creative prayer. The psalmist could have gotten by with saying, "Lord, You are so powerful." But that wasn't good enough for him. He wanted to find the best, most creative way to express God's power that he could think of.

Does God demand that kind of creativity in every prayer? Of course not. Does He appreciate the extra effort that goes into creative prayers? What do you think? (Hint: Look at the kind of prayers He chose to include in His Word.)

Prayer is personal not repeating someone else's idea of prayer

### 2. *Be yourself.*

Your prayers should reflect your unique situation, your unique style of talking, your unique emotional state, your unique way of looking at the world, your unique method of showing gratitude, and so on. Your prayers should reflect exactly who you are, where you're at in your life, and what you want in your relationship with God—without any pretenses or fakeness.

It's okay to pick up prayer tips from other people, but don't try to copy anyone else. Your prayers should be one of a kind, just like you are.

### 3. *Be persistent.*

Most veteran pray-ers will tell you that they have at least a couple of requests that they've been taking to God every day for years—even decades!

If that seems like a bad strategy to you, check out how the psalmists seem to have felt about asking God for the same thing over and over again:

- "May all my enemies be disgraced and terrified. May they suddenly turn back in shame" (Psalm 6:10 NLT).
- "I will call on the Lord, who is worthy of praise, for he saves me from my enemies" (Psalm 18:3 NLT).
- "I trust in you, my God! Do not let me be disgraced, or let my enemies rejoice in my defeat" (Psalm 25:1–2, NLT).

And these are just three random examples. You can't swing a stick in the Book of Psalms without hitting a verse where someone is asking God to do something about his enemies. You'd think that after a while God would say, "Enough of the enemy stuff! I'm tired of hearing about it. Just get on with your life." But that's not what God does. The fact that He includes these prayers in His Word tells us that He doesn't mind repeated requests.

What we need to keep in mind, though, is that God has His own timeline for doing things. When we bring certain requests to Him, He may smile and say to Himself, "That's not going to happen yet, but if you keep asking, you'll get the answer you're looking for in 1,203 days."

We should also point out that there are a couple of instances in which persistent prayer probably isn't acceptable. First, there's the matter of asking for something that goes against God's will. For example, if you're praying every day to win the lottery, God's probably going to get tired of hearing it. The more you dwell on inappropriate prayer requests, the less effective your prayer life is going to be.

Second, there's the matter of laziness. If you're praying every day for your best friend to become a Christian but never make an effort to share your own faith with her, God probably won't be pleased with your persistence.

But if you feel confident that your prayers are within God's will, and if you're willing to back up your requests with action, there's no reason that you can't pray for the same thing day after day until God answers it. Most prayer requests don't have expiration dates.

### 4. *Be generous with your time.*

With your busy schedule, how much time can you set aside for prayer? A half hour a day? Fifteen minutes? The Bible doesn't give us a minimum amount, so we're on our own when it comes to creating a prayer schedule.

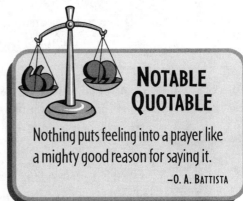

**NOTABLE QUOTABLE**

Nothing puts feeling into a prayer like a mighty good reason for saying it.

—O. A. Battista

David seems to have preferred three-a-days: "Evening, morning and noon I cry out in distress, and he hears my voice" (Psalm 55:17). Of course, that doesn't mean we have to follow his lead. David's schedule may have allowed him to have three uninterrupted times during the day when he could chat with God. We may not have that same luxury.

What's important is that we spend as much *scheduled* time with God as possible. Praying whenever we think of it or whenever we feel like we "need" it just isn't good enough. Instead, we must give prayer the same priority as work, school, exercise, or anything else on our schedule. We must carve out time in our day in which we do nothing but pray. If your relationship with the Lord is a priority in your life, your schedule should reflect that. Obviously, the more time you set aside, the quicker your prayer life will mature and the more positive results you'll see.

In between your scheduled prayer times, too, you can turn to God for quickie conversations or extra boosts of encouragement or peace of mind. And you don't even need to make an appointment!

And if you really want a challenge, look at what the apostle Paul commanded: "Pray without ceasing" (1 Thessalonians 5:17 KJV). In computer terms, that would be like installing a high-speed DSL between you and God. The link would always be open, and information would be continuously flowing back and forth at all hours of the day.

## Two to Grow On

Before we wrap up this chapter, we need to look at two components of prayer that are vital to your continued growth—journaling and fasting. Think of this duo as turbochargers, boosters that can kick your prayer life into high gear. Let's take a look at each of them.

### *Journaling 101*

We mentioned journaling earlier in this chapter as a way of keeping track of answered prayers. But journaling is also a tremendous tool for organizing your prayerful thoughts and for charting God's work in your life and the growth it produces in you.

A journal is a prayer diary, a place to record your adoration, confession, thanksgiving, and supplication—as well as your motivation for bringing them to God. A journal is a place to record the "story behind the story" of your prayers, the personal requests and emotions that trigger your praise and requests.

The most important thing to keep in mind when it comes to journaling is that you're writing for yourself. Your purpose is to create written evidence of God's work in your life, information that you can use as future praise for God and future encouragement for you. For example, when you're facing a discouraging time in your life, imagine how helpful it would be to be able to flip through a notebook with entry after entry of prayers that sprang from similar circumstances—prayers that were eventually answered in ways you never dreamed possible.

### *The Fast Track*

Fasting has long been a secret weapon of prayer warriors. For centuries, veteran pray-ers have used fasting, the discipline of denying food to one's body for a certain period of time as a way of bolstering the urgency of their prayers, purifying their communication with God, and refocusing their personal priorities.

The thinking behind the practice goes like this. We all have natural desires and urges—like hunger—vying for attention every day. Usually these urges take precedence. When we get hungry, we eat. Fasting is a conscious effort to flip those priorities and make the natural desire of hunger secondary to the desire to communicate with God.

If you decide to fast for, say, twenty-four hours, you're determining that, for that period of time, food is less important to you than prayer. Your hunger pangs then become "prayer pangs," causing you not to eat, but to talk to God.

Some people fast during times of crisis, such as when a loved one is seriously ill. Some people fast in conjunction with an organized group prayer effort, such as a church's quest to raise a certain amount of money for missions work. Some people fast on a regular basis simply to keep their prayer life sharp and effective.

Whatever the circumstances or motivation, prayer veterans testify to the fact that fasting makes them feel closer to God and gives them a deeper appreciation for the needs they bring to Him.

## One More Thing

At the beginning of this chapter, we suggested that it's unlikely that you will ever fully understand how prayer works. Please don't let that discourage you. Take comfort in the fact that prayer *does* work. Regardless of the mysteries surrounding the details of prayer, these facts remain:

- You can talk to the almighty Creator of the universe anytime you want.
- He will listen carefully to everything you have to say.
- He will work through your prayers to change your life, the lives of others, and the world!

Amen to that.

## Know What You Believe

How much do you know about prayer? Here's a quiz to test your knowledge.

1. Which of the following is a good reason to pray?
   a. To convince God to trust you, despite His better judgment
   b. To keep God from getting mad at you for ignoring Him
   c. To get the things you want in life
   d. To become a part of God's will or plan

2. Which of the following is not a component of an ACTS prayer?
   a. Thanksgiving
   b. Adoration
   c. Condescension
   d. Supplication

3. Which of the following is not a helpful tip for improving your prayer life?
   a. Be creative.
   b. Be brief.
   c. Be yourself.
   d. Be persistent.

4. Which of the following is not a good reason to keep a prayer journal?
   a. To chart your spiritual growth
   b. To organize your thoughts when you pray
   c. To show your friends what a prayer warrior you are
   d. To keep a record of God's work in your life

5. Which of the following is not true of fasting?
   a. It's a way of reorganizing your priorities.
   b. It's a way of focusing intensely on prayer for a certain period of time.
   c. It can be done in conjunction with a group prayer effort.
   d. It's the only diet program endorsed by God.

*Answers: (1) d, (2) c, (3) b, (4) c, (5) d*

CHAPTER 10

# For Better or Worship

## SNAPSHOT

Charlotte started the car and waited for the digital clock to pop up. "12:45," she muttered. "Forty-five minutes late."

"It didn't really seem that long, did it?" Lindsay said.

"Are you kidding me?" Charlotte asked. "That's the longest church service I've ever sat through."

"What about that time they let the youth group serve communion?" Lindsay reminded her. "That was pretty long."

"Today was longer," Charlotte assured her. "And it makes me mad."

"Is that why you kept clearing your throat during the sermon?" Lindsay asked.

"Hey, someone had to let him know his time was up," Charlotte replied.

"I thought it was a pretty interesting message," Lindsay said.

### SNEAK PREVIEW

1. Worship is giving God His due; what He's due is everything we have.
2. Corporate worship, the kind that takes place in church, involves studying God's Word, praying, singing, giving, and engaging in fellowship with other believers.
3. Personal worship can be done anywhere at any time.

"That doesn't matter," Charlotte replied. "He had *six* points in it."

"What's wrong with that?"

"That should be a two-parter!" Charlotte emphasized. "He should have done three points today and three points next week."

"I never studied sermon law," Lindsay said. "What's the punishment for too many points?"

Charlotte gave her a smirk. "And where did they get that new worship leader?" she asked.

"I think he's a seminary student," Lindsay said. "He's filling in until Mike gets out of the hospital. Why?"

"I think he likes the stage a little too much, if you know what I mean," Charlotte said. "How many songs did he do up there anyway?"

"I wasn't counting," Lindsay said.

"He probably would have done a forty-five-minute encore, if somebody had let him," Charlotte noted.

"Anything else?" Lindsay asked.

"Well, I wasn't going to say anything—" Charlotte began.

"Of course not," Lindsay said. "Someone might think you had a negative attitude toward church or something."

Charlotte ignored her and continued, "—but now that you mention it, I don't think it's a good idea to have visiting missionaries read the Scripture passage before the sermon."

"Why not?" Lindsay sighed.

"Because they always take, like, ten minutes to get around to it," Charlotte explained. "They always do that thing where they say, 'I bring you tidings from Ethiopia, where we are . . . yada, yada, yada.' And then they launch into a long spiel about everything that's ever happened to them in Ethiopia."

Lindsay chuckled.

"What's the matter with you?" Charlotte asked.

"I was just thinking, what if they'd asked *you* to fill in as worship leader," Lindsay said with a grin. "I can just see you up there motioning for the choir to speed up, cutting off the organist if she holds a note too long, and turning off the microphone if Pastor Brian preaches for more than a half hour."

"Laugh all you want," Charlotte said. "But at least people would be in their cars and on their way home by 12:05."

"Better yet," Lindsay suggested. "You could just install a drive-thru worship window, and people wouldn't even have to get *out* of their cars."

* * * * * * * * * * * * * * * *

Worship is the eternal destiny of every Christian. Call it the national pastime of heaven. Even when we're not engaged in worship in heaven, it will be going on nonstop all around us.

Think we're exaggerating? Check out the following quotes from the apostle John's description of heaven in the book of Revelation:

> Day and night they never stop saying: "Holy, holy, holy is the Lord God Almighty, who was, and is, and is to come." (4:8b)
>
> They lay their crowns before the throne and say: "You are worthy, our Lord and God, to receive glory and honor and power, for you created all things, and by your will they were created and have their being." (4:10b–11)
>
> In a loud voice they sang: "Worthy is the Lamb, who was slain, to receive power and wealth and wisdom and strength and honor and glory and praise!" (5:12)
>
> Then I heard every creature in heaven and on earth and under the earth and on the sea, and all that is in them, singing: "To him who sits on the throne and to the Lamb be praise and honor and glory and power, for ever and ever!" (5:13)

The notion of worshiping God forever in heaven probably either thrills you or makes you really nervous, depending on your view of worship. If *worship* to you means singing hymns you don't understand, sitting through one prayer after another on Sunday morning, or trying not to fall asleep during the sermon, you're probably not thrilled with the idea of that scenario repeating itself over and over again throughout eternity.

The good news is that that's not the kind of worship John was describing. The fact is, we're in for a much more . . . *intense* worship experience than anything we've ever participated in.

Think about the most exciting game you've ever seen in person or the best concert you've ever been to. Got it? Now think about the one moment during that contest or performance—whether it was a game-winning shot or the first few notes of a song you never expected to hear in concert—that caused the adrenaline floodgates to open in your body and shot you to your feet, clapping and screaming like a maniac. Think about the exhilaration, the wild excitement, the absolute pandemonium of experiencing such a remarkable event with hundreds (or thousands) of people who appreciated it as much as you do.

**NOTABLE QUOTABLE**

Does not every true man feel that he is himself made higher by doing reverence to what is really above him?

—Thomas Carlyle

Now think about this. If we can appreciate and celebrate such relatively inconsequential things on earth, imagine what worship in heaven will be like when we're finally able to grasp the fullness of God's nature and work.

Worship in heaven, like everything else in heaven, will be perfect. That means it will be free of impurities such as boredom, impatience, wandering thoughts, and personal agendas that interfere with our earthly worship.

And while we may be tempted to sit back and anticipate heavenly worship, we can't lose sight of our responsibility to make our earthly worship a force to be reckoned with. In order to do that, though, we first need to understand what worship is.

# Worship Is . . .

We'll spare you a complex definition from *Webster's* or a long theological discourse on the nature of worship. Instead, we'll simply define the act as "giving God what He is due."-our undivided devotion

Imagine being present the day Michelangelo unveiled his completed work on the ceiling of the Sistine Chapel—arguably one of the most impressive artistic feats in human history. Imagine standing beneath such an awe-inspiring display of artistic genius, rendered in astonishing detail . . . and then walking out without a word or even the slightest reaction.

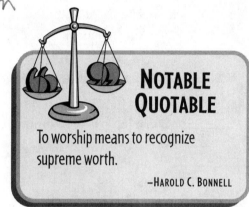

**NOTABLE QUOTABLE**

To worship means to recognize supreme worth.

—HAROLD C. BONNELL

Multiply that scenario by about a billion or so, and you begin to understand the need for worship on the part of all believers. When we consider who God is and what He's done—throughout history and for us specifically—we *have* to respond. To not do so would be unthinkable.

But *how* do we respond? Our "simple" definition of *worship*—"giving God what He is due"—leaves us with two obvious questions: 1. What is God "due" from us? 2. How do we give it to Him?

The answer to the first question can be found in a two-word phrase in 1 Corinthians 7:35. God is due our "undivided devotion." Being devoted to God means committing ourselves to honor Him through our words and our actions. One way we do that is by participating in our church's worship services every Sunday morning. As we'll see later in the chapter, though, that's just the tip of the worship iceberg.

As for *how* we worship God, John 4:24 gives us a good place to start: "God is spirit, and his worshipers must worship in spirit and in truth."

Worshiping God in spirit means the following:

**NOTABLE QUOTABLE**

Those who are wise consider how God responds to their worship.

—DAVID MAINS

- Our worship can and should take place anywhere and everywhere—and not just in church on Sunday mornings.
- Our worship comes from within, as an outpouring of feeling and not simply as an instinct to do what everyone else in church is doing.
- Our focus on God is personal (even in a group setting).

Worshiping God in truth means that we can't fake our devotion to Him. In other words, we need to find a way to worship that's right for us, one that we're comfortable with, and one that doesn't make us feel like we're just going through the motions.

Toward that end, there are two types of worship that we need to acquaint ourselves with: corporate and personal.

**NOTABLE QUOTABLE**

Worship is, in part, listening to what God might say to us, through music, through words, through fellowship. It is also our response to what He speaks. Worship has occurred when life responds with an openness to how God could change our lives.

—C. NEIL STRAIT

## The Corporate Type

Corporate worship generally takes place in church on Sunday mornings. It's the kind of worship Paul described in Ephesians 5:19–21: "Speak to one another with psalms, hymns and spiritual songs. Sing and make music in your heart to the Lord, always giving thanks to God the Father for everything, in the name of our Lord Jesus Christ. Submit to one another out of reverence for Christ."

The corporate worship that goes on in most Christian churches today is based on the practices of the first-century church. Understanding these practices can give us a better idea of how God expects us to worship Him.

Generally, corporate worship of the first-century involved five different practices. Let's take a look at each one.

### *1. Studying God's Word*

Acts 2:42 tells us that first-century church members "devoted themselves to the apostles' teaching" when they got together. That same devotion to God's Word is expected of twenty-first century Christians who gather together to worship God.

Opening our hearts to God's Word and God-honoring teaching—in the form of sermons, dramas, and Scripture reading—is a way of simultaneously discovering and celebrating who God is and what He's done. What better way is there to honor God and show our devotion to Him than to listen intently to His Word in order to find out everything we can about Him?

We worship God by giving Him what's rightfully His—and that includes our undivided attention when His truth is being taught.

### *2. Praying*

When the apostle Paul issued his instructions for church worship in 1 Timothy 2, this is how he began: "I urge, then, first of all, that requests, prayers, intercession and thanksgiving be made for everyone." Prayer came first, as far as Paul was concerned. He understood that communicating with God as one unit helped believers focus their worship attention.

What's more, corporate prayer gives us believers a chance to magnify our personal praise by combining it with the praise of others. Just as the sound of one or two people clapping can escalate into thunderous applause, so too can the prayers of individuals be joined together for a worship experience that is greater than the sum of its individual parts.

#### JUST WONDERING

**How is communion part of our worship of God?**

Communion, symbolically partaking of Christ's body (represented by bread) and blood (represented by wine or juice), is a chance for believers to commemorate Jesus' sacrifice and celebrate what it means for us. What's more, by acknowledging Christ as our spiritual "food," we are indicating that He is the One who sustains and nourishes us. Acknowledging those things with a congregation of fellow believers is a way of building closeness and community.

### *3. Singing*

"When you come together, everyone has a hymn"; "Let the word of Christ dwell in you richly as you . . . sing psalms, hymns and spiritual songs with gratitude in your hearts to God" (1 Corinthians 14:26; Colossians 3:16). Such passages make it clear that music and singing are to play a significant role in our worship of God.

Psalm 100:2 offers these specific instructions: "Worship the LORD with gladness; come before him with joyful songs." You'll notice that it doesn't say "well-sung songs" or even "on-key songs"; just "joyful songs." All God cares about is our attitude in singing, not our talent. That's good news for those of us who couldn't carry a tune if it had a handle on it. Is it so hard to imagine that the Holy Spirit works in our singing in the same way He works in our praying—that is, by transforming our imperfect voices into a beautiful sound to God's ears?

**JUST WONDERING**

**Where does baptism fit in with worship?**

Baptism is a way of sharing our stories as believers with other believers. It is a way of publicly acknowledging our faith in Christ and in God's work of salvation. The water used in baptism represents cleansing, a "washing away" of our sin. Sharing that symbolic cleansing with a group of believers is a way of praising God together for His work.

### *4. Giving*

Second Corinthians 8:5 tells us that giving our individual resources to assist in God's work is a natural extension of giving ourselves to God. And we're not just talking about money, either. Giving, as it relates to worship, also includes our time, energy, and compassion.

What we need to understand, though, is that there's nothing generous or philanthropic about giving our money, time, and energy to God and His work. You see, those things are His already. Remember; worship is giving God what He's due—what He deserves. Most Christians would agree that God deserves nothing less than everything we have. Giving a portion (10 percent or more) of what we have back to Him is simply our way of acknowledging His ownership of them.

It's not a matter of our saying, "Hey, God, look at what I'm giving You." It's more a matter of our saying, "God, after all You've done for me, the least I can do is give this back to You." (We'll talk more about tithing—that's the fancy name for giving our resources back to God—in chapter 17.)

### *5. Fellowshiping*

We'll discuss fellowship, our interaction with other believers, in detail in the next chapter. For now, we need to understand that devoting our time, energy, attention, and commitment to God's people is a way of worshiping God Himself.

Remember, God intends for the body of Christ to function as one unit in order to accomplish His work and promote His glory. As individual believers, our responsibility is to make sure that our part of the body functions in harmony with those parts around us. That involves fellowship—maintaining a loving, caring, strengthening, encouraging, and supporting relationship with the Christians around us.

**NOTABLE QUOTABLE**

One of the acid tests of a Christian is his attitude toward his possessions. Someone has figured out that one out of every four verses in the Gospels is related to this attitude. I think the emphasis can be condensed into a single phrase: What we worship determines what we become. If we worship material possessions, we tend to grow more materialistic. If we worship self, we become more selfish still. That is why Christ continually endeavored to direct men's worship.

—Harvey F. Ammerman

## Getting Personal

Those are the elements that make up corporate worship. But that's not where our worship responsibilities end. You see, there's also the matter of personal worship to consider. When you consider who we're worshiping, it should come as no surprise that one day a week just isn't enough to finish the job.

Lamentations 3:22–23 says, "Because of the LORD'S great love we are not consumed, for his compassions never fail. They are new every morning; great is your faithfulness." Shouldn't our worship be as fresh as God's faithfulness?

Worship is a moving thing it demands our constant attention

The apostle Paul apparently thought so. Look at his instructions in Romans 12:1: "Therefore, I urge you, brothers, in view of God's mercy, to offer your bodies as living sacrifices, holy and pleasing to God—this is your spiritual act of worship." Paul was not describing a one-time offering. Our spiritual act of worship to God, according to the apostle, is a *living* thing, which means it demands our constant attention. In other words, worship is a full-time job—plus weekends.

Worship isn't something that comes naturally to most Christians. The pressures of simply trying to make it through another day/another week/another month often leave us feeling drained. What's more, we usually need a little push to see beyond our self-centered focus.

> **JUST WONDERING**
>
> **Why is Sunday our day of worship?**
> The tradition of going to church on Sunday stretches all the way back to the earliest Christians. The Bible doesn't explain it, but Bible experts have offered a couple of theories. One is that the early Christians wanted to show their faithfulness to God by dedicating the very first day of the week to Him. Another theory is that the first-century Christians chose Sunday because it was the day of Christ's resurrection.

Consider yourself pushed. On the pages that follow, you'll find eight tips for developing a more worshipful attitude in your life. Some of the tips may be more applicable for you than others, but all of them are worth exploring.

### *1. Get rid of your sin.*

Sin interferes with every aspect of our relationship with God—including our ability to worship. If you have unconfessed sin in your life, something that you're aware of, it's important that you confess it and receive God's forgiveness for it before it interferes with your worship. (In chapter 9 you can find tips for confessing sin in prayer.)

The problem of sin in our lives extends beyond our personal worship. Jesus said, "Therefore, if you are offering your gift at the altar and there remember that your brother has something against you, leave your gift there in front of the altar. First go and be reconciled to your brother; then come and offer your gift" (Matthew 5:23–24).

Note the sequence of events there. First, you take care of any sins you've committed against someone else, and *then* you worship at the altar.

For maximum effectiveness, ask the Holy Spirit to reveal any sins that you may have forgotten and then ask for forgiveness for those, too. Remember, the more sins God forgives and forgets, the closer our relationship with Him becomes.

**NOTABLE QUOTABLE**

He worships God who knows Him.

—SENECA

### 2. *Open your eyes.*

The world is full of worship inspiration. All you have to do is recognize it. Of course, that's easier said than done in a culture as busy as ours. That's why you need to train yourself to become an observer of God's work. There are several ways to do this, none of which is very difficult or time-consuming. For example, you might . . .

- spend a Saturday biking or hiking a mountain trail, a forest preserve path, or a country road;
- ask friends and family members to share with you some of the good things that are going on in their lives—things with God's fingerprints all over them;
- spend a few hours under the stars at night, pondering the immensity of God; or
- look for evidence of God's presence in the news events of the day.

Make mental notes of the things you see, hear, experience, and learn. Better yet, make physical notes in a journal or notebook. Be as specific as possible in your descriptions—and in the worship sessions that you use them for. Your strategy should be to continue planning these special "eye-opening" events until your observation skills sharpen to the point of noticing God's handiwork everywhere you go.

### 3. *Take advantage of every opportunity.*

You don't need a church for your personal worship. You don't even need a Bible (although it can be a great help). What's more, you don't need an hour, a half hour, fifteen minutes, or even five minutes. You can have a complete personal worship "session" in the time it takes to sing (silently or audibly, depending on your circumstances) "How Great Thou Art" or some other song of praise, or in the time it takes to offer a sincere prayer of adoration.

In other words, you can offer personal worship any time you have a few spare moments. What better way is there to fill your commute time or the time you spend, say, washing your car or walking on a treadmill than by worshiping God?

The point is, regardless of how packed your schedule may seem, you can always find opportunities to worship God—if you're looking for them.

> **NOTABLE QUOTABLE**
>
> Worship is not a text but a context; it is not an isolated experience in life, but a series of life experiences.
>
> —GARY GULBRANSON

### *4. Get the Holy Spirit involved.*

The most valuable worship resource at your disposal is inside you at this very moment. The Holy Spirit can and will . . .

- offer gentle prods and subtle reminders when you have opportunities for personal worship;
- inspire your personal worship by bringing to mind praiseworthy aspects of God and His work; and
- help you focus your thoughts and words during personal worship.

All you have to do is invite Him to be a part of your personal worship plans and then pay attention to His leading.

### *5. Spend time in the Psalms.*

Say what you want about the psalmists—those guys knew how to worship God. What's more, you may find their obvious love and awe for Him to be contagious. That's why it's a good idea to make the Book of Psalms a regular part of your Bible study. Immersing yourself in individual psalms is like taking a walk through the Worship Hall of Fame.

Check out the emotion and unbridled praise running through these psalm snippets:

> O LORD, our Lord, how majestic is your name in all the earth! You have set your glory above the heavens. From the lips of children and infants you have ordained praise because of your enemies, to silence the foe and the avenger. When I consider your heavens, the work of your fingers, the moon and the stars, which you have set in place, what is man that you are mindful of him,

> the son of man that you care for him? (8:1–4)
>
> The LORD is my shepherd, I shall not be in want. He makes me lie down in green pastures, he leads me beside quiet waters, he restores my soul. He guides me in paths of righteousness for his name's sake. Even though I walk through the valley of the shadow of death, I will fear no evil, for you are with me; your rod and your staff, they comfort me. (23:1–4)
>
> Praise the LORD, O my soul; all my inmost being, praise his holy name. Praise the LORD, O my soul, and forget not all his benefits—who forgives all your sins and heals all your diseases, who redeems your life from the pit and crowns you with love and compassion, who satisfies your desires with good things so that your youth is renewed like the eagle's. (103:1–5)

Many of the psalms are so well-written and so timeless that they can be repeated word for word as personal worship today. If you like a challenge, try memorizing some of your favorite passages from the Book of Psalms. If not, read them aloud to God as part of your personal worship.

### *6. Use sound tracks.*

The right music can go a long way toward setting a mood of worship. Many Christians can name one or two songs or hymns that automatically put them in a worshipful frame of mind. If you can find songs that have that effect on you, you can create a backdrop for your personal worship that will enhance your time with God. The more songs you find, the more diverse your worship accompaniments will be.

If you have a sizable CD collection and a programmable player, you can create hours worth of musical background for your at-home worship. If you have a cassette tape player, buy some worship music tapes or record a personalized worship mix tape (or two) from your existing collection. That way, you'll have portable music accompaniment for personal worship in your car, at the gym, or during long walks.

### *7. Put your God-given talents and abilities to work.*

This is where you can put the *personal* in personal worship. Earlier in this chapter, we explored the five common elements of corporate worship. Where personal worship is concerned, there are no common elements. *Anything* that expresses your devotion to God in a way that honors Him is worship. The more personal and heartfelt that expression is, the more meaningful it is to God.

Think about your talents, abilities, and interests. How can you put them to work in a context of worship? Here are a few ideas to get you started:

- If you're blessed with artistic talent, draw or paint a picture that expresses your feelings about who God is, what He means to you, or why He deserves your praise and devotion.
- If you enjoy photography, capture on film various images from nature or the world around you that inspire feelings of worship. Create an album or gallery that you can use for your personal worship time.
- If you're a writer, try your hand at creating your own psalm of praise and worship. Write a short story in which worship is a central theme. Write an essay about the overlooked aspects of God's work in the world. Write a poem that captures the essence of your feelings about God.
- If you're a tech head, create a worship web site. Start an online worship community in which visitors to your site can add their own thoughts and experiences regarding worship.

Better yet, come up with your own ideas for personalizing your worship.

### 8. *Find a church that encourages your worship.*

Ideally, much of your personal worship will spring from your corporate worship on Sundays. The worship themes, Scripture references, and biblical truths that you absorb at church can be used to fuel your personal interaction with God throughout the week. That's why it's vital that you find a church that inspires and fulfills your need for worship.

**ON A PERSONAL NOTE**

Schedule an appointment to talk to your church's worship leader. Find out how songs and hymns are chosen for a particular service and how closely the worship leader works with the pastor to make sure that the music complements the message. If you're comfortable with the idea, volunteer your talents and services to assist the worship team.

Let's get this straight. There is no "right" way to worship God. There are traditional and nontraditional ways, but if the worship is sincere and God-honoring, we can't claim that one way is better or more effective than another. What it comes down to is personal preference. The key to successful worship is finding a church whose approach lets you focus on genuine, heartfelt worship. What you need to do is figure out what type of corporate worship you prefer. If you get nothing out of singing traditional songs or reciting responsive readings, look for something a little less traditional. If you find comfort in "old time" hymns and a traditional worship setting, look for a church that meets those requirements.

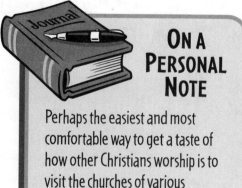

**On a Personal Note**

Perhaps the easiest and most comfortable way to get a taste of how other Christians worship is to visit the churches of various Christian friends and neighbors.

If your worship needs are being met in your current church, there's no need to look elsewhere. If, however, you find that your worship—corporate or personal—is lacking something, you might want to start exploring other church options.

How you choose to worship is up to you. All that matters is that your efforts are sincere and God-honoring. Remember, this isn't empty ritual we're talking about. Worship is not a matter of reciting a few things that we think God wants to hear and then moving on. Worship is about recognizing how much we owe God, not only for our salvation but for the way He sustains and blesses us every day of our lives, and attempting to repay that debt the only way we can—with a life of devotion to Him.

## Know What You Believe

How much do you know about worshiping God? Here's a quiz to test your knowledge.

1. Which of the following best describes worship?
   a. Pretending to be holier than you are
   b. Striving to make a good name for yourself in church
   c. Giving God His due
   d. Doing what comes naturally

2. Which of the following is not true of worship?
   a. It's overdone in most churches.
   b. It's the eternal destiny of every Christian.
   c. It comes in at least two varieties—corporate and personal.
   d. It's commanded in Scripture.

3. Which of the following is not a part of corporate worship?
   a. Giving
   b. Praying
   c. Singing
   d. Judging

4. Which of the following is not a helpful tip for developing a worshipful attitude?
   a. Open your eyes to worship opportunities.
   b. Don't try to worship unless you have at least a half hour to devote to it.
   c. Get the Holy Spirit involved.
   d. Spend time in the Book of Psalms.

5. Which of the following is not necessarily a hindrance to worship?
   a. Music
   b. Insincerity
   c. Selfishness
   d. Unconfessed sin

*Answers: (1) c, (2) a, (3) d, (4) b, (5) a*

CHAPTER 11

# All Together Now

## SNAPSHOT

"You missed a great service this morning," Dewey said as he took off his tie and unbuttoned his shirt.

Todd sat up in bed and rubbed the sleep from his eyes. "Actually," he said with a yawn, "I didn't miss it a bit."

Dewey looked at his roommate's rumpled bedclothes and shook his head. "I see you attended Bedside Baptist again this morning," he said.

Todd flopped back on his mattress with his arms outstretched. "What can I say?" he sighed. "I'm comfortable with Pastor Sheets."

"Don't think you should be in church, instead of in bed, on Sunday mornings?" Dewey asked.

"Why?" Todd asked. "What can I get from church that I can't get from having my own Bible study, praying by myself, and jamming to Christian tunes

### SNEAK PREVIEW

1. For Christians, fellowship is more than a social obligation; it's a necessity for our spiritual health.
2. Finding the right church for fellowship involves not just choosing one that will meet your needs, but choosing one in which you can use your spiritual gifts to minister to others.
3. Fellowship isn't a passive phenomenon, something that you feel; it's an active process, something that you create.

in my car—on my own time?"

"What about fellowship?" Dewey asked.

"I get all of that I need from you and my other Christian friends," Todd replied.

"It's not the same," Dewey insisted.

"Why not?" Todd asked. "You're a Christian, and I'm a Christian. In my book, that means anytime we have a conversation, I'm having fellowship."

"But it's not *church* fellowship," Dewey said.

"It's more natural than church fellowship," Todd insisted.

"Are you saying that church fellowship is *fake?*" Dewey asked.

"Not fake, just forced," Todd said. "It's like you're expected to have a deep and abiding relationship with someone just because you happen to be in the same church building at the same time."

"That's not true."

"Sure it is, and I'll give you an example," Todd replied. "Remember the last time I went to church with you? There was an old woman who sat at the end of our row."

"Mabel," Dewey said with a smile.

"That's right, Mabel," Todd said. "Remember how, after the service, she cornered us and started sharing her entire medical history?"

"You were the one who asked, 'How are you?'" Dewey reminded him.

"How long did we listen to her goiter problems?" Todd asked. "Twenty minutes, easy."

"What's your point?" Dewey asked.

"Think about this," Todd said. "What if you met Mabel for the first time somewhere else—say, the subway—and she started talking about herself that way? What would you do?"

"Well, that's tough to say," Dewey began.

"I know exactly what you'd do," Todd said. "You'd say, "No habla Ingles," and move to another car."

Dewey smiled and nodded toward the bed. "You're awful cynical for someone who spent the morning in church."

Todd grinned. "Hey, like I said before, arguing with you is fellowship for me."

* * * * * * * * * * * * * * * *

Is there a word more exclusively Christian than *fellowship?* Think about it. Have you ever heard anyone use that word outside of a church context?

Imagine the conversation: "Dirk's parents are out of town, so he's planning to throw an all-night *fellowship* for the football team and cheerleaders." Or: "If anybody asks for me, tell them I'll be *fellowshiping* at the beach this afternoon." Or: "I don't usually *fellowship* with coworkers, but I was wondering if you'd like to have dinner with me on Friday."

It's not a word that gets thrown around casually, that's for sure. If you're a new believer, or new to the church, you may have only a vague notion of what *fellowship* even means.

The *American Heritage Dictionary* calls it "the condition of being together or of sharing similar interests or experiences." But that's *everyday* fellowship they're talking about. When you put the word into a Christian context, its meaning expands dramatically.

Christian fellowship starts out as a connection based on common beliefs, a common purpose, and a common goal. But from there it takes on a life of its own. Those who test the water of Christian fellowship find that they are complemented, strengthened, and, to a certain extent, *completed* by their fellow believers.

The concept of fellowship—meeting the needs of others while having your own needs met by them—may seem out of step in a society that prizes individualism and self-reliance. But, as we'll see in the pages that follow, our individual experiences, gifts, and talents are what make fellowship so vital.

# All Aboard the Fellow-ship

**JUST WONDERING**

**Isn't it possible to have fellowship with other Christians without going to church?**

Yes, but that's like asking, "Isn't it possible to find fuel for my car without going to a gas station?" Theoretically, it is possible. You could probably siphon enough gas from your neighbors' lawn mowers and generators to keep you going for a while, but it wouldn't be enough to sustain you full time. From a practical standpoint, it wouldn't make much sense. The same applies to fellowship. Technically, anytime Christians get together, whether it's for Bible study or bowling, there's a potential for fellowship. And that may be enough to sustain you for a while. But it doesn't make sense to rely on those dribbles of fellowship when the main supplier is as close as your local church.

There are three compelling reasons to make fellowship with other believers a priority in your life. Let's take a look at each one.

### *1. God gave us an innate desire for fellowship.*

God created humans with a need to be connected to and involved with other people. In Genesis 2:18, God said, "It is not good for the man to be alone." Granted, the context of that verse is the creation of woman, but the point remains. Humans are wired in such a way that we find fulfillment in interacting with other people.

When the Lord created the foundation of His church in Acts 2:42–47, He set up a similar interdependence among believers. Members of the first-century church actually . . .

- ate daily meals together,
- shared necessities such as food and shelter, and
- sold their possessions and donated the proceeds to the church in order to help other believers.

That's some pretty extreme fellowship. Not only was their spiritual well-being tied to each other, so was their physical, financial, and social well-being.

We could argue that cultural changes have eliminated the need for money pooling among Christians today. But the model of mutual dependence and support still applies. Just as man was incomplete without woman, a Christian is incomplete without fellow believers.

### *2. Our relationship with the Lord suffers without fellowship.*

Look at the things God's Word commands Christ's followers to do:

- "A new command I give you: Love one another. As I have loved you, so you must love one another. By this all men will know that you are my disciples, if you love one another." (John 13:34–35)
- Warn those who are idle, encourage the timid, help the weak, be patient with everyone (1 Thessalonians 5:14)
- Bear with each other and forgive whatever grievances you may have against one another. Forgive as the Lord forgave you. (Colossians 3:13)
- Each of you should look not only to your own interests, but also to the interests of others. (Philippians 2:4)

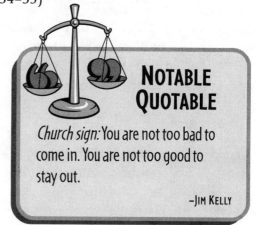

> **NOTABLE QUOTABLE**
>
> *Church sign:* You are not too bad to come in. You are not too good to stay out.
>
> —JIM KELLY

Notice how all of these instructions assume personal relationships on the part of believers. And not just casual, "Hi, how ya doin'?" relationships, either. Love, compassion, encouragement, forgiveness, and accountability are hallmarks of deeply committed relationships. Such relationships are . . .

- long-term
- time consuming
- sometimes inconvenient
- occasionally confrontational
- uniquely fulfilling
- ultimately life-changing

In other words, the kind of relationships that are built through fellowship.

What you'll also find is that fellowship with other believers gives you a broader perspective of the Lord and His work. It's one thing to catch glimpses of the Lord's work here and there in your own life. It's quite another thing to hear testimony from fellow believer after fellow believer of the things God's done—and continues to do every week—in their lives.

That's the idea behind community praise and worship. With a whole congregation of people sharing experiences, the sheer volume of things to praise God about increases dramatically.

What it comes down to is this: If we're serious about our commitment to Christ, we must open our lives to our fellow believers and allow them to open their lives to us.

### *3. The body of Christ depends on fellowship.*

The Bible describes the church as the body of Christ, and individual believers as parts of that body (1 Corinthians 12:12–31). And it's that image, perhaps more than anything else, that drives home the importance of fellowship.

Keep in mind that there's no such thing as a stand-alone Christian. If you believe in Christ, you are part of His body. The choice you face is whether you want to be an active limb (or organ) or a useless appendage. In other words, do you want to work together with the rest of the body or make the rest of the body work around you?

**NOTABLE QUOTABLE**

God calls us not to solitary sainthood but to fellowship in a company of committed men.

—DAVID SCHULLER

Think about it. If you're, say, a "thumb" on the body of Christ, and the person in the pew in front of you is an "index finger," you've got to learn to work together; because if you can't, the entire body will suffer. First Corinthians 12:26 puts it this way: "If one part suffers, every part suffers with it; if one part is honored, every part rejoices with it." Like it or not, there are people in the church depending on you and the contributions you can make to their lives. They may not even know who you are yet, but they're depending on you. So if you choose to ignore opportunities for fellowship, you're not only hurting yourself, you're hurting a lot of other believers, as well.

Whether we fully understand fellowship or not, the Lord has determined that it's vital to the spiritual health and growth of all believers. That means it's our responsibility to treat fellowship as seriously as He does and to make it a high priority in our lives.

# The Church Shopping Network

Maybe you don't attend church regularly—or ever. Or maybe you do attend, but you feel disconnected and wonder if it's the right church for you. If either of those scenarios describe you, read on. If not, skip ahead to the next section, "Ask Not What Your Church Can Do for You . . ."

The first step in making sure that you get your recommended daily (or weekly) allowance of fellowship is finding a church. But how do you find one? After all, churches generally aren't known for their aggressive marketing campaigns or high-pressure sales pitches. You probably won't find a lot of self-serving church ads in your local Yellow Pages. Neither will you find rival churches "slashing costs" to bring in new member. ("Join today and take advantage of our low 8 percent tithing rates!") In fact, you'll probably find that most of the church representatives you encounter will care more about your finding the *right* place of worship and fellowship for you than about "getting your business" themselves.

Obviously your ultimate choice in a church will depend primarily on your personal preferences. There are, however, some general principles you need to consider when choosing a place to worship and have fellowship.

> **JUST WONDERING**
>
> **Should I just stay in the church I grew up in?**
> There's a lot to be said for spending your life in one church—as long as it's the right church for you. Having a shared history with people certainly can enhance fellowship. The longer that history is, the deeper the fellowship can become. However, you need to keep in mind that tradition is not a legitimate reason for choosing a church. If you don't believe your spiritual needs are being met in the church you grew up in, it's time to find a new place to worship.

### *1. Make sure the church's doctrine is sound.*

A church without sound biblical doctrine is teaching heresy. And it's your responsibility to make sure that you're not seduced by false, heretical teachings in your quest to find the right church for you. God left us with a certain amount of leeway in interpreting various passages in His Word and applying them to our lives and our style of worship. That's why certain church beliefs and practices vary from denomination to denomination. Those differences are based on different emphases and interpretations of Scripture, and are to be expected.

There are, however, *absolute* teachings or "boundaries" in Scripture that we are not free to cross in our interpretation of God's Word. These "core beliefs" are shared by *all* Christian churches and must be present in any church that you seriously consider for yourself. Here are some of the biggies:

- The Bible is the absolute authority when it comes to matters of the Christian faith. It is sufficient and trustworthy for providing guidance, wisdom, and direction for our lives.
- God exists in three persons—the Father, the Son, and the Holy Spirit—all of whom are equal, yet distinct.
- Christ is fully God and fully human.
- Christ died to pay the punishment for our sins, rose from the dead, and ascended to His Father in heaven.
- Putting one's faith in Christ and His work is the *only* way to be reconciled to God and receive eternal life.

An easy way to find out if a church holds these beliefs is to look at its doctrine statement. In most churches, copies of the doctrine statement are readily available for the asking. If you encounter a church that doesn't have a written doctrine statement or one that refuses to show it to you, let the red flags fly.

After you've read the church's doctrine statement, listen carefully to Sunday school lessons and sermons to make sure that they adhere to the statement. If everything checks out doctrinally, you can move on to a closer inspection of the church's internal dynamics.

### *2. Observe the way the church members interact.*

When you visit congregations, you'll want to keep your ears open to the content of the Sunday school lessons and sermons. But you'll also want to keep your eyes open to the interaction of the people around you. Specifically, you'll want to ask yourself some important questions:

- Is there a welcoming spirit in the church?
- Can you sense a loving attitude among the members?
- Is there noticeable interaction or support among various age groups in the church?
- Do the people seem to enjoy worshiping together?
- Is their love for the Lord apparent?

Obviously, you're not going to find a "perfect" congregation. Every church has its problems and challenges. What's more, in any large group, you're bound to find people you click with and people you don't. That's only natural. In addition, your attitude going into a church is going to affect your judgment. Make sure that you keep an open mind during this process. Don't go into a church looking for a reason to dislike it. Remember, you're trying to find a place where you can fulfill your responsibility for providing and receiving Christian fellowship.

**JUST WONDERING**

**How much of a difference is there between various church denominations?**
Depends on the denominations you're comparing. If you visit an Episcopalian church one week and a Pentecostal church the next, you'll find that the differences can be like night and day. If you were to compare a Baptist service with an Evangelical Free service, you might have a hard time spotting a difference between the two. You see, not only do different denominations emphasize different practices and teachings, but individual churches within those denominations add their own emphases and practices to the mix. You can use denominations to narrow your search, but ultimately it comes down to choosing the right church for you.

### ***3. Make sure the church's style of worship coincides with your personal preferences.***

Some churches prefer a formal approach to worship, favoring structured services, specific rituals, and stained-glass surroundings. Other churches opt for a much more casual approach, preferring a spontaneous service structure, singing songs and testifying to the Lord's goodness as the Spirit leads them. Most churches fall somewhere between the two extremes.

Likewise, some churches prefer traditional music in their services—four-stanza hymns, accompanied by stately organ music. Other churches view themselves as rock venues, complete with their own house bands. Most churches try to accommodate a variety of musical styles in their services.

And then there's the matter of Sunday dress. Formal or informal? Some people view dressing up for church as part of their responsibility to set aside a day of worship to the Lord. In other words, they feel led to do things on Sunday that they don't normally do the rest of the week. Putting on their "Sunday best" is not a matter of trying to impress anyone; it's simply a matter of making the day of worship special. Other people argue that getting dressed up affects their comfort level in church. They point out that the more comfortable they are, the better able they are to focus their thoughts on God. For that reason, they prefer to dress casually when they attend church.

**NOTABLE QUOTABLE**

A church is a hospital for sinners, not a museum for saints.

—ABIGAIL VAN BUREN

The point is not that one type of church, one approach to worship, is good and another is bad. The point is, you can find churches that match your preferences in worship style, music, and dress. But first you have to give some serious thought as to what your preferences are.

***4. Make sure that the church has ministries that coincide with your needs.***

If you're a college student, look for a church with a thriving college-age group. If you have a heart for helping the needy, make sure that you find a church that shares your passion—perhaps even one with an established outreach ministry. If you have young kids, find a church that offers exciting children's Sunday school or children's church programs.

## Ask Not What Your Church Can Do for You . . .

Keep in mind that finding a church home is only a first step. It doesn't guarantee automatic fellowship any more than enrolling in college guarantees an automatic education. Fellowship is something you have to work at.

You'll find that one of the biggest obstacles to meaningful fellowship is an inward focus, or plain ol' self-centeredness. What happens is that we go to church expecting to have *our* needs catered to. We view the ministry and the purpose of the church as a one-way street that dead-ends at our door. We treat church as a spiritual "grocery store," gathering the information and encouragement we need to sustain us during the week and then taking it home with us. When that runs out, we come back the next week for a refill.

But that's not even close to the model God had in mind when He created His church. He envisioned a structure in which believers give back to the church and their fellow worshipers every bit as much as they receive. Some of that giving back takes the form of ministry, volunteering your time and energy to serve others in an organized capacity; some of it takes the form of tithing, supporting the church and its ministries with your finances (a practice we'll cover in detail in chapter 17); and some of it takes the form of fellowship.

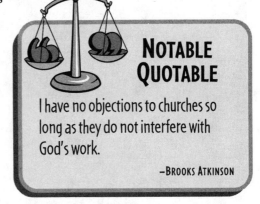

**NOTABLE QUOTABLE**

I have no objections to churches so long as they do not interfere with God's work.

—BROOKS ATKINSON

Jesus gave His followers these instructions: "Love one another" (John 13:34). We've made this point in a couple other places in this book, but it bears repeating here. Jesus wasn't talking about a *feeling;* He was talking about *action.* You can't make yourself feel love for another believer. But you can decide to treat that person in a loving way.

That's the nature of fellowship. You don't wait until you have warm, fuzzy emotions—until you feel "fellowship-y"—to get involved in the lives of your fellow church members. Instead, you take an active approach toward building fellowship and then let the feelings develop from there.

Granted, fellowship does grow and take on a life of its own over time. However, when it comes to initiating fellowship and giving it a chance to grow, there are three steps you need to take.

### *1. Mingle.*

Let's be honest here. It is possible to go to church anonymously. You can establish a routine of slipping in just before the service begins, sitting in the back row for easy exit access, and slipping out as soon as the benediction is over. The larger the church, the easier it is to maintain your privacy.

It is possible to worship God that way. It is possible to grow in your knowledge of Scripture that way. It is possible to be moved to make some life-changing decisions that way. But it is not possible to experience true fellowship that way.

### JUST WONDERING

**Are shy people at a disadvantage when it comes to fellowship?**

Not necessarily. Creating fellowship with other believers doesn't require an extroverted personality. You don't have to become a politician, shaking every hand and kissing every baby in the congregation. Simply putting yourself in the right places at the right times will go a long way toward establishing fellowship. The more that people see your face around the church, the more likely it is that they will begin to talk to you. In worst-case scenarios, however, when you are required to break out of your shell and approach others, think of fellowship as a sacrifice for Christ. In other words, be prepared to sacrifice your personal comfort to achieve the fellowship He calls you to.

In order to enjoy the kind of fellowship God has in mind for His people, you need to learn to invest yourself in the lives of others. And if that sounds like a complex, time-consuming process, you don't know the half of it.

The good news is that there's nothing terribly difficult about it. In fact, the first step is no more complicated than hanging around after Sunday school or the worship service to introduce yourself to others.

Spend at least a few minutes each week getting to know your fellow worshipers. Find out who they are, where they come from, what they do, how long they've been attending the church—anything that might be helpful in striking up future conversations with them. Your goal is to open lines of communication and create familiarity with as many people as possible.

### *2. Get involved.*

The next step in building fellowship is to expand your personal involvement in the church. Increase your allotment of weekly "church time" from an hour or so (the length of a Sunday school class or worship service) to three or four hours or more. Give the church calendar priority in your date book.

Clear your schedule for picnics, potlucks, fun fairs, family nights, concerts, or any other fellowship opportunities your church offers.

If that sounds about as exciting as attending a paint-drying exhibition, remind yourself to keep your eyes on the prize. The time you spend doing "churchy" things is an investment in your future. The more quality time you spend with people, the closer you will grow to them. The closer you grow to people, the more opportunities for fellowship you have. The more fellowship you have with fellow believers, the stronger your relationship with Christ becomes.

> **NOTABLE QUOTABLE**
>
> The first Sunday I sang in the church choir, two hundred people changed their religion.
>
> —FRED ALLEN

Earlier in this chapter, we emphasized the importance of finding a church with ministries that fit your particular needs. It's also important that you find a ministry (or ministries) in the church that you can get involved in. (We'll talk more about how to find the right ministry for you in chapter 17.)

In addition to giving you a chance to put your God-given skills and spiritual gifts to use, volunteering for a ministry gives you a chance to serve side by side with a variety of people in the church. And that's where fellowship *really* blossoms. Let's put it this way: If spending time with someone rates as a good way to build fellowship, serving and ministering with that person is off the fellowship charts.

Find a ministry to serve in, and you will find fellowship.

### 3. *Make yourself vulnerable.*

It's one thing to have people you can say "Hi" to every week and maybe joke around with; it's quite another thing to have people in the church who will take an active interest in your spiritual growth and hold you accountable to Christian standards while allowing you to do the same thing in their lives.

The key ingredient to developing relationships of depth—not to mention fellowship that can change lives—is openness. Openness involves sharing . . .

- concerns
- questions

- doubts
- past failures
- goals

However, with openness comes vulnerability, and with vulnerability comes uneasiness. You can't expect others to work through that uneasiness without being willing to do the same yourself. That's why it's important for you to take he initiative in opening up to your fellow believers. Don't wait for someone else to break the ice; you'll miss valuable fellowship time.

Obviously, you'll want to be careful not to be too open too quickly. You don't want to overwhelm others with your vulnerability. Share just enough to encourage others to do the same. Take a few tentative steps, get some reaction, and then take a few more steps.

When people open up to you, reward them with your full attention. Listen to what they say. Offer your prayers, your encouragement, and your empathy. Hold back your opinions and judgments. Remember, your goal is to increase each other's openness and vulnerability.

**ON A PERSONAL NOTE**

Once you've selected a church to call home, create a résumé for yourself that you can present to your pastor or a church leader. On it, list any talents, abilities, experiences, or interests that you could apply to ministry in the church. Based on that information, ask your pastor or church leader to help you find a ministry within the church that suits you.

Keep in mind that fellowship doesn't happen overnight. It's not something that can be forced or rushed. If you want it, you've got to dedicate your time, energy, patience, and effort to the cause.

## Membership Has Its Privileges

Once you've chosen a church to call home and begun the process of building fellowship, there's another issue to consider. Should you join the church and become an official member?

Some would argue that actually becoming a member of a church is an unnecessary step or a mere formality. After all, there are no passages in Scripture that demand church membership, and it's not like your salvation depends on it.

Consider this, though: Applying for church membership and fulfilling the requirements for it demonstrate your commitment to the people in your congregation, much in the same way that getting married demonstrates your commitment to your loved one. Church membership is a way of saying, "For better or worse, I am a part of this group of people. This is where I will focus my worship and fellowship energy. This is where I will channel my tithes. Instead of ditching when things get bad, I am committing myself to working to make them better."

**ON A PERSONAL NOTE**

One of the keys to fellowship is an encouraging spirit. To help foster such a spirit in your church, develop a habit of writing encouraging notes to church leaders and ministry volunteers. In your notes, be specific and sincere in the praise you offer. Identify one or two things that you really appreciate about the person and his or her ministry. You may be surprised by the response you get.

If you want to think about future benefits, here's one. Having a church home provides stability for your family. Growing up in a congregation among people who know and love you is incredibly grounding for a child. The more comfortable kids are in church settings, the more likely it is that they will continue attending church when they become adults.

In short, the arguments for joining a church seem to outweigh the arguments against it. The bottom line is, taking the steps to become an official member of your church demonstrates your commitment, and commitment strengthens fellowship.

## It's Refining

A popular stereotype suggests that church members are a bunch of judgmental hypocrites, pretending to be something they're not on Sundays and then living like non-Christians the rest of the week. Maybe that's a gross exaggeration, or maybe there are kernels of truth in it. As far as our fellowship is concerned, however, none of that matters. We are responsible for creating fellowship with other believers, specifically the believers we worship with each week. There are no guidelines as to who's "worthy" of our fellowship and who isn't.

Fellowship isn't something that exists exclusively between upstanding members

**NOTABLE QUOTABLE**

The Christian church is the only society in the world in which membership is based upon the qualification that the candidate shall be unworthy of membership.

—CHARLES C. MORRISON

of the church community or between Christian role models and their eager protégés. Remember, everyone who calls Jesus Savior is part of His body—the moral strugglers as well as the moral pillars. Fellowship must exist among all of us.

In fact, the Bible tells us that there's a "refining" element to fellowship. Actually, it says, "As iron sharpens iron, so one man sharpens another" (Proverbs 27:17). The idea is that as we come into contact and interact with each other, we sharpen each other's dull edges and rough patches. In other words, fellowship has the power to change us, to make us better and more useful.

That means our job is not to figure out who we want to have fellowship with, but to figure out how we can create fellowship with as broad a range of people as possible—personalities and backgrounds notwithstanding.

Don't forget, the book of Revelation tells us that we're going to be fellowshiping together for *eternity*. We might as well get started now.

## Know What You Believe

How much do you know about Christian fellowship? Here's a quiz to test your knowledge.

1. Which of the following is not true of Christian fellowship?
   a. It involves meeting the needs of others.
   b. It involves having your own needs met.
   c. It involves pretending to like people you can't stand.
   d. It involves a significant investment of time and energy.

2. Which of the following should be the least compelling reason for making fellowship a priority in your life?

a. You never know when a church contact might become a business contact.
b. God created us with a need for it.
c. Our relationship with the Lord suffers without it.
d. The body of Christ depends on it.

3. Which of the following is the least important thing to consider when looking for a church?
   a. The doctrine that's taught there
   b. The way members interact with each other
   c. The number of services to choose from on Sunday
   d. The style of worship

4. Which of the following is not a recommended method for initiating fellowship?
   a. Mingling
   b. Asking people to share with you their worst sins of the past week
   c. Getting involved in church ministries
   d. Making yourself vulnerable in your relationships with people at church

5. Which of the following is not an actual instruction from God's Word?
   a. Love one another.
   b. Encourage the timid.
   c. Forgive as the Lord forgave you.
   d. Reject those who make you uncomfortable.

*Answers: (1) c, (2) a, (3) c, (4) b, (5) d*

Chapter 12

# Can I Get a Witness?

## SNAPSHOT

"Believe me, I'm not the guy you want trying to lead other people to Christ," Barney grunted as he chipped at the ice on his windshield with the corner of his scraper.

Colin worked to free one of the snow-encrusted wiper blades. "Why not?" he asked. "You've been a Christian for, what, five years now?"

"Yeah, five years in April," Barney replied.

"And we've had the Bible study for three years," Colin continued. "So at least you know what you're talking about."

"I wouldn't go that far," Barney laughed. "Don't you remember when I said I didn't agree with corporate prayer because I didn't like the way big business worked?"

"That's okay," Colin said. "The first time I ever tried

### Sneak Preview

1. Sharing our faith with unbelievers is the responsibility of every Christian.
2. Actions (that is, a God-honoring, service-based lifestyle) and words (that is, a coherent verbal presentation of the good news of Christ) are both essential to our Christian witness.
3. The Holy Spirit will use our sincere faith-sharing efforts to effect changes in the lives of unbelievers.

to share my faith with someone, I ended up telling him that if he accepted Christ, his kids would automatically get into heaven, too."

"You mean, like a Magic Kingdom family pass?" Barney asked.

"Yeah, something like that," Colin said. "I got a little carried away. I had to go back to him a couple days later and do a retraction."

"Yikes," Barney said. "I guess that pretty much ended that, huh? Do you still see that guy around?"

"Actually, I do," Colin said. "He was sitting next to you at Bible study tonight."

Barney's jaw dropped. "Billy?" he asked.

Colin smiled and nodded.

"You led Billy to Christ?" Barney asked.

"I'd say it was more like the Holy Spirit led Billy to Christ *through* me," Colin replied. "Or *in spite* of me."

* * * * * * * * * * * * * * *

- ➤ Clean up the activity room after the youth group's annual Fun with Chocolate Pudding Night.
- ➤ Volunteer for the women's ministry's Mothers of Colicky Babies' Day Out program.
- ➤ Transcribe the entire hymnbook into Mandarin for any Chinese visitors to the church.
- ➤ Lead a year-long Bible study on the Book of Leviticus.
- ➤ Disinfect every toy in the nursery by hand—including those disgusting teething rings.

This is just a partial list of the things most Christians would rather do than share their faith in a one-on-one setting. It's not that we're ashamed of our Christianity. It's not that we don't have concern for the souls of unbelievers. It's just that, well, there are so many legitimate reasons for us *not* to share:

1. We might stumble over our words so badly that no one knows what we're talking about, least of all *us*.
2. We might get asked a question we can't answer.
3. We might get rejected in a really humiliating way.
4. We might get branded as religious fanatics.
5. We might have to defend our faith if we encounter people of other religions.

Of course, on the other side of the argument, we've got Romans 10:14: "How, then, can they [unbelievers] call on the one they have not believed in? And how can they believe in the one of whom they have not heard? And how can they hear without someone preaching to them?"

The official name for it is *evangelism*, and if you think it's something that should be left to evangelists, you're right . . . you evangelist, you.

# *No Habla* Christianity?

Sharing our faith with unbelievers isn't a spiritual gift issue. We can't sit back and wait for someone who's "good" at evangelism to do the job for us. The fact is, witnessing to unbelievers is something all Christians are expected to do.

Remember, there are no "assigned" parts in the body of Christ. There are no "mouth Christians" who are responsible for doing all the talking. Instead, we're all part of Christ's mouth. We are all given the job of communicating the Good News to people who aren't familiar with it.

If that's not incentive enough, consider this: There are people in this world that *you* can reach for Christ more effectively than even someone like Billy Graham could. Some people will listen to the things

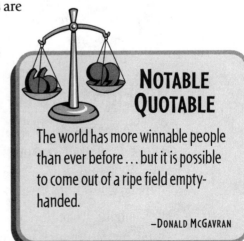

**NOTABLE QUOTABLE**

The world has more winnable people than ever before . . . but it is possible to come out of a ripe field empty-handed.

—DONALD MCGAVRAN

*you* have to say for no other reason than the fact that they come from you. Some people will take your message to heart simply because of who you are.

No matter how many communication skills you lack, the fact remains that you have a message to deliver. More than that, you have people waiting to hear what you have to say. They may not *know* they're waiting for you, but they are. And when they hear what you have to say, they'll *realize* that they've been waiting for you.

If you're still not convinced that sharing your faith should be at the top of your To Do list, we're going to have to haul out the big guns—the words of Paul and Jesus Himself:

> All this is from God, who reconciled us to himself through Christ and gave us the ministry of reconciliation: that God was reconciling the world to himself in Christ, not counting men's sins against them. And he has committed to us the message of reconciliation. We are therefore Christ's ambassadors, as though God were making his appeal through us. (2 Corinthians 5:18–20)

> Therefore go and make disciples of all nations, baptizing them in the name of the Father and of the Son and of the Holy Spirit, and teaching them to obey everything I have commanded you. And surely I am with you always, to the very end of the age. (Matthew 28:19–20)

> But you will receive power when the Holy Spirit comes on you; and you will be my witnesses in Jerusalem, and in all Judea and Samaria, and to the ends of the earth. (Acts 1:8)

## Walking the Talk

Actually, the first step in creating an effective Christian witness is relatively "safe." It involves living in such a way that people recognize something different in you—something that's appealing, something that's worth investigating, and something that's missing in their lives.

We're talking about bringing Matthew 5:14–16 to life: "You are the light of the world. A city on a hill cannot be hidden. Neither do people light a lamp and put it under a bowl. Instead, they put it on its stand, and it gives light to everyone in the house. In the same way, let your light shine before men, that they may see your good deeds and praise your Father in heaven."

Those "good deeds" should spring not from a desire to be admired, but from a commitment to follow Christ's example of serving others. If you dedicate yourself to meeting the needs of the people around you—to "loving your neighbor as yourself"—you will find more natural opportunities to share your faith than you ever dreamed possible.

> **NOTABLE QUOTABLE**
>
> Christians are to *be* good news before they *share* the good news.
>
> —JOE ALDRICH

When it comes to sharing our faith, or *witnessing*, words without actions are empty. On the other hand, actions without words are incapable of explaining the gift of salvation and the benefits of making Jesus Lord. Living a godly life will get the attention of unbelievers, but sooner or later, you've got to open your mouth.

## Prep School

When you decide to speak, you'd better make sure that you know what you're talking about. Or, as 1 Peter 3:15 puts it, "Always be prepared to give an answer to everyone who asks you to give the reason for the hope that you have."

The way to prepare yourself for the "test" that unbelievers will present is the same way you've been preparing for tests since grade school—by hitting the books. Obviously, that means acquainting yourself with God's Word, particularly those passages related to our sin, Jesus' sacrifice, and God's work of salvation. We highlighted a number of such passages in chapter 1 of this book.

Beyond that, though, you need to familiarize yourself with specific principles and strategies for sharing your faith. We will provide an outline in this chapter to get you started. However, you shouldn't stop here. You need to become an expert on the subject of witnessing. Fortunately, there have been dozens of great books written on the topic, so you shouldn't have any problems finding at least one or two that are right for you.

If your church has a library, that should be your first stop. If not, check out your local Christian bookstore for titles on witnessing and sharing your faith. Ask knowledgeable Christian friends to recommend books for you. You might even want to check with your pastor, to see if he has any books on his shelves that he'd be willing to lend to you.

Pore over the books and jot down any information that seems helpful or important to you, along with any supporting Bible references. Your goals are two:

- Become comfortable in your knowledge of God's Word, particularly passages that shed light on His plan of salvation.
- Begin to assemble the information that you will explain to unbelievers.

We'll talk about the specifics of what you need to know and communicate later in this chapter. For now, though, we'll simply emphasize the importance of reading anything you can get your hands on that will help you prepare or inspire you to share your faith.

Having said that, we need to point out that you may never know enough to feel completely at ease with the idea of telling others about Christ. There will likely be nagging doubts in the back of your mind about whether you're qualified to share your faith. Don't let those doubts dictate your actions.

The fact is, it doesn't matter when *you* think you're ready to witness. What matters is when *God* thinks you're ready. At some point, you're going to have to move beyond "book learning" and start accumulating "on-the-job training."

**NOTABLE QUOTABLE**

Far too many Christians have been anesthetized into thinking that if they simply live out their faith in an open and consistent fashion, the people around them will see it, want it, and somehow figure out how to get it for themselves.

—BILL HYBELS

## Making Contact

If your initial goal is to talk to friends and family members about Christ, you don't have to worry about how to strike up a conversation with them. If, however, you're considering talking to . . .

- a coworker you don't know very well,
- a woman you see on the train every morning,

- a guy who works out at your gym,
- someone you get paired up with at the golf course, or
- the stranger next to you in line at the movies

. . . you're going to need an opening, a way of making yourself known in an effective, nonthreatening way. There are three things you need to keep in mind as you search for this elusive opening.

### *1. Keep things casual.*

The last thing you want to do is weird people out by coming on too strong or sending the wrong signals. A simple, "Hi, how ya doin'?" followed by a quick comment about the weather or some other harmless topic is a good start. A casual, friendly tone is the key to starting a good conversation.

If the person chooses to respond, great. If not, at least you will have established contact, something you can build on the next time you see the person.

### *2. Read the signs.*

You can't force camaraderie. If a person looks at you as though you're contagious with a flesh-eating bacteria, respect feelings and give space. Learn to read body language and recognize verbal clues. It's important that you not overstay your welcome. You don't want to become a person that others try to avoid. For example, if you notice a person looking past you when you talk, it might be a sign that he's not interested in listening to you at that moment. If so, that means it's time for you to excuse yourself.

**NOTABLE QUOTABLE**

The evangelistic harvest is always urgent. The destiny of men and of nations is always being decided. Every generation is strategic. We are not responsible for the past generation, and we cannot bear the full responsibility for the next one; but we do have our generation. God will hold us responsible as to how well we fulfill our responsibilities to this age and take advantage of our opportunities.

—BILLY GRAHAM

### *3. Look for common ground.*

The circumstances of your encounter will dictate your common ground. If you're office mates, you can talk about work or your commute. If you work out at the same gym, you can talk about your exercise routine or diet regimen. Otherwise, you should probably just look for something about the person that you can make an intelligent remark about.

Here are a couple of ideas for opening a conversation.

- "I noticed the Michigan State bumper sticker on your car. That was a great game they played against Purdue last week."
- "Is that your son who's always waiting for you at the station every evening?"
- "That's a great jacket. Did you get it at Von Maur?"

This is really just a matter of finding a way to be sociable. Your goal is to establish at least a passing acquaintance with the person so that you're comfortable saying, "Hi" and making small talk when you see each other.

## Making the Transition

This is where you make the switch from small talk to meaningful conversation. We won't lie to you. This is the step in sharing your faith that has the most potential for awkwardness and embarrassment. However, neither of those possibilities should prevent you from doing what you're expected to do.

The keys to making a good transition are timing and flow. You want to make sure that your transition comes at a logical point in your conversation. Otherwise, you're going to come off like an overanxious telemarketer, giving the person the impression that you have a hidden agenda in talking to them.

### Just Wondering

**How should I respond to someone who tells me to "get lost"?**

Out of respect for that person, you should probably "get lost." Apologize for your imposition, wish the person well, and make your exit. If you carry business cards, and if you think it's appropriate, given the circumstances, hand the person one of your cards and invite them to call you anytime they feel dissatisfied or as though something is missing in their lives. (You'll want to be sure to emphasize that you're not trying to pick up the person, romantically speaking.) If you have time, you might write on your card something like, "Call me if you ever need a listening ear" or "Call me if you're ever curious about what God can do in your life."

Here are a few ideas for making the transition that you might want to consider.

### *1. Refer to your church.*

This is probably the easiest transition of all because you can work it into almost any situation. For example, if you're talking about another person, you might say, "He reminds me of a guy I go to church with." If you're talking about the location of a store or business, you might say, "That's not too far from my church." Or, if you're talking about restaurants, you might say, "There's a place that my friends and I go every Sunday night after church that serves the best fried onion platter I've ever tasted."

Obviously, the response you're looking for is, "You go to church?" That question gives you an opportunity to talk comfortably about what you think of your church and why it's different from the stereotypical image of churches that many people have.

### *2. Talk about a personal situation in which the Lord figures prominently.*

This doesn't have to be a heavy theological presentation. You can use a news story to trigger a discussion. For example, you might ask, "What do you think about the latest terrorist threat?" After the person responds, you might say something like, "I don't know what I'd be thinking if I wasn't sure how everything is going to end."

When the person asks you what you're talking about, you can mention your faith in God's sovereignty (using words other than *sovereignty*, of course) and the fact that God will ultimately make things right.

Another great transition opportunity presents itself when the person shares some personal difficulties with you. After listening empathetically, you might say something like, "When I'm in situations like that, the only thing I've found that's consistently helpful is talking to God about it."

### *3. Ask a point-blank question.*

You should probably make sure that you have a comfortable rapport with the person before you try

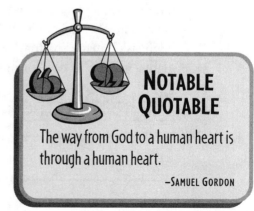

**NOTABLE QUOTABLE**

The way from God to a human heart is through a human heart.

–SAMUEL GORDON

this strategy, because it involves starting a conversation cold. Some people aren't comfortable with that, which means there's an increased risk of resistance and rejection.

When it works, though, nothing is more effective in making the transition to spiritual topics. For example, you might ask . . .

- Have you ever thought about what happens to us after we die?
- What would you say is your number-one priority in life?
- Do you ever feel like there's something missing in your life?
- What would it take to make you content?
- What do you think of Jesus?

The more openly and honestly the person responds to your questions, the more likely it is he or she will be receptive to the Good News you have to share.

Whatever method you choose, the transition stage is vital in focusing attention on the gospel presentation to come. Once you've steered the conversation to spiritual ground, you should probably ask for permission to move on to the next step. The way you phrase your question will depend on your transition. For example, if you mentioned something about a personal situation in which the Lord helped you, you might ask, "Would you mind if I told you a few things about the Lord and what He's done for me—and what He can do for you?"

If the person agrees, move on to the next step. If the person resists, ask if the two of you can talk at a later time. If you think the person would be okay with it, you might ask him to explain why he's hesitant to talk about spiritual things. Make a mental note of his objections so that you can address them later.

## The Heart of the Matter

Let's say the person gives you the go-ahead. What do you do next? How do you actually explain something as complex as spiritual salvation to someone who probably knows nothing about it?

Complicating the scenario further is the fact that you're also facing a ticking clock. After all, a person's only going to stay interested in what you have to say for so long. Depending on the person's attention span, your window of opportunity may be anywhere from two minutes to two hours. And you need to be prepared for both extremes.

The key to making the most of your opportunity is to eliminate everything but the absolute essentials in your explanation (at least, to begin with), and then divide the rest into bite-sized chunks of information. Not only does that make the material easier to present, it also makes it easier to learn.

Chapter 1 of this book contains an example of the condensing process. In that chapter, we managed to pare down the story of salvation to twelve major points:

1. God is holy.
2. God created humans with free will.
3. God had a perfect plan for the human race.
4. Humans are sinful.
5. Sin separates us from God.
6. God is just.
7. The punishment for sin is physical and spiritual death.
8. We can do nothing to save ourselves.
9. God loves us.
10. Jesus defeated sin.
11. Jesus paid the price for our sin.
12. Jesus defeated death.

We could pare the list down even further by combining some of the points:

**ON A PERSONAL NOTE**

Develop a habit of praying just before you share your faith with someone, whether the encounter is planned or spontaneous. Ask the Holy Spirit to calm your nerves, focus your thoughts, give you the words to say, help you recognize verbal and nonverbal clues from the person you're talking to, and assist you in maintaining a listening ear. Ask Him also to give you the wisdom to know how to end your encounter.

1. God is *holy*, which means He is completely separate from sin, and *just*, which means He demands punishment for sin.
2. God could have created us as robots programmed to obey Him, but instead He gave us a choice in the matter and created us with free will.
3. Our decision to disobey God separated us from Him and made us subject to His punishment, which is death.
4. As sinners, we can do nothing to save ourselves from God's punishment.
5. Instead of punishing us like we deserve, God loved us so much that He sent His Son in human form—the only sinless human who ever lived—to take the punishment for our sin.
6. After Jesus was executed for the sins we committed, He rose from the dead to defeat death once and for all.
7. Jesus is the only way to God; if we believe in Him, we will have eternal life.

And there you have the absolute essentials. Any presentation of the gospel should include those points in some form or another.

One witnessing approach that covers all of the essentials is the "Romans Road" method, so named because it's based on three verses from the New Testament book of Romans. If you're a beginner, you might want to give the Romans Road approach a try. It's simple—just three steps—and straightforward.

Here's how it goes:

1. Read Romans 3:23: "For all have sinned and fall short of the glory of God." Explain that anything that goes against God's Word or His will for our lives—including lying, losing control of

### JUST WONDERING

**What should I do if someone from another religion tries to witness to me?**

That depends on how much time you have available and how comfortable you are with debating and discussing spiritual matters. (If you're not very comfortable with it, check out chapter 16 for tips on how to defend your faith.) If you have the time and the confidence, agree to listen to the person's testimony if he will listen to yours. If you don't have the time at that moment, simply announce that you're a Christian and that you'd like to talk to the person sometime later.

our anger, and lusting after another person—is sin. Facing that definition of *sin*, most people will admit that they are sinners.

2. Read Romans 6:23: "For the wages of sin is death, but the gift of God is eternal life in Christ Jesus our Lord." Explain that even one sin is enough to earn God's death penalty. Then draw attention to what some people call "the biggest 'but' in the Bible." Point out that God's gift can't be earned; it can only be received. Explain that the gift was paid for by Jesus' sacrifice on the cross. You could then take the person to another (optional) stop on the Roman Road, Romans 5:8. Explain this gift was motivated by God's love: "God demonstrates his own love for us in this: While we were still sinners, Christ died for us."

3. Read Romans 10:13: "Everyone who calls on the name of the Lord will be saved." Explain that all we have to do in order to receive God's free gift of salvation is recognize and admit our situation—that we are powerless to save ourselves from the punishment we deserve for our sin—and then ask God for forgiveness and salvation.

Keep in mind that the information you're providing—whether it's divided into twelve points, seven points, or three points—is simply raw material. Your responsibility is not only to learn it, but also to shape it and present it in a way that's comfortable to you and interesting to the people you talk to.

As long as you cover the essentials, you can arrange the points in any order you choose. For example, if you use the question, "What do you think about Jesus?" as your transition, you might want to lead off your presentation by asking, "Do you want to know what Jesus thinks of you? He loves you so much that He died to save your life."

In order to feel truly comfortable with this material, though, you need to make sure that you understand each of the essential points inside and out. If there's anything in your presentation that doesn't make sense to you, get it cleared up as soon as possible. You can count on getting thrown for a loop by an off-the-wall question every now and then, but you shouldn't blank out on the basic points of the gospel.

## Getting Autobiographical

After you present your points from Scripture, take a few minutes to get personal about your faith. Share some recollections about the doubts and questions you had when you heard the gospel message for the first time. Explain in detail how you finally responded to the message—what you did, what you said, how you felt, and so on. Walk the person you're talking to through the whole conversion process. When you're finished, spend a few minutes talking about the things you've experienced since becoming a Christian.

There's no need to go overboard here. Remember, authenticity is the key. Resist the urge to dramatize or embellish the events of your conversion. Don't set expectations that probably won't be met if and when the person makes a decision for Christ.

**On a Personal Note**

Contact the person who was primarily responsible for leading you to Christ. Ask him or her to recall some of the questions you asked, some of the objections you had, or some of the doubts you expressed about your decision. Then talk about how the person responded to your questions, objections, and doubts. Not only will it help you empathize with the people you share your faith with, it may provide you with some valuable tips for sharing your own faith.

## Feedback

After you've finished sharing the gospel and your own experiences, it's important that you put the ball back in the listener's court by asking for a response to what you shared. Some people may respond with questions, such as:

- How do you know the Bible is true?
- Isn't it boring to be a Christian?
- Will God forgive me if I've done some *really* bad things in my life?
- How much will I have to change if I become a Christian?
- Will I have to stop smoking?
- What happens if I mess up? Will God take back His salvation gift?

Questions—even really tough ones—are a great response, because they demonstrate an interest in what you've shared, as well as a willingness to talk more about it. You may not have all the answers the person is looking for, but you can get them. Schedule a time to get together with the person again. Then, in the meantime, consult your pastor or other mature Christians to get the answers you need.

Some people may respond to your witness with indifference or even outright rejection. When they do, you may be shocked and disappointed—maybe even a little angry—especially if you thought you really nailed your presentation.

This is where you need to keep a cool head, though, because your response will go a long way toward determining whether you get a second chance to share your faith with the person. Don't be afraid to ask for a reason for the rejection ("So what did you hear that you didn't like?"), but don't press the issue. Make a mental note of the person's objections and move on. With the Holy Spirit on the job, odds are good that you'll get another opportunity to witness to them. And, when you do, you can be ready for it.

**ON A PERSONAL NOTE**

Come up with a list of three to five people with whom you will commit to sharing your faith. Then keep a running account of your encounters with each person, including an updated status of where the person is, spiritually speaking. For example, you might write something like, "Starting to ask questions" or "Says he wants to wait until he gets older to think about Christianity." With that information, you can plan how to approach the people the next time you talk to them.

Some people may respond to your witness by asking you how they can have what you have—that is, the assurance of salvation and a personal relationship with the Lord. And that's when the real excitement begins.

## Sealing the Deal

You'd think that having a person respond positively to your witness and decide to make a commitment for Christ would cause you to relax and heave a big sigh of relief. But that's not usually the way it works. Usually what happens at that point is that the pressure gets cranked *up* two or three notches. Maybe it's the responsibility. Or the thought that the person's eternal fate is somehow resting in your hands, and that if you do something wrong . . .

Keep in mind that you're *not* doing this alone. The Holy Spirit is right there with you, every step of the way, making sure that nothing gets overlooked or misinterpreted. Before you do anything else, then, it might be a good idea to say a quick prayer, asking the Holy Spirit to give you the right words to say.

Afterward, there are three things you'll need to do for your seeking friend or acquaintance.

### 1. Review

Briefly go over the major points of God's salvation one more time to make sure that the person understands them.

### 2. Pray

There are no hard-and-fast rules about how this prayer should go, but there are a couple of things you should keep in mind. For one thing, it should be a joint venture. You should start, praying aloud, to give the person an idea of how praying is done. Thank the Lord for the person and the decision that's about to be made.

When you're done praying, yield the floor to the person making the decision. He or she may stutter and stammer all the way through a prayer, but that's okay. It will sound like pure poetry to God. If you sense that the person is really struggling, gently guide him in asking for God's forgiveness and salvation.

### 3. Invite

What you don't want to do is shake hands with the person after the prayer, offer your congratulations, and hit the road. It's important that you take responsibility for helping your new Christian friend begin to grow as a believer. Your best strategy is to offer a standing invitation for the person to go to church with you. If they accept, you can introduce them to your Christian friends and maybe even get them involved in a Sunday school class or a new believers' Bible study.

# Six to Grow On

It would be impossible for us to walk you through a "typical" faith-sharing encounter, because there's no such thing as a typical faith-sharing encounter. Every conversation you have with an unbeliever will have its own unpredictable rhythms, tangents, and peculiarities. Learning to "go with the flow" is an essential skill when it comes to sharing your faith. There are, however, some tips that generally apply to most faith-sharing situations. We've listed a half dozen of them.

> **JUST WONDERING**
>
> **How long should I wait before I bring up the topic of Christianity again to someone who's already rejected it?**
> You might want to consider giving the person a chance to bring up the topic to you again. Continue to "let your light shine" in the way you go about your daily business; maintain regular, casual contact with the person; keep praying for another faith-sharing opportunity; and let the Holy Spirit prepare the way for a second encounter.

### *1. Keep a Bible handy.*

Nine times out of ten, the people you share your faith with won't question Scripture passages when you quote them. They won't even think about whether or not you might be manipulating God's Word just to prove a point (which, of course, none of us should ever do).

However, it's important for you to be prepared for that tenth person. Always have a Bible nearby when you share your faith, so that if someone asks to see a verse you're quoting or accuses you of taking biblical statements out of context, you can support your claims with visual evidence.

Keep in mind that it's possible to overuse your Bible, too. What you don't want to do when you're sharing your faith is keep flipping back and forth between Scripture passages. You'll lose your listener's interest faster than you can say "Philippians."

### *2. Don't let your ego get in the way.*

Sharing your faith isn't about proving that you're right and other people are wrong. And it's not about proving your moral superiority. If you approach witnessing from an egotistical perspective—that is, if you act like it's your responsibility to "show poor heathens the light"—you're going to create walls of resistance before you even get started.

Along those same lines, you need to make sure that you don't take it personally when someone doesn't respond to your witness in the way you'd like. There's a good chance that your role may be the "introducer" of the gospel message in that person's life. God may use you to lay the groundwork and then use someone else to complete the conversion process. It doesn't matter where you're at in the process, as long as you're involved.

**3. *Practice on other Christians.***
Test out new ideas and ways of presenting the gospel on your Christian friends. Ask them to respond as an unbeliever might. Use your practice time to work out kinks in your presentation and anticipate possible responses on the part of actual unbelievers.

**4. *Always be prepared to seize the moment.***
Second Timothy 4:2 says, "Preach the Word; be prepared in season and out of season." You never know when an opportunity to share your faith is going to present itself, so you have to be ready when it does. You can't always say, "Let's talk about this next Thursday." Sometimes people will be most receptive to your message on the spur of the moment. If you're prepared to take advantage of that, you've got a good shot at leading them to Christ.

**5. *Keep things one-on-one.***
You'll find that people are much more likely to ask questions, share their real feelings, and respond to your message honestly if you're alone with them. Having other people present not only tends to be a distraction, it also causes the people you're sharing with to become embarrassed and self-conscious about opening up.

**6. *Avoid soliloquies.***
Don't preach; share. What you want is a dialogue, not a monologue. Make a point

**JUST WONDERING**

**Does God reward us for leading people to Christ?**
Bible passages such as 1 Thessalonians 2:19-20 suggest that God does single out people who faithfully share His gospel with others for praise and reward. To receive a "crown" from God in heaven is one of the highest honors we can hope for. On top of that, we'll have the pleasure of greeting people in heaven that we assisted on earth. Imagine how incredible that will be!

of asking questions ("Do you understand how God can be loving, holy, and just at the same time?") and inviting feedback ("Am I explaining this clearly enough?") while you share. Encourage a give-and-take exchange.

These are just a few tips to get you started. You'll find that as you begin to share your faith, you'll come up with other tips to add to this list. The more often you present your Christian witness, the more comfortable you'll become with it. The more comfortable you become, the better your communication will be.

Before long, you may even start thinking of yourself as an evangelist.

## Know What You Believe

How much do you know about sharing your faith? Here's a quiz to test your knowledge.

1. Which of the following quotes about witnessing does not come from the Bible?
   a. "He has committed to us the message of reconciliation."
   b. "Go and make disciples of all nations."
   c. "You will receive power when the Holy Spirit comes on you."
   d. "Let every man find his own path to the Father."

2. What does it mean that Christians are the "light of the world" (Matthew 5:14)?
   a. We are "brighter"—that is, more intelligent—than unbelievers.
   b. We need to be careful about who we share our faith with because our light dims every time we fail to lead someone to Christ.
   c. We will always be looked up to and admired by non-Christians.
   d. We show others the way to Christ.

3. Which of the following is not an essential point in the story of salvation?
   a. As sinners, we can do nothing to save ourselves from God's punishment.
   b. After Jesus was executed for the sins we committed, He rose from the dead to defeat death once and for all.
   c. One of Jesus' own disciples refused to believe in His resurrection.
   d. God is *holy*, which means He is completely separate from sin, and *just*, which means He demands punishment for sin.

4. Which of the following is not one of your responsibilities in responding to a person who wants to accept Christ as Savior?
   a. Inviting the person to attend church with you.
   b. Asking the person to tithe.
   c. Leading the person in prayer.
   d. Reviewing the main points of salvation to make sure the person understands.
5. Which of the following is not an important tip to keep in mind when it comes to sharing your faith?
   a. Don't let your ego get in the way.
   b. Never try to talk to an unbeliever by yourself.
   c. Practice with other Christians.
   d. Avoid soliloquies.

*Answers: (1) d, (2) d, (3) c, (4) b, (5) b*

CHAPTER 13

# Where There's a Will . . .

## SNAPSHOT

"I was upset about it for a while," Bill said as he jogged past the two-mile marker. "But then I realized it was—"

"God's will," Ray finished.

"Yeah," Bill said. "How did you know I was going to say that?"

Ray broke pace to jump over a mud puddle but quickly fell back into rhythm next to Bill. "Because that's your explanation for everything," he huffed. "When Dottie broke up with you, you said it was God's will. When you lost your job at Nicholson Brothers, you said it was God's will. When you broke your collarbone, you said it was God's will."

"So?" Bill said.

"So, if I were you, I think I'd ask God to let me go freelance for a while," Ray said. "His will doesn't seem to be working for you."

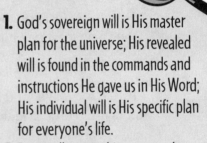

### Sneak Preview

1. God's sovereign will is His master plan for the universe; His revealed will is found in the commands and instructions He gave us in His Word; His individual will is His specific plan for everyone's life.
2. Practically everything we need to know about God's will for our lives can be found in the Bible.
3. Discovering God's individual will for our lives involves taking stock of our God-given spiritual gifts, abilities, and personality traits.

"No, that's not true," Bill said, as he picked up the pace a little. "With God's will, every day is something new. Good or bad, I wouldn't trade that for anything. Besides, eventually everything's going to end in perfection."

"I don't know," Ray said, "I'm not convinced that *God's will* isn't just the Christian term for 'random luck.'"

"You don't think God is capable of having a plan for everyone's life?" Bill asked.

"It's not a matter of being *capable*," Ray replied. "It's a matter of logical extremes."

"What do you mean?"

"I'm just asking how far you go in looking for God's will in your everyday life," Ray said. "Here, try this. I caught three green lights in a row on the way here this morning. Was that God's will?"

"Yeah, I think so," Bill answered.

"Okay, but the last light turned yellow before I got to the intersection," Ray explained. "So what if I'd stopped instead of speeding up? Would that have gone against God's will?"

"Hey, way to focus on the big picture," Bill said sarcastically. "I'm talking about God's plan for your entire life, and you're obsessing over a traffic light."

"Hey, if the question's too tough for you, just say so," Ray said.

"It's not too tough for me," Bill snapped. "Just give me a minute to organize my thoughts." He opened his mouth to say something else, but didn't. Then he glanced at Ray and furrowed his brow. Finally, after a minute or so, he shook his head. "Look, man, I'm already starting to tighten up in both legs. The last thing I need now is a brain cramp, too."

* * * * * * * * * * * * * * *

For many believers, God's will is the "lost ark" or the "holy grail" of the Christian life—the ultimate prize for the faithful. They imagine His will as a hidden map that, when discovered, will show them exactly where their future leads and what God has in store for them.

If that's how you picture God's will, we've got some news for you, Indiana Jones. That's not how it works. God does have a will for your life, and it's important for you to understand it. But what that will is—and, more specifically, what it isn't—may surprise you. So take off your fedora, toss aside your whip, and keep reading, because adventure and discovery await.

## Three Kinds of Will

The first thing we need to do when we talk about "God's will" is define our terms. You see, God's will can actually be divided into three different categories:

- His sovereign will
- His revealed will
- His individual will

Let's take a look at each one.

## God's Sovereign Will

Think of God's sovereign will as His master plan for the universe—the one that's been in effect since before time began. His sovereign plan includes everything from the order in which the stars in the universe will implode to the order in which the hairs on your head will fall out.

We're not privy to the details of God's sovereign will because, well, we're not deity. God chooses not to test our reactions to His all-encompassing plan before He implements it. With the exception of biblical prophecies, He doesn't make the details of His sovereign will known before they occur.

We can do nothing to change God's sovereign will or prevent it from occurring. In fact, our only logical response to God's sovereignty is worship. We can and should give honor and glory to God for the fact that He controls everything in the universe.

## God's Revealed Will

God's revealed will . . . otherwise known as *the Bible.* As Christians, we instinctively nod our heads when someone mentions the importance of God's Word. We emphatically assert that of course Scripture is vital to the good health of . . . harumph, harumph, harumph.

Here's the deal. If your question is, What does God want me to do with my life? your answer is in the Bible.

We don't have to tell you that God's Word is full of instructions. On any casual read through, you're likely to stumble onto such commands as:

- "Do not worry about your life" (Matthew 6:25).
- "Love one another" (John 13:34).
- "Serve one another" (Galatians 5:13).
- "Give thanks in all circumstances" (1 Thessalonians 5:18).
- "Let us not give up meeting together" (Hebrews 10:25).

The mistake many people make in searching for God's will is to assume that those instructions, and the hundreds more like them in Scripture, don't have any direct bearing on the specific details of their lives. In other words, they treat God's instructions as noble principles to live by, but not much help in finding a career, a spouse, or a direction in life.

And that's too bad. You see, that way of thinking lies about 180 degrees from reality. In fact, committing ourselves to understanding and obeying God's commands in Scripture puts us in the position of discovering His will for our lives.

### Just Wondering

**Where do sin and imperfection fit into God's sovereign will for the world?**
God did not create sin as part of His plan for the universe. However, because He is omniscient (all-knowing), He created a plan that takes sin and imperfection into account–and still results in ultimate glory for Himself. To put it a little less theologically, if you give God lemons, He knows how to make lemonade.

For example, who's to say that . . .

- your whole perspective on your future won't be changed when a certain Scripture passage touches your heart during your Bible study?
- an unexpected career opportunity won't develop from a chance encounter when you're sharing your faith?
- your future spouse won't be serving next to you at a soup kitchen sponsored by your church?

We're not suggesting that that's how God's will *always* makes itself known. God's work is usually much more subtle and impressive than that. By oversimplifying the process, though, we can connect the dots between our obedience and our future.

# God's Individual Will

Let's talk about that future—specifically, about whether God has an individual one picked out for each of us. In other words, does God keep some kind of portfolio on us that reveals . . .

- the perfect college for us to attend?
- the perfect person for us to marry?
- the perfect career for us to pursue?
- the perfect city for us to live in?
- the perfect house for us to buy?
- the perfect car for us to drive?
- the perfect friends for us to hang out with?
- the perfect way for us to spend our weekends?
- the perfect names for us to give our kids?

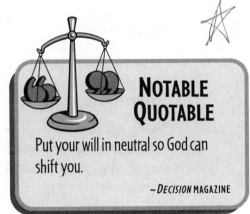

**NOTABLE QUOTABLE**

Put your will in neutral so God can shift you.

—*DECISION* MAGAZINE

Depends on who you ask. Some Christians believe that God has a specific, perfect plan for every area of our lives. That's not to say they believe we have no choice in the matter, or that God will necessarily intervene if we try to enroll at the "wrong" university or exchange vows with the "wrong" person. We were created with free will, after all. Instead, they believe that we simply suffer the consequences of our hasty, ill-considered choices. In other words, though we may be content with the spouse we choose, if that person is not God's intended spouse for us, we won't be as content as we could be.

Some Christians believe that God gave us His Word in lieu of a detailed individual plan for our lives. They argue that God expects us to weigh every decision we make in our lives against the instructions and truths of Scripture in order to make sure that it coincides with His revealed will. They contend that as long as a life decision falls within the parameters of His Word, God will approve of it and bless it.

> **NOTABLE QUOTABLE**
>
> The best thing about the future is that it comes only one day at a time.
>
> —ABRAHAM LINCOLN

Some Christians take a middle position on the issue, believing that God has specific plans for certain areas of our lives but leaves other areas to our discernment—within His revealed will, of course.

Let's assume that God *does* have some specific plans for your future—an individual will for your life beyond His revealed will. The obvious question then becomes, How do you discover or recognize it?

### *Taking Inventory*

The first place to look is to the obvious clues God has left in your life. In chapter 4, we examined the spiritual gifts God's Holy Spirit gives to all believers. By looking at your own personal gifts, you may be able to pick up some vital information about His plans for you. You may find that God has conditioned you to enjoy and thrive on certain types of interaction and challenges.

In chapter 4, we identified eighteen spiritual gifts (compiled from individual lists found in Romans 12, 1 Corinthians 12, and Ephesians 4), but we also noted that some of them were intended to fulfill specific, unique needs of the first-century church and are no longer necessary. For the purposes of this chapter, we're going to focus on eleven *active* spiritual gifts, which are summarized as follows:

1. ***Evangelism.*** This is the ability to proclaim the gospel so that people understand and respond to it.
2. ***Pastoring.*** This gift involves shepherding, caring for, and protecting God's people—usually in a leadership position. This gift is often tied in with teaching.
3. ***Serving.*** This gift involves meeting people's physical and emotional needs in a hands-on way, by getting personally involved in their lives and doing things that other people may be unwilling to do.
4. ***Teaching.*** This gift involves being able to explain God's truth to other people in ways that they understand and respond to. It's closely related to the gift of wisdom and knowledge.
5. ***Faith.*** This is the ability to rely on God to have one's needs met—and to serve as an example to other believers of what faith can accomplish.
6. ***Encouraging.*** This gift involves providing encouragement and comfort to people—spurring them on to achieve what God has in store for them.
7. ***Distinguishing spirits.*** This gift involves being able to tell the difference between true and false teaching.
8. ***Mercy.*** This gift involves a special ministry of kindness and assistance to the needy, particularly those who are sick or suffering.

**ON A PERSONAL NOTE**

One of the best ways to ease anxiety over God's plans for your future is to look at His work in your recent past. Take some time to think of things that have happened in your life in the past year or so–things that you couldn't have predicted, or even imagined, a year ago. Consider the ways in which God has matured you, guided you, and prospered you. Once you've got a sizable list, thank God for His work in your life, and ask Him to help you recall that work when you start to fret about the future.

9. *Giving.* This gift involves the ability to be generous with what you have, no matter how much or how little that may be.

10. *Administration.* This gift involves overseeing the day-to-day operations of the church.

11. *Wisdom and knowledge.* This gift involves being able to understand God's truth and explain it to others who need help.

Do one or two of those descriptions seem familiar to you? Have you been told since you were a kid that you're generous or a good helper? Do your friends come to you when they have a question about spiritual things? Do you feel comfortable sharing your faith with others? Are you a natural encourager?

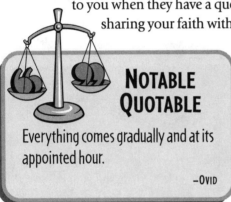

**NOTABLE QUOTABLE**

Everything comes gradually and at its appointed hour.

—OVID

If you answered "Yes" to any of those questions, chances are you're already familiar with at least one or two of your spiritual gifts. What you need to understand, though, is that regardless of which gifts you've been given, you have a responsibility to put them to use.

In fact, activating your spiritual gifts is one of your first steps in discovering God's will for your life. That's not to say that as soon as you start teaching a Sunday school class or offering encouragement in a ministry setting, the door to your future will swing wide open. It's simply one step in a long process.

Recognizing your spiritual gifts will give you valuable *ministry* direction. And that's a great start in discovering God's will for your life. Never underestimate the importance of finding the right ministry for yourself.

### *Looking at Talents, Abilities, and Preferences*

In addition to your spiritual gifts, you have other God-given talents that come in to play when you're searching for God's will. The fact is, God has wired you in a certain way for a reason. Whether your skills, talents, abilities, knowledge, or interests involve . . .

- writing computer programs,
- repairing cars,

- ➤ drawing or painting,
- ➤ making music,
- ➤ playing sports,
- ➤ teaching,
- ➤ crunching numbers, and/or
- ➤ working with kids,
- ➤ marketing,
- ➤ writing,
- ➤ performing,
- ➤ working with your hands,

. . . they will likely play a big role in helping you discover God's will for your career, your ministry, your social life, or your personal time. Who knows what doors may be opened simply by making your talents and abilities known?

In addition to your spiritual gifts and your talents and abilities, you've got your personal preferences to consider. For instance, some people enjoy being around other people; some people have an intense need for personal time. Similarly, some people prefer to spend their time outdoors, staying active; some people prefer to spend their time behind a desk or in front of a computer screen. And some people thrive in pressure-filled situations; others thrive in more sedate surroundings.

### On a Personal Note

If you're not sure about your interests and skills, try taking some personality and career-aptitude tests. (You can probably find at least a few such tests at your local library.) You may or may not be surprised by the results, but they can be useful in suggesting or reaffirming things about yourself that you need to know.

Consider your own personality—your unique preferences, tendencies, and quirks. Chances are you'll find some valuable clues as to what God has prepared for you. After all, if He expects something of you, it only makes sense that He will equip you for it.

If all of these personal examination instructions seem a little obvious to you . . . well, you're starting to get the picture of what God's will is really about. Chances are, you already have an inkling of what God's future for you holds. You may not know who you'll marry, what your career will be, or where you'll live, but you probably know that certain things are givens.

And those "givens" are Exhibit A of what God has planned for your future.

# A Half-Dozen Don'ts

In your quest to discover the specifics of God's will for your life, there are some principles you'll need to keep in mind. Here are six tips designed to help you in your search.

### *1. Don't misunderstand what it means to discover God's will for your life.*

We're not talking about the Christian equivalent of a psychic reading here. God is not some cosmic fortune-teller, giving people quick glances at His crystal ball. Neither is He going to send you a package of information, listing . . .

- the realtor who's going to sell you your dream house,
- the personnel director of your ideal employer,
- the people you're supposed to lead to Christ, and
- the amount of money you're required to donate to your church's missions.

If you want to cut to the chase, we could just say that God is not interested in sharing the details of our future with us. And for good reason, too. If God were to reveal the specifics of what lay ahead of us, our relationship with Him would change immediately. For one thing, we wouldn't have to rely on Him anymore.

Obviously, that's not what God wants. His desire is for us to draw closer to Him, to depend on Him to see us through each day. That's why He generally reveals His will for our lives a little at a time. Any more than that would simply be too much for us to handle.

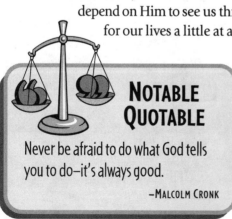

**NOTABLE QUOTABLE**

Never be afraid to do what God tells you to do—it's always good.

—MALCOLM CRONK

### *2. Don't look for divine patterns or evidence of God's will where they don't exist.*

If you look hard enough, you can convince yourself that you see God's will in every . . . cold you suffer, telemarketing call you receive, shirt that shrinks in the dryer, and cavity your dentist finds. The problem with such an encompassing view of

God's will is that it diverts your focus from what's really important. It's possible to get so wrapped up in looking for "cosmic connections" that you lose sight of the fact that your responsibility is to actually do God's will. Remember, this is all about making sure that God's work gets done—in and through your life.

### 3. *Don't confuse waiting on the Lord with wasting time.*

One of the great myths associated with God's will is that your life is supposed to be in some kind of "holding pattern" until you figure out what it is God wants you to do. Some people point to passages such as Psalm 27:14—"Wait for the LORD"—to defend their minimal efforts.

The fact is, regardless of how little you know about God's individual will for your life, you still have your plate full with His revealed Word. The Bible has something new to teach you every day. Why not focus your time and energy on discovering its truths? Why not make your waiting as productive as possible?

### 4. *Don't miss God's will when He reveals it.*

The Old Testament prophets Samuel and Elijah both learned from personal experience that God doesn't always make Himself known in obvious or expected ways. In fact, God had to call Samuel *four* times before the young prophet realized who was talking to him! (You can check out the prophets' stories for yourself in 1 Samuel 3:1–10 and 1 Kings 19:9–18.)

There's a lesson in those encounters for those of us seeking God's will for our lives. If we're busy looking for a bold, dramatic revelation, there's a good chance we will miss indications of God's will when they're *actually* revealed.

Keep in mind that God doesn't just use the things that *happen* in our lives to reveal His will; He also reveals it through the things that *don't* happen. For example . . .

- the college application that's denied,
- the loan that doesn't come through,
- the job interview that bombs, or

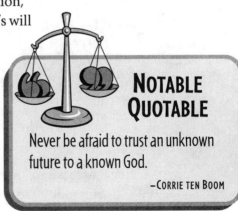

**NOTABLE QUOTABLE**

Never be afraid to trust an unknown future to a known God.

—CORRIE TEN BOOM

- the dream date that turns out to be a nightmare

. . . can all be revelations of God's will. We just need to recognize them for what they are.

### *5. Don't expect something out of character for God.*

Repeat after us: God's individual will never contradicts His revealed will. In other words, God will not suspend the commands and instructions in His Word for the sake of your convenience or "happiness." Anyone who believes that it's God's will for them to . . .

- divorce their spouse and marry someone else,
- take revenge on a nemesis at work,
- exaggerate qualifications for a job, or
- withhold information on their tax return

. . . is dangerously wrong. Not only will the person miss out on God's *actual* will in those errors, that believer will damage his or her relationship with Him in the process.

That's why it's absolutely essential to know exactly what God's Word says before we start making hasty conclusions about His will for our lives.

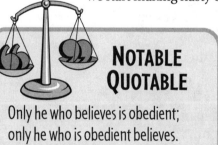

**NOTABLE QUOTABLE**

Only he who believes is obedient; only he who is obedient believes.

—Dietrich Bonhoeffer

### *6. Don't let other people tell you what God's will for your life is.*

Proverbs 15:22 tells us, "Plans fail for lack of counsel, but with many advisers they succeed." You need to recognize two things about this verse: 1. It can and should be applied to your search for God's will for your life. 2. The word is *advisers*, not *dictators*.

Mature Christians who point you to relevant Scripture passages and offer their sincere prayers in your search for God's will are a valuable commodity. On the other hand, people who *tell* you what God's will for your life is based on their own experiences and understanding of Scripture may do more damage to your cause than good. What's more, a closer inspection of the advice you receive from overanxious counselors will likely reveal hidden agendas or ulterior motives on their part.

Ultimately, *you* are the one responsible for carrying out God's will in your life. *You* are the one who will face the consequences for misunderstanding or ignoring that will. So while it's commendable to seek input and advice from Christians you trust, you can't accept their advice at face value. You have a responsibility to make sure that their counsel is biblically sound and God-honoring.

## No Need for Treasure Hunts

Don't make the mistake of turning your search for God's will in your life into some grand treasure hunt. God isn't hiding the plan for your ultimate happiness and fulfillment from you. He's not going to punish you with a mediocre life because you failed to heed one of the twelve tips in this chapter. That's not God's style.

We'll leave you with this assurance: If you . . .

- commit yourself to growing every day in your relationship with God,
- assign Bible study and prayer top priorities in your life, and
- determine to learn as much as you can from your pastor, your Sunday school teacher, your mentor, and other trusted Christians

. . . you will discover God's will for your life.

And you'll like it, too.

**JUST WONDERING**

**Can I pray to change God's will for my life?**

Technically, you can take any request to God—and expect an answer from Him. In this case, the answer will be "No," but it will be an answer. Instead of praying to change God's will, try praying to change your attitude toward it. Ask the Holy Spirit to help you understand what God's will can accomplish in your life and in the lives of those around you.

## Know What You Believe

How much do you know about discovering God's will? Here's a quiz to test your knowledge.

1. Which of the following is not one of the three categories of God's will?
   a. Living will
   b. Sovereign will
   c. Individual will
   d. Revealed will

2. Which of the following is not true of God's revealed will?
   a. It's found in Scripture.
   b. It can help us discover the secrets of God's sovereign will.
   c. It can help us discover our individual will.
   d. There's always something new to learn about it.

3. Which of the following does not play a major role in helping you discover God's will for your life?
   a. Your spiritual gifts
   b. Your talents and abilities
   c. Your TV viewing habits
   d. Your personality traits

4. Which of the following is true of God?
   a. His preference is to reveal our entire future to us at one time.
   b. He expects us to do His will but doesn't equip us for it.
   c. He has no specific will for anyone's life but allows us to think He does.
   d. He wants us to draw closer to Him every day.

5. Which of the following is the least helpful tip for discovering God's will for your life?
   a. Don't bother trying to figure out what God may or may not want you to do; ultimately, it doesn't matter.
   b. Don't look for divine patterns where they don't exist.

c. Don't let other people tell you what God's will for your life is.
d. Don't expect something out of character for God.

*Answers: (1) a, (2) b, (3) c, (4) d, (5) a*

CHAPTER 14

# Blessed Reassurance

## SNAPSHOT

Amy rinsed the plate she'd just washed and handed it to her mother. "Remind me again why we spend every Thanksgiving in the worst neighborhood of the city, fixing food for people we've never met," she said.

Ann snapped her dish towel playfully at her daughter. "The short answer is that we're doing what Jesus told us to do by serving others."

"You mean we're doing what the *Bible* says Jesus told us to do," Amy corrected.

Ann raised her eyebrows. "I was just getting ready to ask whether you've learned anything interesting in your world religion class," she said. "I guess I just found out."

"I'm not trying to be a radical," Amy explained. "I'm just saying we don't know what really happened

### SNEAK PREVIEW

1. Occasional doubts and questions are evidence of an active faith in God.
2. God is not offended by our sincere doubts and questions; in fact, He invites us to investigate His truth for ourselves.
3. If you're committed to finding answers to your questions, God will bless your efforts and give you the peace of mind you seek.

when the Bible was being written."

"Give me a scenario," Ann said.

"Okay, here's one a guy in class used," Amy explained. "Picture this: One day Jesus sees a crippled man fall down by the side of the road. Jesus can't get to the guy Himself, because of the crowd, so He tells His disciples to help the guy up. But Matthew is too far back to see what's going on. Later, when he asks about it, all he hears is that Jesus wanted His disciples to help a guy in need."

"I think I know where you're going with this," Ann said.

Amy continued. "So when the time came for Matthew to write his gospel, he remembered what he'd heard that day and mistakenly turned Jesus' one-time request into an all-time commandment."

"And that explanation makes sense to you?" Ann asked.

"Not really," Amy said. "But if you think about it enough, it can raise some doubts."

Ann thought for a moment. "So, for all we know, murder and adultery aren't really sins," she concluded.

"What are you talking about?" Amy asked.

"Well, Moses was an old man when he climbed Mount Sinai to get the Ten Commandments from God. Maybe his hearing was shot, too. Maybe he misunderstood what God really said and just wrote down words that sounded close."

"Okay, you're not taking this conversation seriously," Amy said. "Let's just drop the subject."

Ann ignored her and continued. "Maybe what God actually said was, 'You shall not . . . *till*,' but Moses heard the word *kill* instead. Maybe God didn't want us tilling the dirt in our gardens."

"Okay, Mom, I get the point," Amy sighed.

Ann grinned at her. "I think as long as we're talking about doubts, we should get all of the possibilities out there," she said.

"Is there any chance I'll hear the end of this conversation before I go back to school?" Amy asked.

"I *doubt* it," Ann replied.

* * * * * * * * * * * * * * * *

God's Word asks us to accept a lot of things that common sense, conventional wisdom, natural laws, political correctness, and the beliefs of others would tell us to reject. Think about it.

- People walking through the middle of a sea on dry ground?
- A man surviving a night alone in a pit with starving lions?
- A man spending three days in the stomach of a giant fish and then being vomited back onto shore, alive and well?
- God singling out the Israelites for preferential treatment and special blessings?
- God demanding blood sacrifice as payment for sin?
- Deity taking human form?
- A carpenter who turns out to be the Messiah?
- People rising from the dead?
- Only one set of spiritual beliefs that actually leads to eternal life with God?
- The Creator of the universe taking an active interest in the details of our daily lives?

You've got to admit, some of those stories call for a lot of open-mindedness—especially thousands of years after the fact.

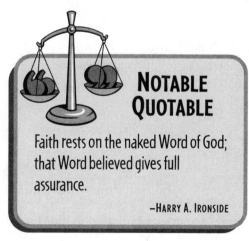

**NOTABLE QUOTABLE**

Faith rests on the naked Word of God; that Word believed gives full assurance.

—HARRY A. IRONSIDE

Jesus Himself recognized the difficulty of our position, especially compared to that of His disciples. After all, Jesus' followers had physical evidence to help them believe that He is who He says He is and that He can do what He says He can do. The disciples and the crowds who followed Jesus during His time on earth only had to trust their senses.

In John 20:29, Jesus says to one of His disciples, "Because you have seen me, you have believed; blessed are those who have not seen and yet have believed." That would include us. And while it's certainly comforting to know that we're blessed because of our sightless belief, that doesn't make our faith any easier to maintain.

**ON A PERSONAL NOTE**

Make a list of the things you put your faith in on a daily basis. For example, when you sit down, you put your faith in the fact that your chair can hold you. When you eat a hamburger, you put your faith in the fact that it's not tainted by harmful bacteria. When you drive on a two-lane highway, you put your faith in the fact that the drivers coming toward you will stay in their lane. Ask yourself whether any of those items are more trustworthy than God and His Word.

## Faith Value

Mark Twain once wrote, "Faith is believing what you know ain't so." The author of Hebrews 11:1 wrote, "Faith is being sure of what we hope for and certain of what we do not see."

The differences between those two statements may seem subtle at first glance, but are, in fact, enormous. Faith is not . . .

- a leap into the realm of the far-fetched and fanciful.
- the opposite of intellect.
- a naive response to the world around us.
- wishful thinking.

Faith is actually a gift from God that allows us to see possibilities beyond our limited perspective—that is, beyond our five senses. Faith is also an attitude we choose to adopt—not in spite of the evidence but because of it. In other words, we have faith because we have decided, based on experience, that God and His Word are worthy of our trust.

As we mentioned in the opening paragraph, objections to the Christian faith and God's Word are often based on . . .

- common sense,
- conventional wisdom,
- natural laws,
- political correctness, or
- the beliefs of others.

Under normal circumstances, these things might be helpful in reaching a conclusion about what is and isn't "believable." But we're a long way from "normal" here.

The events that form the foundation of our faith—specifically Jesus' birth, life, death, and resurrection—are difficult for many people to believe because the world has never experienced anything like them before or since. Because Christ's coming is unprecedented and unparalleled, common sense and conventional wisdom can't be applied to it. There's simply nothing *common* or *conventional* about what Jesus did during His time on earth.

Don't forget, we're talking about deity in human form here. That means all bets are off. The laws of time, space, and dimension—not to mention those of physics and natural science—that govern our lives and shape our impressions of the world simply don't apply to God and His work. That means our normal criteria for determining whether to believe or not believe in something don't apply, either.

**NOTABLE QUOTABLE**

Doubt makes the mountain which faith can move.

—*DECISION* MAGAZINE

No mere human can raise someone from the dead. Jesus Christ, the One who gave humans life to begin with, can. No mere human can stop a storm in its tracks simply by saying, "Be still." Jesus Christ, the One who set the entire universe in motion in the first place, can. No mere human can change our eternal destiny. Jesus Christ, our loving God in human form, can.

No mere human can claim to be the only way to God. Jesus Christ, the One who lived a sinless life and conquered death, can.

Believing that Jesus is who He says He is doesn't require us to *suspend* our intellect and common sense; it requires us to *expand* them.

## Ego Check

How shortsighted and narrow-minded is it to believe that . . .

- our body of knowledge is complete, that we know everything there is to know about everything?
- our five senses are the only useful tools for discovering ultimate truth?
- nothing can exist outside the realm of what we decide is possible?

Research indicates that, on average, humans use approximately 10 percent of their brain's capacity. Ten percent—now think about that. With 90 percent of our cranial precincts not reporting, don't you think it's a little early for us to be making projections about what is and isn't possible as far as God is concerned?

**NOTABLE QUOTABLE**

A faith which does not doubt is a dead faith.

—MIGUEL DE UNAMUNO JUGO

We don't have to suspend our critical thinking in order to have faith; we have to suspend our ego. We have to rid ourselves of the notion that we sit atop the intellect chain. That's just not the case. As finite human beings, we will *always* have a lot to learn. Faith is simply a matter of opening ourselves up to the learning process.

Think about it this way. A wise freshman undergraduate isn't going to challenge his professor's lectures based on his high-school-level knowledge of a subject like, say, microbiology. Instead, that student is going to have faith in the fact that the professor knows what he's talking about and that he's telling the truth.

The same principle applies to the Christian faith. If we're wise, we're not going to challenge the accounts or principles in God's Word based on our limited knowledge of the world around us. Instead, we're going to accept the fact that God knows what He's talking about and that He's telling us the truth in His Word.

That's reasonable faith.

# Believe It or Not

That's not to say that faith should come automatically or even easily to us. We live in a skeptical age. We live in a society that prizes individual thought. At the same time, we're inundated with false claims and wild hyperbole from marketers and advertisers seeking to gain our trust and loyalty. We can hardly be blamed for having at least occasional reservations or questions when it comes to our spiritual beliefs.

What does that mean for those of us who call ourselves Christians? Actually, there are three things we need to understand about doubt.

***1. Doubt is normal.***

Do you remember who led you to Christ? That person wrestled with occasional doubts about his or her faith.

Do you remember the first Christian whose life made an impact on you? That person had questions about God and His will that would shock you.

Do you remember the best sermon or the most inspiring testimony you ever heard? The person who gave it has been battling doubts and fears on and off for most of his or her Christian life.

You know the Bible character, other than Jesus, that you most admire? That person occasionally questioned whether God's work was worth the trouble it caused.

How can we be so sure about other people's inner workings? Because *every*

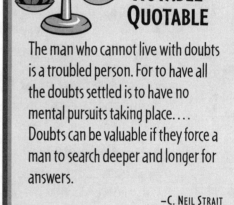

**NOTABLE QUOTABLE**

The man who cannot live with doubts is a troubled person. For to have all the doubts settled is to have no mental pursuits taking place.... Doubts can be valuable if they force a man to search deeper and longer for answers.

—C. Neil Strait

committed Christian wrestles with doubt and tough questions occasionally. (Some wrestle with them frequently.)

### *2. God isn't offended by doubt.*

Let's make this clear. There is nothing sinful or disobedient about having doubts. No one in the Bible is condemned for wavering in his or her spiritual certainty. No one is struck down for asking a legitimate question about God.

There's nothing wrong with debating and questioning the finer points of Christianity. That's the way we make our faith our own. God created us with the ability to reason. Why shouldn't we apply that skill to our spiritual beliefs?

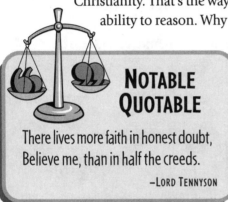

**NOTABLE QUOTABLE**

There lives more faith in honest doubt,
Believe me, than in half the creeds.

—LORD TENNYSON

God isn't threatened, displeased, or dishonored by the sincere questions and doubts of His people. In fact, He welcomes scrutiny. Psalm 34:8 invites us to "taste and see that the LORD is good." In other words, come experience the Lord's goodness so that you can believe in it.

God won't wilt under the glare of the spotlight. There are no vulnerable parts of His plan for us that will be exposed under intense scrutiny. There are no loose ends in the Christian faith that He's hoping we won't notice. God knows that the closer we look at His Word and His work in the world, the stronger our faith in Him will grow.

### *3. Doubt must inspire action.*

We should add one exception to the previous point. God will not have patience with people who use doubts and questions as a smoke screen to cover up their stubbornness, laziness, disinterest, or noncommitment. It's one thing to say, "I'm having a hard time understanding why my Muslim friends won't go to heaven when they die, especially since they worship the same God I do. That's why I asked Pastor Sorensen to recommend a book about the differences between Christianity and the other major religions." It's an entirely different thing to say, "I just can't believe God would send people to hell for going to the wrong church. Period."

Both statements reflect doubt. However, in the first approach, the person recognizes that the doubt is an obstacle to a closer relationship with God. As a result, the person is making a legitimate effort to understand the problem. In the second approach, the person is simply refusing to accept a truth about God because it doesn't fit his or her preconceived notions. What's more, the person seems content to remain in doubt indefinitely.

The Pharisees were full of doubts and questions about Jesus and His teachings:

> "Why does your teacher eat with tax collectors and 'sinners'?" (Matthew 9:11)
>
> "Teacher, we want to see a miraculous sign from you." (Matthew 12:38)
>
> "Why do your disciples break the tradition of the elders? They don't wash their hands before they eat!" (Matthew 15:2)

But they weren't seeking the truth. They were looking for opportunities to prove their own superiority to Jesus. They weren't interested in learning about Him; they were looking for reasons not to believe in Him.

Look at some of Jesus' responses to their questions:

> "Go and learn what this means: 'I desire mercy, not sacrifice.'" (Matthew 9:13)
>
> "A wicked and adulterous generation asks for a miraculous sign!" (Matthew 12:39)
>
> "You hypocrites! Isaiah was right when he prophesied about you: 'these people honor me with their lips, but their hearts are far from me.'" (Matthew 15:7–8)

It's pretty apparent that Jesus wasn't much interested in engaging the Pharisees in debate simply for the sake of proving His intellectual superiority. When someone had a legitimate question, Jesus was careful to address it. When someone used

**NOTABLE QUOTABLE**

Faith in God makes a person undaunted, unafraid, undivided, and "unflappable." Real faith results in active response, responsive action, and willing obedience... Faith is focusing on God's promises, and cropping out the world's discouragements.

—William A. Ward

questions as a defense against His teaching, Jesus was careful to dismiss it.

Many people put off making a decision for Christ or pursuing a personal relationship with Him by using their doubts and questions as an excuse. That's not acceptable. If you have doubts, you have a responsibility to do something about them. You have to move from the realm of the intellectual and theoretical and into the realm of the practical and applicable. If you have questions, you have to take the initiative to get them answered.

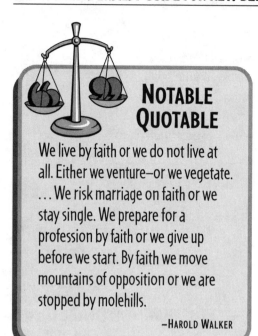

**NOTABLE QUOTABLE**

We live by faith or we do not live at all. Either we venture–or we vegetate. . . . We risk marriage on faith or we stay single. We prepare for a profession by faith or we give up before we start. By faith we move mountains of opposition or we are stopped by molehills.

–HAROLD WALKER

# Profiles in Doubt

Obviously, one of your first stops should be the Bible. God's Word has a lot to teach us about doubt—particularly in the experiences of faithful and not-so-faithful Bible characters. Let's take a look at three stories in particular to see what we can learn.

### *Liquid Courage: The Story of Peter*

Our first lesson is found in the story of Peter's late-night stroll on the Sea of Galilee. Matthew 14:22–33 tells us that Peter was in a boat with the other disciples late one night when they saw a figure walking toward them on the surface of the water. Thinking it was a ghost, the disciples panicked until they heard Jesus' voice say, "Take courage! It is I. Don't be afraid" (verse 27).

For reasons that aren't fully explained, Peter asked Jesus for permission to join Him on the sea. When Jesus said it was okay, Peter climbed out of the boat and walked toward Him—on top of the water! As he walked, though, Peter began to notice the howling wind and choppy waves all around him. He got scared, started to sink, and cried out, "Lord, save me!" And Jesus did, safely escorting Peter back to the boat.

This is a great illustration of the power of faith and the impact of doubt. Notice that Peter's first response to the unbelievable situation that confronted him was faith. Something deep inside told Peter that believing in Jesus at that moment would pay off big time.

So Peter acted on his faith and was rewarded with an incredible personal experience with the Savior. Unfortunately, Peter allowed himself to become distracted by the things around him. He became aware of his vulnerable position and began to second-guess himself and his faith. Worse than that, though, he took his eyes off Jesus.

And he began to sink.

That's the way doubt works in the lives of believers. When we hear God's truth, whether it's a Bible story or a command about how we should live, something deep inside—the Holy Spirit, to be exact—tells us that believing in that truth will ultimately pay off for us.

And that's when the distractions start:

- the voices of conventional wisdom insisting that our faith in things we can't explain makes us naive and laughable
- the voices of political correctness suggesting that our rigid views make us narrow-minded and unreasonable
- the voices of friends and acquaintances hinting that our spiritual beliefs make us dull and unlikable

When we start to pay attention to those voices, we become aware of our vulnerable position. We second-guess our faith. We lose sight of Jesus, and we begin to sink.

This is where it's important to mention that Jesus didn't punish Peter for his doubt. He didn't leave His disciple to drown. He didn't even make him find his own way back to the boat. Instead, Jesus responded immediately to Peter's cry and helped him regain his footing.

Jesus is ready to do the same thing for us when we call out to Him. When our doubts and fears begin to overwhelm us, Jesus will respond immediately to our prayers and help us regain our spiritual footing.

### *Put Your Hand in the Hand: The Story of Thomas*

Our second lesson can be found in the adventures of Thomas, one of Jesus' disciples, following the Savior's resurrection. John tells us that the first time Jesus appeared to His disciples after rising from the dead, Thomas was absent (20:19–29).

**ON A PERSONAL NOTE**

Come up with a list of resources that you can give to someone else who is struggling with doubts. Write down Bible references, the names of Christian books and videos, and any other resources that you've found helpful in combating doubt. Keep a copy of the list handy. You never know when you might have a chance to give it away!

Later, when the other disciples told Thomas the good news, he thought they were crazy. He said, "Unless I see the nail marks in his hands and put my finger where the nails were, and put my hand into his side, I will not believe it" (verse 25).This despite the fact that Thomas had seen Jesus raise people from the dead and had heard Jesus predict that He would rise from the grave!

A week later, Jesus appeared to His disciples again—and this time Thomas was present. Jesus said to him, "Put your finger here; see my hands. Reach out your hand and put it into my side. Stop doubting and believe."

With a mixture of guilt, shock, amazement, and joy, Thomas managed to utter five words in response: "My Lord and my God!" (verses 27–28).

This is a revealing illustration of how Jesus responds to our doubt. You'll notice that He didn't get mad at Thomas or humiliate him for his lack of faith. He didn't burst into the room and shout, "All right, which one of you guys thinks I'm not real?"

Instead, Jesus was quite matter-of-fact about the situation. He said, in essence, "Okay, Tommy, you say you need to touch My wounds in order to believe? Go ahead; touch them. Do what you need to do to get past your doubt. I've got big plans for you, and I need you to believe."

Jesus treats our doubts the same way. He doesn't get mad at us or make our lives miserable until we come to our senses. Instead, He gives us what we need to work through our doubts. He won't make us the same offer He made Thomas—that is, physical, tactile proof of His resurrection—because we live in an era of faith.

However, if we're committed to overcoming our doubts, Jesus will provide us with the means of doing just that. It might come in the form of . . .

- a Bible passage that speaks directly to our hearts in a way we've never experienced before,
- a supernatural sense of peace about our concerns, or
- a mentor who's struggled with and overcome similar doubts and knows how to help us work through them

. . . but it will come. And when it does, we have a responsibility to respond as Thomas did—with an overwhelming, heartfelt acknowledgment that Jesus is God and Lord of our lives.

> **JUST WONDERING**
>
> **How can I help other people who are struggling with doubt?**
>
> One of the best things you can do is provide a sympathetic ear and a nonjudgmental attitude. Resist the urge to scream, "Infidel!" when people confide in you about their doubts and questions. If you think it's appropriate, share your own struggles with doubt, as well as the methods you used to overcome them. If you know of any helpful resources–human, video, or written–be sure to recommend them.

### *Trial by Fire: The Story of Shadrach, Meshach, and Abednego*

Our third lesson is found in the Old Testament story of Shadrach, Meshach, and Abednego, three young Jewish men who were taken into captivity when Babylon conquered Israel. Daniel 3 tells us that Nebuchadnezzar, the king of Babylon, erected a giant statue in the province and proclaimed that anyone who did not fall down and worship it at an appointed time would be thrown into a blazing furnace. When the appointed time came, everyone in the province fell to the ground to worship the king's statue—everyone except Shadrach, Meshach, and Abednego, that is.

As followers of the true God, they were forbidden to worship idols. So they remained standing. And they got caught. The king gave them a second chance, and they still refused to bow. That made the king furious, so he ordered the furnace to be heated seven times hotter than usual before having the three young men tossed inside.

As they were being led to the furnace door, Shadrach, Meshach, and Abednego made one final statement. They said, "If we are thrown into the blazing furnace, the God we serve is able to save us from it, and he will rescue us from your hand, O king. But even if he does not, we want you to know, O king, that we will not serve your gods or worship the image of gold you have set up" (verses 17–18).

Look at those words again and consider this: It takes a strong faith to be able to say, "Even if you throw us into a raging fire, we know God will protect us." But it takes a truly remarkable faith to be able to say, "Even if the Lord allows us to burn to death, we will trust and serve Him because His will is more important than our lives."

Notice the lack of self-interest in Shadrach, Meshach, and Abednego's testimony. Their faith wasn't about believing that God would ultimately make their lives happy. Their faith wasn't about them at all. Their faith was only in the perfection of God's will.

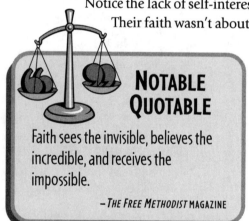

**NOTABLE QUOTABLE**

Faith sees the invisible, believes the incredible, and receives the impossible.

—*THE FREE METHODIST* MAGAZINE

We're not relating this story to make anyone feel like a loser for having doubts. It's safe to say that Shadrach, Meshach, and Abednego wrestled with their share of doubts and questions before developing their remarkable confidence in God. Our purpose in telling you this story is to give you a model of faith to shoot for in your own life.

You see, the selfless faith we're talking about—the kind that Shadrach, Meshach, and Abednego displayed thousands of years ago in Babylon—not only changes lives; it changes entire communities. The story of Shadrach, Meshach, and Abednego ends with God protecting them from harm in the fiery furnace, and the amazed king declaring God to be the one true deity of Babylon.

Imagine what that same kind of faith could do among your friends, family, coworkers, and acquaintances.

# When in Doubt . . .

Of course, in order to reach that level of faith, we first need to take care of our nagging doubts. If you're struggling with persistent doubts and questions, there are some specific steps you can take to address and overcome them.

### *1. Identify your doubts.*

Don't just say, "I'm having a hard time with my faith right now." Identify exactly what's shaky in your mind. Do you doubt that . . .

- God exists?
- the Bible is true?
- God loves you?
- God has a plan for your life?
- you're sinful?
- Jesus is the only way to God?
- giving your life to Christ is worth the sacrifice?

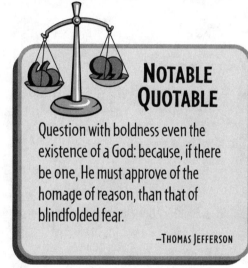

**NOTABLE QUOTABLE**

Question with boldness even the existence of a God: because, if there be one, He must approve of the homage of reason, than that of blindfolded fear.

—THOMAS JEFFERSON

As you identify your doubts, write them down in your journal or in a notebook that you keep handy. Update your list periodically to reflect your progress in getting answers and assurances for your problem areas.

### *2. Identify the cause of your doubts.*

Think about the things going on in your life that might be contributing to your skeptical frame of mind. For example, are you . . .

- hanging around with other people who are questioning Christianity?
- going through a rough stretch in your life?
- mad at God and trying to punish Him for something?

- trying to stall for time before making a commitment to Christ?
- having trouble understanding God's Word?

Once you've identified one or more potential causes for your doubt, think of some ways to combat their influence. For example, if you decide that you've been susceptible to the doubts and cynicism of other people concerning your faith, you may want to seriously consider cutting down on the amount of time you spend with those people.

**3. *Pray.***

One of the best prayers ever recorded on this subject is found in Mark 9:24: "I do believe; help me overcome my unbelief!" This short-but-sweet request acknowledges that belief and unbelief, faith and doubt, are often combined in us.

Ask the Holy Spirit to work in and through your thought processes and attitudes in order to strengthen your belief and lessen your unbelief. Ask Him to reveal any problem areas that you're not aware of and then give you the wisdom to deal with them effectively.

**4. *Talk to mature Christians about your doubts.***

Make an appointment with your pastor or Sunday school teacher to talk about your struggles. You may find that they too have wrestled with similar doubts and can offer practical suggestions. If that's not the case, they should be able to refer you to some Bible passages or other resources that can get you started in the right direction. At the very least, it never hurts to have another person praying for you.

**5. *Live as though you believe.***

Don't get stuck in a rut of doubting the same thing

### JUST WONDERING

**How should I respond to Christians who think I'm weak or immature because I have doubts?**

With love. But you knew that was coming, didn't you? Keep in mind that the only person you have to please with your spiritual growth is the Lord. Remember the distractions that caused Peter to sink during His faith exercise on the Sea of Galilee? The opinions of others would qualify as a distraction for you. If you allow the comments and judgments of others to negatively affect your quest to resolve your doubts, you'll have taken your eyes off Jesus—and you'll be heading for trouble.

over and over again. If your intellect isn't allowing you to grasp something, let experience drive it home. Here's how: Accept whatever it is you're doubting at face value and start living as though you believe it's true. In time, you'll find that the Lord will solidify that belief in your heart.

**NOTABLE QUOTABLE**

Faith speaks when hope dissembles:
Faith lives when hope dies dead.

—ALGERNON CHARLES SWINBURNE

For example, let's say you struggle with questions about whether God really loves you, based on your regrettable past. You can . . .

- read Bible verses about God's love,
- identify the reasons for your feelings of unlovability,
- ask the Lord to make you feel more loved, and
- listen to trusted Christian acquaintances assure you that you're loved.

But at some point, you need to start living your life like you're loved. That means treating yourself with dignity and respect so that others will do the same. It means refusing to damage your body with harmful substances and habits.

## Life Assurance

If you're serious about getting answers to your questions and assurance for your doubts, God will provide them for you. But He may not do it on an intellectual level, in the way you might expect. Instead, there's a good chance that He will give you the assurance and faith you need at a gut level—an inexplicable sense of peace that you can live with . . . and grow on.

**NOTABLE QUOTABLE**

Faith grows only in the dark. You've got to trust Him where you can't trace Him. That's faith. You just take Him at His Word, believe Him, and grip the nail-scarred hand a little tighter. And faith grows.

—LYELL RADER

# Know What You Believe

How much do you know about faith and doubts in the Christian life? Here's a quiz to test your knowledge.

1. Why did Jesus call believers of future generations "blessed" in John 20:29?
   a. They wouldn't have to deal with the Pharisees.
   b. They would believe in Him without having seen Him.
   c. They wouldn't be faced with the disgusting task of washing each other's feet all the time.
   d. They would have access to religious broadcasting on cable TV.

2. Which of the following is true of faith?
   a. It's a gift from God that allows us to see possibilities beyond our limited perspective.
   b. It never makes any rational sense.
   c. It's just another name for wishful thinking.
   d. It's greater than charity and love, according to 1 Corinthians 13.

3. Which of the following is not true of doubt?
   a. God isn't offended by it.
   b. Almost all Christians experience it occasionally.
   c. It can ultimately be beneficial in helping us make our faith our own.
   d. According to the book of Romans, it's the only thing that can separate us from God's will.

4. Which of the following characters did not experience a faith-growing incident in the Bible?
   a. Meshach
   b. Horshach
   c. Peter
   d. Thomas

5. Which of the following is not a recommended step for overcoming doubts?
   a. Identify the cause of your doubts.
   b. Pray about your doubts.

c. Never admit to having doubts about God or His Word.
d. Talk to mature Christians about your doubts.

*Answers: (1) b, (2) a, (3) d, (4) b, (5) c*

CHAPTER 15

# Crawling from the Wreckage

## SNAPSHOT

"Who did you get to sub at shortstop?" Roger asked as he stretched his throwing arm behind his head.

Marv looked up from lacing the webbing on his mitt. "A guy I work with named Greg," he replied. "He's never played in a church league before, but he's played for the same park district team for ten years."

"Greg?" Roger asked. "That's not the guy who had the affair with the intern and then left his wife and kids, is it?"

"Well, that's probably not how I'll introduce him; but, yeah, that's the guy," Marv said. "Why, is that a problem for you?"

"I wouldn't say it's a problem," Roger replied. "But I am a little uncomfortable with the idea."

"What if I told you that he bats clean-up and that I saw him go deep three times in one game?" Marv asked.

### SNEAK PREVIEW

1. God has a history of using decidedly imperfect people to accomplish great things as part of His will.
2. God intends for us to live free of the guilt and shame of failure.
3. A repentant heart is all that's required to have our sins and failures forgiven and forgotten by God.

"I don't know," Roger said, "I just think that if you get too chummy with those people, you end up sending the wrong message."

"What people?" Marv asked. "Shortstops?"

"No," Roger said. "You know, people who've made a mess of their lives."

Marv sighed. "And what's the wrong message that you send out?" he asked.

"You know, that it's okay to be a sinner," Roger replied.

"If it will make you feel any better, we could draft a resolution before the game, stating that, for the record, our team is opposed to sin," Marv offered. "We could all sign it and present it to the umpire with the lineup card."

"Come on," Roger said. "I'm being serious."

"Look," Marv said, "the guy made one horrible mistake. He'll be the first to admit it. I know how sorry he is, so I don't think it's fair to hang that 'sinner' tag on him for the rest of his life."

"I'm just afraid that if people find out, it might hurt our testimony as a team," Roger explained. "Remember, this is a *church* league."

"I see," Marv said. "And is that the same concern you had last year when you got suspended for three games for taking a swing at that umpire?"

"Hey, I apologized for that!" Roger objected. "I paid my debt. How long are you going to keep throwing that in my—" He stopped, looked at Marv, and chuckled in recognition.

"So you say this guy's a power hitter, huh?" Roger asked.

* * * * * * * * * * * * * * * * * * *

"Be perfect, therefore, as your heavenly Father is perfect" (Matthew 5:48). Those are Jesus' words, His instructions to us.

Perfect? For some of us, it takes everything we have just to be marginally tolerable. On our good days, we may achieve decency. On rare occasions, we might even come close to admirability. But it never lasts. We always do something stupid, something ill-advised, something sinful to mess everything up.

Our quest for perfection goes out the window. We fail ourselves, we fail others, and we fail God. And we do it over and over again.

"Be *perfect*"? What was Jesus thinking?

## Join the Club

And what about the role models God gave us in the Bible—people like Noah, Moses, David, and Peter? Are we expected to measure up to *them?*

### *Noah*

Take Noah, for instance. Genesis 6:9 says that he was "a righteous man, blameless among the people of his time." In fact, if it hadn't been for Noah's righteousness, God would have destroyed all life on this planet in the Great Flood. Noah was the only person on earth who didn't displease God. For his sake, God allowed the human race, not to mention the animal kingdom, to continue.

How can we possibly hope to measure up to someone with a legacy like that—someone who was "blameless"?

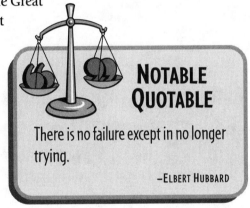

**NOTABLE QUOTABLE**

There is no failure except in no longer trying.

—ELBERT HUBBARD

Of course . . . there was that embarrassing incident that occurred sometime after Noah and his family left the ark. Genesis 9:21 tells us that one day, for reasons known only to himself and God, Noah got crazy with some homemade wine and ended up passing out naked in his tent. (That may not seem like a big deal today, but in Old Testament times, when modesty was of the utmost importance, Noah's actions were positively scandalous.)

But that's not all. When Noah's youngest son, Ham, discovered his father's nakedness, he did something he shouldn't have. (The Bible isn't clear on exactly what he did, though the son did gaze on his uncovered father.) As a result, Ham and his descendants were cursed forever.

You could make the point that if Noah hadn't gotten blasted, his son wouldn't have sinned. Furthermore, hundreds of thousands of Ham's descendants would have been spared the consequences of Ham's curse if Noah had only known when to say when.

In short, Noah's failure resulted in a life of misery for his son and his descendants.

### *Moses*

And what about Moses? When God told him to rescue the Israelites from their cruel slavery in Egypt, Moses obeyed, even though it put his life in jeopardy. When God told him to lead the Israelites back and forth across a barren wasteland for *forty years,* Moses obeyed, even though it meant decades of unpleasant living conditions and even less pleasant traveling companions. When God told Moses to climb Mount Sinai alone, Moses obeyed, even though he was an old man at the time.

How can we possibly hope to measure up to Moses' standard of obedience?

Of course . . . there was that incident in the Desert of Zin. According to Numbers 20:1–13, the Israelites were desperate for water, so God told Moses to speak to a rock, and He (God) would cause water to pour from it. Moses, frustrated by the Israelites' constant complaining, struck the rock with his walking stick instead. Water gushed out, and the Israelites were satisfied—temporarily, at least.

**NOTABLE QUOTABLE**

Most successes are built on failures.

—CHARLES CROW

Moses' life was never the same again, however. God punished Moses' disobedience by forbidding him to ever enter the Promised Land.

Because Moses failed, he was doomed to die in the wilderness, close enough to see the goal he had worked forty years to achieve, but not close enough to experience the satisfaction of having achieved it.

### *David*

Let's not forget David. Dedicated enough as a shepherd to fight—and defeat—bears and lions with his bare hands in order to protect his flock. Courageous enough to confront—and defeat—the fearsome giant-warrior Goliath without any protective armor. Talented enough to have his songs and prayers included in God's Word. Wise enough to be tapped by God to serve as the king of Israel.

What chance do we have of achieving that level of obedience, courage, and faithfulness?

Of course . . . there was that incident that started on the roof of the palace. Second Samuel 11 tells us that David was enjoying the cool evening air one night when he spied a woman taking a bath in a nearby home. David liked what he saw, so he asked around and discovered that the woman's name was Bathsheba and that she was married to Uriah, a soldier in David's army who was away at war.

David sent for Bathsheba and . . . well, slept with her. Shortly thereafter, he received news that Bathsheba was pregnant. Hoping to cover up his sin, David sent for Uriah and tried to get him to sleep with his wife, so that it would appear that Uriah had gotten her pregnant. But Uriah refused, out of loyalty to his fellow warriors back at the battle.

That's when David . . . well, arranged to have Uriah killed. The king instructed his general to put Uriah in the thick of the heaviest fighting and then pull back the rest of the troops, leaving him to die battling all alone. The general did as he was told, and Uriah was killed. When Bathsheba's grieving period for her husband ended, she married King David, moved into his palace, and gave birth to his son.

David got what he wanted—but at an awful cost. God punished the king by allowing his newborn son to die.

Because David failed to control his lust one night, countless lives were disrupted, a marriage was destroyed, and two people ended up dead (Uriah and the child born from the affair).

**NOTABLE QUOTABLE**

To err is human, to forgive divine.

—ALEXANDER POPE

### *Peter*

In the New Testament, you've got the likes of Peter, a man so earnest, loyal, and dedicated that Jesus chose him to be part of His "inner circle." Under Jesus' teaching and guidance, Peter seems to have emerged as a leader among the disciples. His extraordinary faith and resolve were bolstered by the countless miracles he saw Jesus perform. He boldly proclaimed, "Lord, I am ready to go with you to prison and to death" (Luke 22:33). When the soldiers came to arrest

Jesus, it was Peter who pulled out his sword, ready to fight to the death to protect his Master.

How can we hope to even come close to that kind of dedication and courage?

Of course . . . there was that incident that occurred a few hours after Jesus was arrested. Luke 22:54 tells us that Peter secretly followed the soldiers who took Jesus away. He ended up outside the home of the chief priest, where Jesus was put on trial. A crowd had gathered outside the building, and one of the women there recognized Peter as one of Jesus' disciples. "This man was with him," she said (verse 56).

**NOTABLE QUOTABLE**

Failure should be our teacher, not our undertaker. Failure is delay, not defeat. It is a temporary detour, not a dead-end street.

—WILLIAM A. WARD

What an opportunity for Peter to take a bold stand for Christ! What a chance for him to discuss the things he had seen the Savior do and heard Him say! What an invitation to share the life-changing work of the Lord!

Seizing the moment as only he could, Peter looked the woman in the eye, and said . . . "Woman, I don't know him" (verse 57). Huh?

We might be tempted to argue that Peter misunderstood the question or that his mind was preoccupied at that moment. But, the thing is, he gave the same response two more times that night. That's right, in the hours that Jesus needed His followers the most, His closest friend on earth denied *three times* that he even knew who Jesus was!

Luke 22:61 even suggests that Jesus witnessed Peter's final denial. Verse 62 describes Peter's reaction when he realized what he had done: "He went outside and wept bitterly."

### *And the Beat Goes On*

Four major Bible characters, four major personal failures. And the list doesn't stop there. Abraham, the father of the Jewish nation, slept with his wife's servant. Jacob, the father of the twelve tribes of Israel, cheated his older twin brother out of his inheritance. Then there's Thomas, one of Jesus' own disciples, who refused to believe that Christ had risen from the dead until he saw physical proof. Don't forget the apostle Paul, the man who wrote most of the books in the New Testament; he made his name in the early days of the church as a torturer and murderer of Christians. And Mark, the author of one of the four definitive biographies of Christ, deserted Paul and Barnabas in the middle of an important missionary journey.

Explore the life of any major Bible character—other than Jesus Christ, that is—and chances are you'll find a failure every bit as noteworthy as that person's greatest accomplishment.

If this were a tabloid exposé about the seamy underbelly of the biblical world, we could end it here and congratulate ourselves for a job of character assassination well done. But that's not the aim of this chapter. You see, those all-too-human Bible "heroes" knew something that set them apart from their peers, not to mention from many Christians today.

They knew what true repentance and forgiveness really mean. And they knew that God can use anyone—regardless of background or history—to accomplish His will.

**ON A PERSONAL NOTE**

Here's a question for you to think about: Which Bible character do you most identify with, failures and all? Take a look at the capsule descriptions in this chapter and then do some investigating of your own in God's Word. Once you've chosen your scriptural counterpart, do some additional research to discover how God ultimately used that person to accomplish His will. You may just stumble onto a preview of the kind of things He has in store for you!

## Second Wind

The hard-earned knowledge and wisdom of these heroes of the faith gave them the determination and encouragement to move past their sins and beyond their downfalls. The men of God we've listed in this chapter refused to be defined by their failures.

### *Noah: The Rest of the Story*

Noah isn't remembered as a drunken exhibitionist today. His legacy is found in Hebrews 11, which is known as the "Faith Hall of Fame" because it celebrates the lives of Old Testament men and women who were judged to be ultimately faithful by God and held up as role models for the rest of us to follow.

Verse 7 says, "By his faith he [Noah] condemned the world and became heir of the righteousness that comes by faith." Notice there's no mention of Noah's failure or the havoc it wreaked on his family. His faith and righteousness were all that God remembered.

### *Moses: The Rest of the Story*

Moses isn't known today as the guy who clubbed the rock in the desert. He's known as the faithful servant of God who parted the Red Sea, received the Ten Commandments, and led God's people on one of the most remarkable journeys ever taken.

Moses' epitaph can also be found on the roll of honor in Hebrews 11. (In fact, Moses rates a full seven verses of coverage.) Verse 27 says, "He [Moses] persevered because he saw him who is invisible."

### *David: The Rest of the Story*

You won't often find the words "adulterous murderer" attached to David's name today. You will, however, find the words "Son of David" attached to Jesus' name. (See Matthew 9:27, for example.) God determined that it was necessary for His Son to be a human descendant of David. He wanted David's name to be closely associated with the Messiah. As honors go, you can't do much better than being named a major branch of Jesus' family tree.

As you might expect, David is also mentioned in the Faith Hall of Fame. Hebrews 11:32–33 describes him as one "who through faith conquered kingdoms, administered justice, and gained what was promised."

### *Peter: The Rest of the Story*

Peter's life didn't become a sad testament to "what might have been." His commitment to Christ didn't end with his three denials. Obviously, Jesus understood that. After He rose from the dead, Jesus made a personal visit to Peter in order to restore His relationship with the remorseful disciple. Jesus renewed His promise to make Peter a cornerstone on which He would build His church. Today, Peter is widely recognized as one of the two most important figures (along with Paul) in early church history.

Tradition has it that many years later, Peter was given another chance to deny Christ—just before his *own* crucifixion. Peter declined the opportunity, but he did make a final request. Peter didn't believe he was worthy to be executed in the same manner as the Son of God. So he asked for, and was granted, permission to be crucified . . . upside down.

## Coming Back from Failure

Four major personal failures, four praiseworthy endings.

The secret of these eventual success stories? A healthy perspective on failure. These men of God neither underestimated nor overestimated its impact on their lives. They viewed failure as the beginning of a difficult road back to God and not as the end of their usefulness to Him.

By examining what these heroes of the faith did and didn't do in the wake of their devastating lapses of faithfulness and good judgment, we can develop a game plan for dealing with our own failures.

### *Sorry Seems to Be the Smartest Word*

The first step in recovering from failure is having the right attitude toward it—namely, a repentant spirit. And the first step in developing a repentant spirit is recognizing that it involves a lot more than saying, "Oops, my mistake."

Take another look at our biblical examples—especially David and Peter. Notice their reaction to their failure. When they blew it, they weren't merely sorry; they were sorrowful. In fact, they were devastated.

Look at some of the phrases David used in his prayer of forgiveness in Psalm 51:

> Against you, you only, have I sinned and done what is evil in your sight. (verse 4)
>
> Create in me a pure heart, O God, and renew a steadfast spirit within me. (verse 10)

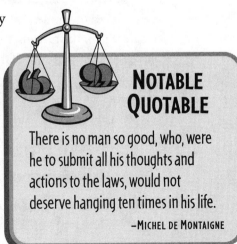

**NOTABLE QUOTABLE**

There is no man so good, who, were he to submit all his thoughts and actions to the laws, would not deserve hanging ten times in his life.

—MICHEL DE MONTAIGNE

> Do not cast me from your presence or take your Holy Spirit from me. (verse 11)
>
> Restore me to the joy of your salvation. (verse 12)

David wasn't sorry that he got caught. He wasn't worried about how his reputation might be affected. He wasn't concerned about the example he was setting for other people.

He was sorry for disrupting and damaging his relationship with God.

The same thing goes for Peter. As he "wept bitterly," he wasn't thinking about his lost opportunity to share his faith outside of the high priest's house. He wasn't thinking about the shame he brought on the fledgling Christian movement. He wasn't thinking about how the other disciples would treat him when they heard what he'd done.

He was sorry for letting down his Savior and Lord.

Those same feelings of remorse and sorrow should be our first reaction to failing God. Those are the feelings that will ensure a proper attitude on our part when we seek His forgiveness.

## Forgive and Forget

We explored the hows and whys of confessing sin and praying for forgiveness in chapter 9. For the purposes of this chapter, we'll simply remind you that the process isn't something that's done quickly, casually, or halfheartedly.

When you come to God for forgiveness, you need to carefully consider . . .

- what you did wrong,
- why you did it, and
- how it affected your relationship with your heavenly Father.

The first part, admitting what you did wrong, requires you to shine a light on details of your failure that you may prefer to keep hidden. It's important to demonstrate to the Lord that you understand the full extent of what you've done wrong.

We're talking about the difference between David saying, "Hey, God, I'm sorry I messed up with Bathsheba—period," and David saying . . . well, what he said in Psalm 51. A prayer of forgiveness is not the place for a partial confession. You need to make sure that you come clean about every aspect of your failure. Keep in mind that there are no details too gory, no specifics too offensive to take to God.

Working your way step by step through the events of your failure will help you avoid the temptation of downplaying your sin or remembering it as less serious than it actually is.

The second part of your prayer, owning up to *why* you failed God and yourself, will help you better understand your heart attitudes, the personal weaknesses and character flaws that motivate you. This is not a place for superficial analysis or excuse-making. Remember, God is aware of everything that's going on inside you. He knows *exactly* why you did what you did.

This is about learning from your mistakes. It's about helping yourself recognize the early signs of impending failure, so that you can avoid repeating that failure in the future.

The third part of your prayer, examining how your failure has affected your relationship with God, is about recognizing His holiness and making yourself aware of how offensive sin is to Him. This is about developing the kind of sensitivity to God and His will that will act as an alarm when potentially damaging situations present themselves.

### Just Wondering

**What if I don't *feel* as sorrowful about sin as people like David and Peter did? Does that mean there's something wrong with me?**

Nothing that the Holy Spirit can't fix. The Bible describes a condition known as "hard-heartedness," in which people aren't as affected by their sin as they should be. The Holy Spirit is the perfect person to address hard-heartedness in believers because He's already on the premises–that is, He already lives in our hearts. Ask the Holy Spirit to do some "softening" work in your heart, to make you more aware of your sin and the full consequences it brings with it. Ask Him to give you a deeper understanding of what your sin does to you, to others, and to your relationship with God.

Once you've completed these steps—once you've presented your confession and expressed your repentance to God—it's time to listen. (Remember, prayer is a conversation with God, and good conversation always involves speaking *and* listening.)

While you listen for God's answer to your prayer, consider the following two promises found in His Word:

1. "If we confess our sins, he is faithful and just and will forgive us our sins and purify us from all unrighteousness" (1 John 1:9).
2. "For I am convinced that neither death nor life, neither angels nor demons, neither the present nor the future, nor any powers, neither height nor depth, nor anything else in all creation, will be able to separate us from the love of God that is in Christ Jesus our Lord" (Romans 8:38–39).

If you genuinely want forgiveness from God, you've got it. That's a fact. Yet applying that fact to your everyday life can be quite a challenge. It's one thing to *know* you're forgiven; it's quite another thing to live like it's true, to avoid the temptation of becoming discouraged or giving up after your umpteenth failure.

### *Living Free*

Galatians 5:13 sums up the diceyness of the situation nicely: "You, my brothers, were called to be free. But do not use your freedom to indulge the sinful nature." God's intent is for us to live free from sin and all of the entanglements that go with it. Living free means not being weighed down by guilt and shame, not being crippled by memories of previous failures.

Living free also means dealing wisely with the sins we commit and the failures we experience. By God's

## JUST WONDERING

**Will God actually answer me when I ask for forgiveness?**
Probably not verbally. But He will make you aware of His response. He may give you a sense of relief about being forgiven or a sense of peace about your relationship with Him. He may reveal an unmistakably fitting Bible passage in your daily devotions. He may cause you to overhear a snippet of a sermon or song that speaks directly to your situation. Keep your eyes and ears open, and you'll know when God answers you.

grace, we are forgiven for the things we repent of. As we said earlier, that's a fact. However, we must never try to take advantage of that grace by falling into the pattern of sinning now and repenting later.

Nowhere in the Bible does God endorse a blasé attitude toward sin or failure. Every sin we commit, every failure we experience, must become a learning experience for us. Specifically, we must learn how *not* to do the same thing again.

There are two major obstacles to living with the kind of freedom God intends: a bad past and problem sins. Let's take a look at what to do with each one.

## Facing the Past

Some people have skeletons in their closets; some people have entire graveyards. Rahab, the Old Testament woman who faithfully hid Israelite spies in Jericho—and who is listed in the Faith Hall of Fame in Hebrews 11—was a prostitute. Jacob had to live with the fact that he cheated his older twin brother out of his inheritance and destroyed his family in the process. David and the apostle Paul had to live with the knowledge that they were responsible for the death of another person.

Those aren't the kind of incidents that you just shake off.

Many Christians have found that a notorious or shameful past is like a "freedom clog" that prevents them from enjoying the life God has in store for them. They can't get beyond what they've done, so they live with one foot in the past and one foot in the present.

If you've got a past that just won't quit—that is, if who you used to be is affecting who you are—there are steps you can take to free yourself from the problem.

### *1. Turn it over to God.*

Barring any sudden advances in time-travel technology, it's safe to say that you can't change your past. You can, however, give your past to God and let Him take care of it once and for all.

Your first step in escaping the clutches of your past is to bring your entire sordid history to God and ask for His forgiveness. As we mentioned earlier, the more comprehensive you are in laying out your sins before God, the more meaningful

His forgiveness will be to you. Depending on your circumstances and how complete you choose to be in laying our your situation to God, your prayer may take fifteen minutes or it may take all day.

That's okay. God's not going anywhere. He's going to listen carefully to every word you say. When you finish, He's going to forgive you.

And when He forgives you, He will never think about your past sins again. As far as His judgment is concerned, they never happened.

### *2. Make amends.*

If your past failures hurt other people, you'll also need to seek forgiveness from them and make any necessary restitution. James wrote that confession is good for the body—the body of Christ, that is: "Confess your sins to each other" (5:16).

If your past failure involved, say, emotional mistreatment or inappropriateness in a relationship, talk to the person or persons who were affected by your actions—regardless of whether or not they're as guilty as you are. Apologize for what you did and ask for forgiveness. Don't try to make excuses. Accept full responsibility for your failure.

If your failure involved, say, theft, whether from a person or an institution (such as your employer, a department store, or even the IRS), you'll need to repay the debt you owe in full. The way you do it is up to you, but it's important that you make full restitution. Otherwise, it's still theft.

Of course, how people respond to your apologies and requests for forgiveness is up to them. Ideally, everyone you talk to will welcome your efforts to make good on your past failures and happily give you their forgiveness. Realistically, there's a chance that some people might spit in your face, depending on the circumstances. That's their business. You're not responsible for the responses of other people. If you've done everything you can to receive forgiveness and achieve closure, rest easy. God doesn't expect anything more than that from you.

You need to recognize, however, that God doesn't magically remove the consequences of our past sins when we repent. He will forgive us, but He won't erase the damage that we do.

The apostle Paul is a good example. A few pages back, we mentioned that in the early days of the church, Paul (or "Saul," as he was known then) gained a reputation as an enemy of Christians. A Jewish religious leader with impeccable credentials, Paul was zealous in his attempts to quash the Christian faith before it grew. In some cases, that meant torturing and even killing Christians who refused to deny their faith. Acts 7:58 tells us that Paul (Saul) was part of the group who murdered Stephen, an early church leader and the first known person to be killed because of His faith in Christ.

Obviously, Paul received forgiveness for his sinful past. Otherwise, he wouldn't have been given such a vital role in the history of the Christian faith. But that forgiveness didn't change the way certain people viewed him. Acts 9:26 tells us that Paul tried to join the apostles after he became a Christian, but they refused to even meet with him because they were afraid that his conversion was fake and that he was plotting to arrest them.

The disciples eventually came around, but it's a good bet that there were others who didn't. Paul's early failure was probably horrific enough to have *permanently* alienated some first-century believers and nonbelievers alike. (How do you think Stephen's immediate family felt about Paul?) Those people who weren't able to see beyond Paul's past missed out on the blessings of his ministry.

You should do everything in your power to make amends to the people who were hurt by your failure. However, you can't expect the consequences of your failure and the emotions surrounding it to disappear overnight.

### *3. Acknowledge God's forgiveness.*

The third step in dealing with past sins is allowing yourself to experience God's forgiveness. If you need some help in doing that, check out the following Bible passages: "For as high as the heavens are above the earth, so great is his love for those who fear him; as far as the east is from west, so far has he removed our transgressions from us" (Psalm 103:11–12). "I, even I, am he who blots out your transgressions, for my own sake, and remembers your sins no more" (Isaiah 43:25).

Don't forget that God has infinitely more reasons than you do to hold a grudge for the things you've done. If He's willing to forget them, you should be, too.

Don't try to be stricter on yourself than God is. The only thing you'll accomplish is making yourself miserable.

Accepting God's forgiveness means refusing to pigeonhole yourself as an "ex" something or other. It means refusing to find identity in what you used to be. It means turning your focus on what lies ahead instead of what lies behind.

## Facing a Problem Sin

Some sins are harder to shake than others. Some sins are too enjoyable, too thrilling, or too deeply embedded in our daily routine for us to overcome on our first try—despite our best intentions. The longer a sin remains a problem, the more damage it can do to our relationship with the Lord—not to mention our feelings of self-worth.

The apostle Paul understood the confusion and frustration that comes from wrestling with the same sin over and over again. Look at his words in Romans 7:15: "I do not understand what I do. For what I want to do I do not do, but what I hate I do." Sound like a familiar dilemma to you?

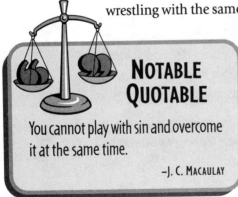

> **NOTABLE QUOTABLE**
>
> You cannot play with sin and overcome it at the same time.
>
> –J. C. MACAULAY

Obviously, no two problem sins are alike, since no two problem *sinners* are alike. Every problem sin has its own specific solution. There are, however, a few general guidelines and suggestions that can be applied to all recurring sins.

***1. Recognize the problem sin for what it is.*** Don't try to downplay or explain away your repeated failures. Whatever else your problem sin may be—a psychological compulsion, an addiction, an attempt to escape reality or block memories—it is still a sin. And it's important that you recognize it as such.

Toward that end, find a Bible passage that applies to your recurring failure. For example, if you're struggling with substance use (or abuse), you might want to check out 1 Corinthians 6:19–20: "Do you not know that your body is a temple of the Holy Spirit, who is in you, whom you have received from God? You are not your own; you were bought at a price. Therefore honor God with your body."

If you're struggling with sin of a sexual nature, you might want to look at 1 Corinthians 6:13: "The body is not meant for sexual immorality, but for the Lord, and the Lord for the body." You might also want to check out Jesus' words in Matthew 5:28: "Anyone who looks at a woman lustfully has already committed adultery with her in his heart."

Don't leave room for doubt in your mind about whether your habitual behavior is sin. Call it what it is.

If you're not sure where to find a passage that addresses a particular sin, try the subject index in the back of your Bible. If that doesn't work, ask a trusted Christian friend, or even your pastor, to recommend some passages to you.

### *2. Confess, confess, confess.*

Problem sins make for some awkward prayer moments: "Hey, God, remember that sin I asked You to forgive me for yesterday . . . and the day before that . . . and twice on the day before that? Well, um . . ." Don't allow that awkwardness to keep you from taking your sin to God as many times as you need to. If you're sincere about your remorse, God will forgive you . . . time and time again.

If you don't stay close to the Lord in prayer, you've got very little chance of overcoming your problem sin. It's natural to feel embarrassment or shame about a sin that you can't control; it's foolish to allow that embarrassment or shame to make you shy away from the only One who can help you overcome your problem.

### *3. Change your patterns of behavior.*

Many recurring sins become matters of habit. We indulge in certain wrongdoings because they're convenient or available to us. Common sense, then, would suggest that making sin opportunities inconvenient and unavailable can go a long way toward loosening that sin's grip on us.

The best, and most difficult, way to make sin inconvenient and unavailable is to change your behavior patterns, the places you go and the way you spend your time. For example, if getting drunk is your problem sin, stay away from bars, clubs, or anywhere alcohol is served. If nicotine addiction is your problem, stay away from the smoker's break room at work. In other words, don't put yourself in a position to sin.

### *4. Change your friends.*

If the people you hang out with encourage or facilitate your recurring failure, it's time to find a new circle of friends. If that seems like a rash solution, keep in mind that Jesus once said, "If your right eye causes you to sin, gouge it out and throw it away. . . . And if your right hand causes you to sin, cut it off and throw it away" (Matthew 5:29–30). It seems that the Lord has a fairly strict attitude toward sin.

It follows that if our eyes and hands are expendable, our friends should be, too. Remember, when you sign on with Christ, you must be prepared to give up everything—including lifelong friends, if necessary—for the sake of your relationship with Him.

### *5. Talk it over with someone you trust.*

The more secret a sin is, the easier it is to return to it. That's why it's important to enlist a few of your most trusted friends in your struggle against your problem failure. Create a mini-network of accountability for yourself. Explain to your friends what's going on in your life, offering as much detail as you're comfortable with. The purpose of this sharing exercise is to give other people a vested interest in your spiritual well-being.

If you know that you're going to have to answer openly and honestly to other people about your actions—and if you know that those people will be disappointed by your failure—you may be less likely to give in to your problem sin. Sharing your business with others and giving them the right to ask how you're doing may feel like an invasion of privacy at times, but that minor irritation pales in comparison to the joy that results from successfully overcoming a problem sin.

**On a Personal Note**

Create a "failure testimony" that you can share with hurting people. Think of a past circumstance in which you experienced failure in a big way. Try to recall how you responded to the failure initially and how you felt about yourself afterward. Think about how God worked through the situation to eventually produce positive results in your life. Once you have details of your testimony clear in your mind, share your experience with other people who are struggling with failure.

### *6. Consider professional help.*

If your desire to commit a sin becomes a compulsion, you may need the help of someone who's professionally trained to help you with your problem. If you find that you can't control your actions, talk to a qualified Christian counselor about your situation. If you're not sure where to look for a counselor, ask your pastor or a trusted Christian friend to recommend one for you. Granted, this is a major step, but it could mean the difference between lifelong problems and spiritual freedom.

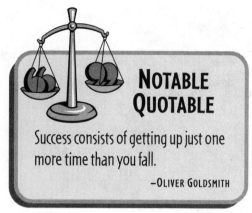

> **NOTABLE QUOTABLE**
>
> Success consists of getting up just one more time than you fall.
>
> —Oliver Goldsmith

Once you've developed a successful strategy for overcoming your problem sin, stick with it. Keep your eyes peeled for the return of old, dangerous habits. When you spot them, put an end to them immediately. Whatever you do, don't get cocky. The minute you start to believe that you've overcome a sin for good, you make yourself vulnerable to another fall.

## One More Thing

Remember that command of Jesus that we quoted at the beginning of this chapter—"Be perfect, therefore, as your heavenly Father is perfect"? We weren't using it simply to make a point about failure or to illustrate the difference between Jesus' righteousness and ours. Jesus meant exactly what He said.

Perfection should be the goal of every Christian. And the fact that we haven't achieved it yet—even the fact that we will *never* achieve it in this lifetime—should not deter us from pursuing it with everything we've got.

None of us will achieve perfection today. But we can give it our most intense effort. When we fall short, we can repent of our shortcomings and try again. And we can move a little closer to perfection than we were yesterday. The key to our pursuit of perfection is learning from our mistakes—that is, learning how not to make them again.

## Know What You Believe

How much do you know about the biblical view of failure? Here's a quiz to test your knowledge.

1. Which of the following Bible characters learned firsthand just how devastating lust can be?
   a. Peter
   b. David
   c. Noah
   d. Moses

2. What can we learn about failure from the examples of biblical heroes?
   a. There are certain people who can escape God's punishment just because God has a special place in His heart for them.
   b. If you want to be remembered as an effective disciple, you'd better be prepared to live a sinless life.
   c. God can and will use repentant "failures" to achieve great things, according to His will.
   d. Giving in to certain temptations means the end of your usefulness to God.

3. Which of the following is not true of God's forgiveness?
   a. It is temporary.
   b. It is gained through prayer.
   c. It is guaranteed in Scripture.
   d. It is available time and time again.

4. Which of the following suggestions is not a recommended strategy for overcoming a sinful past?
   a. Acknowledge God's forgiveness.
   b. Make amends.
   c. Turn it over to God.
   d. Ask God to punish the person who introduced you to the sin.

5. Which of the following is not a good idea when it comes to dealing with problem sins?
   a. Recognize that you will simply outgrow them in time.
   b. Consider professional help.
   c. Change your friends.
   d. Keep your guard up.

*Answers: (1) b, (2) c, (3) a, (4) d, (5) a*

CHAPTER 16

# Objection!

## SNAPSHOT

"Oh, man, did I get ambushed last night," Ron said as he loaded the last two holiday gift baskets into his van.

"What happened?" Caleb asked.

"We went to Maria's Christmas party," Ron said. "And we were having a really good time—until some jerk from the regional office showed up.

"They had music playing in the background . . . and when 'Joy to the World' came on, this guy *freaked*—absolutely freaked. He started yelling to turn it off because it was a Christian song and demanding to know who was in charge of the music."

"His first name wasn't Ebenezer, was it?" Caleb asked with a chuckle.

"Wait; it gets worse," Ron said. "They finally ended up giving in to the guy and turning off the music. I guess they were afraid of a lawsuit or something."

### Sneak Preview

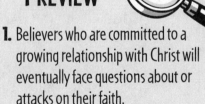

1. Believers who are committed to a growing relationship with Christ will eventually face questions about or attacks on their faith.
2. The Christian faith can be discussed rationally and intellectually.
3. Maintaining a spirit of loving truthfulness is the key to successfully defending one's faith.

"Obviously, they've never seen *Miracle on 34th Street,*" Caleb said. "The good guys never lose lawsuits at Christmas."

"Yeah, well, you can imagine how popular that made him at the party," Ron said. "But this guy didn't care. It was like he was feeding on the negative vibes. Anyhow, that was about the time they started seating us for dinner."

"Don't tell me—" Caleb began.

Ron nodded grimly. "There he was—right across the table from me."

Caleb let out a low whistle.

"The first thing he asked was whether there were any Christians at the table," Ron said.

"Sounds like he was angling for a fight," Caleb observed.

"Where was that wisdom last night when I needed it?" Ron asked. "I figured if I said yes, he'd keep his mouth shut."

"And you were wrong?" Caleb asked.

"He was practically foaming at the mouth, ready to attack," Ron said. "He started off by asking, 'What makes you so conceited that you believe your little religion is better than Buddhism or Hinduism?'"

Caleb smiled. "Did you explain to him how those religions are dependent on human works and how they don't even offer assurance of heaven when you die?"

"Well, not in those exact words," Ron said. "I think what I actually said was, 'Why don't you just chill out and have a bread stick.'"

"That's from Ephesians, isn't it?" Caleb asked.

"Drop the sarcasm. I know it was a stupid thing to say," Ron said. "It didn't even slow the guy down. He proceeded to tell me that Christians are a bunch of losers because we put our faith in a dead guy."

"What did you say?" Caleb asked.

"I told him the truth," Ron said, "That everyone at the table was getting sick of hearing him talk."

Caleb shook his head. "So how did it all end?" he asked.

Ron smiled. "I finally told the guy that if he really wanted to get my reaction to the things he was saying, it would have to be in a one-on-one setting."

"Good strategy," Caleb said. "You took yourself out of a confrontational situation."

"No, I challenged him to a fight in the parking lot," Ron said.

Caleb covered his face with his hands. "Please tell me you didn't beat up someone for questioning your faith," he said.

Ron smiled. "I didn't have to; the guy never showed up," he said, as he raised his arms in triumph. "Chalk up another win for God's side!"

* * * * * * * * * * * * * * * *

History tells us that:

- The apostle Peter was crucified upside down.
- The apostle Paul was beheaded.
- The apostle Thomas was run through with a spear.
- The author of the Gospel According to Mark was dragged to death.
- the author of the Gospel According to Luke was hung.

Countless other believers have been stoned to death, buried alive, sawed in half, devoured by wild beasts, locked in boxes and tossed into the sea to drown, thrown headfirst from great heights, and tortured in other ways too disturbing to mention.

Opposition to the Christian faith has existed since before people even started calling themselves "Christians." A peek at the book of Revelation confirms that opposition will continue as long as believers and unbelievers share this planet. In fact, according to some estimates, as many as 425 Christians worldwide are murdered *every day* because of their faith.

When faced with extreme opposition, millions of believers have stood firm and paid the ultimate price for their faith. Do you ever wonder how you would fare under similar circumstances?

How about under less extreme conditions?

The fact is, we may never face life-threatening hostility as a result of our belief in Christ. However, as Christians, we *will* encounter opposition and challenges to our faith. At least, we will if we're living it right. Our opposition will come in such forms as:

- being stereotyped by people who don't know us,
- being accused of intolerance or narrow-mindedness,
- losing relationships with people who can't accept our faith,
- being made fun of, underestimated, or dismissed because of the way we live, and
- having our core beliefs questioned.

**ON A PERSONAL NOTE**

Check out *Foxe's Book of Martyrs* from your local library. Though you may find some of the descriptions and illustrations in this Christian classic too disturbing for your taste, the book will give you a sense of what it meant for early Christians to stand up for their faith. It may also inspire you to stand up for your faith with boldness and courage.

You see, the kind of life God calls us to puts us at odds with the world around us. Some people appreciate the differences they see in Christians; some people don't. We should expect to hear from the ones who don't.

In fact, God's Word tells us not only to *expect* opposition, but to *celebrate* it. In Matthew 5:11–12, Jesus says, "Blessed are you when people insult you, persecute you and falsely say all kinds of evil against you because of me. Rejoice and be glad, because great is your reward in heaven, for in the same way they persecuted the prophets who were before you."

# Be Prepared

If you haven't faced opposition yet as a Christian, you will. So you need to be prepared for it. Obviously, we can't anticipate the exact kind of opposition that will come your way. We can, however, prepare you for a few of the most common faith-related questions and challenges Christians get.

### *Challenge #1: How do you even know God exists?*

Many unbelievers argue that since there's no way to scientifically prove God's existence, believing in Him is illogical. The challenge may be phrased in different ways—for example, someone might ask, "Do you ever wonder whether there's anyone listening to your prayers?"—but the argument is the same.

Since this argument almost always involves a discussion of the origin of the universe, let's start there in responding to it. What it comes down to is this: Either the universe was created or it's the result of pure chance. If you believe the universe was created, you believe in a Creator. (If you believe in a Creator, you pretty much believe in God.)

Since none of us has ever seen this Creator in person and since no photographic evidence of the Creation exists, our belief in Him technically requires faith—assurance without physical proof. As Christians, we put our faith in the following statements:

> **NOTABLE QUOTABLE**
>
> When I'm getting ready to reason with a man, I spend one-third of my time thinking about myself and what I am going to say–and two-thirds thinking about him and what he is going to say.
>
> –Abraham Lincoln

- ➤ There is a Being who has existed forever.
- ➤ This Being is powerful enough to have created an entire universe from complete nothingness.
- ➤ This Being is intelligent enough to have mapped out every detail of our existence, from the exact distance of the sun required to sustain life to the subatomic workings of our bodies.

We can find passages in the Bible to support each of these claims, but we can't offer conclusive visible proof of them.

By the same token, those who believe that the universe is the result of pure chance have their own set of faith requirements. Remember, no one has any physical proof of what happened at the beginning of the world. The "Big Bang" was not recorded for posterity. Therefore, those people are required to put their faith in the following:

- There is a molecular mass that has either existed forever or that spontaneously came into existence.
- This mass, over infinite time, expanded and separated in such a way to form the entire universe.
- By pure coincidence, one piece of this mass developed the exact elements and conditions necessary for the spontaneous emergence of rudimentary life-forms.
- Those rudimentary life-forms flourished and evolved into the diverse array of creatures and plant life currently in existence on this planet.

Supporters of this explanation can point to plenty of theories to support their conjectures, but when it comes to conclusive evidence, they've got zilch.

**NOTABLE QUOTABLE**

I have carefully examined the evidences of the Christian religion, and if I were sitting as a juror upon its authenticity, I would unhesitatingly give my verdict in its favor.

—ALEXANDER HAMILTON

That's why we can dispense with the argument that the existence of God is a matter of faith versus reason. The fact is, atheism requires every bit as much faith as Christianity does. The odds against the universe coming into existence as the result of pure chance are beyond astronomical. They are . . . well, unbelievable.

So the question is not, "Do you rely on faith or not?" The question is, "What do you put your faith in?"

No one looks at a painting such as the *Mona Lisa* or *The Last Supper*—or even the dogs playing poker—and says, "Obviously, that's the result of a bunch of different colors accidentally being spilled on a canvas." Instead, we look at it and say, "Obviously, that was created by an artist." How much more ludicrous is it to argue that our impossibly intricate universe is the result of one big molecular mass spill?

Psalm 19:1 points to the natural world as evidence of God's existence: "The heavens declare the glory of God; the skies proclaim the work of his hands." As far as the Bible is concerned, everything in the natural world is like a neon sign advertising the work of God.

What's more, Ecclesiastes 3:11 suggests that to deny God's existence is to deny something deep within ourselves. The verse tells us that God "has also set eternity in the hearts of men"—that is, He's given us a deep-seated awareness that something greater lies beyond us. Mathematician Blaise Pascal called it a "God-shaped vacuum" that everyone is born with.

> **NOTABLE QUOTABLE**
>
> It takes no brains to be an atheist. Any stupid person can deny the existence of a supernatural power because man's physical senses cannot detect it. But there cannot be ignored the influence of conscience, the respect we feel for moral law, the mystery of first life . . . or the marvelous order in which the universe moves about us on this earth. All these evidence the handiwork of the beneficent Deity. For my part that Deity is the God of the Bible and of Jesus Christ, his Son.
>
> –DWIGHT EISENHOWER

That's why you'll find that most of the people you encounter who have a problem with acknowledging God's existence aren't actually *atheists* but, rather, *agnostics*. They don't necessarily deny the existence of God so much as they shrug it off as something that can't be understood and, therefore, doesn't make much of a difference in their lives. They reason that even if God does exist, He's too far away for us to be concerned about—or to be concerned about us.

The evidence we need to respond to this argument—firsthand accounts of the Lord's intervening in human lives in unmistakable ways—is found in God's Word.

And that brings us to our second challenge.

### *Challenge #2: How do you know the Bible is true?*

The objection to the Bible's reliability can also be raised in any number of ways:

- "How can a book that was written thousands of years ago still be relevant?"
- "What if the Bible doesn't really say what you think it says?"
- "How do you know that the Bible writers weren't making it all up as they went along?"

On the surface, these may seem like some pretty reasonable arguments. But there's one problem. If someone doesn't believe that the Bible is God's Word, he or she still has to explain it somehow. And that's not an easy thing to do. There are several facts about the Bible that are hard to dismiss. We explored them in detail in chapter 5. Here's a brief sampling of them.

- Forty or so different authors, from widely diverse backgrounds, wrote the Bible over a period of about 1,600 years—with most of the authors having little or no interaction with each other. Logic suggests that such a patchwork approach to literature would yield sixty-six books with little or nothing in common. Yet what emerges in Scripture is one amazingly unified whole that focuses on one continuing theme: God's work on behalf of the human race, and our response to Him.
- Fulfilled prophecies can be found throughout the Book. We're not just talking about four or five lucky guesses that paid off, either. We're talking about hundreds of specific, clearly stated Old Testament prophecies that were fulfilled in and through the life, death, and resurrection of Christ.
- Where history, geography, and archeology are concerned, the Bible has proven startlingly accurate—occasionally even leading the way to new discoveries and causing experts to rethink long-held views.
- At least six of the eight known New Testament writers—Matthew, Mark, Luke, Paul, James, and Peter—were executed because of their Christian beliefs and the things they taught about Christ. If those men had just been making the stuff up, they certainly would have said so in order to escape death. Certainly no one would ever die for what he knew to be a lie. So, as far as the Bible authors were concerned, they were telling the truth—cross their hearts and hope to die.

If the Bible is just another book, how can these facts be explained? We're actually faced with the same choice we had regarding the universe. Either God is responsible for it, or we're talking about enough coincidences to defy all logic.

**NOTABLE QUOTABLE**

There are more sure marks of authenticity in the Bible than in any profane history.

–Sir Isaac Newton

### *Challenge #3: How do you know Jesus is who He claimed to be?*

This third objection is often phrased as a backhanded compliment to Jesus. It usually goes something like this: "Jesus was a great teacher and a great man, and the world would be a better place if everyone lived like He did. But it's wrong to try to make Him anything more than that. He wasn't supernatural. He wasn't a Savior. And He certainly wasn't the Son of God."

The problem with that position is that it's impossible to take a middle ground where Jesus is concerned. In other words, He can't be *just* a great teacher and a great role model.

Jesus Himself eliminated that possibility when He claimed to be the Son of God. If you have any doubts that Jesus taught that He was God's Son (and some people do), check out the following passages:

- The woman said, "I know that Messiah" (called Christ) "is coming. When he comes, he will explain everything to us." Then Jesus declared, "I who speak to you am he" (John 4:25–26).
- "I and the Father are one" (John 10:30)
- The high priest said to him, "I charge you under oath by the living God: Tell us if you are the Christ, the Son of God." "Yes, it is as you say," Jesus replied (Matthew 26:63–64).

C. S. Lewis, the great Christian author, points out that Jesus' words and actions in the Bible—our primary source of information about Him—leaves us only four options regarding Him. Specifically, Jesus is either . . .

- a liar,
- a lunatic,
- a legend, or
- Lord of the universe.

If Jesus was a *liar*, that means He *knew* He wasn't the Son of God, yet purposefully chose to deceive people into giving up their lives and following Him. The problem with this option is that most people, regardless of their spiritual beliefs, recognize Jesus as a great moral teacher. Yet if He was lying about the central part of His message—His own identity—that pretty much renders the rest of His words moot.

**NOTABLE QUOTABLE**

If we desire an increase of faith, we must consent to its testings.

—UNKNOWN

If Jesus was a *lunatic*, that means He actually believed He was the Son of God but was mentally deranged. The problem with this option is that there's nothing in Scripture that suggests Jesus was, shall we say, a few verses short of a chapter. In fact, Jesus showed remarkable composure under circumstances that would have sent most people over the edge. Look at the way He responded to the authorities who put Him on trial for his life (Luke 22:66–23:12).

If Jesus was a *legend*, that means He never claimed to be the Son of God—that His followers made up tales of His miracles, teachings, claims of deity, and resurrection after His death. The problem with this option is timing. You see, the Gospel writers completed their manuscripts while the people who saw and heard Jesus personally were still alive. Those people could have said, "Wait a minute; I had front-row tickets to the Sermon on the Mount, and I didn't hear Jesus say anything like that," or "That's not what happened at Lazarus' tomb." But no one did. What's more, as we've pointed out a couple of times in this book, most of Jesus' disciples and the authors of the New Testament were executed as a result of their belief in Christ. And no one would die for something he knew to be a lie.

So that leaves us with one option—that Jesus is *Lord*. To back up that claim, we have the evidence of His teachings, His miracles, and His life. Let's take a quick look at each one.

Jesus' *teachings* quite literally changed the world. Concepts such as loving one's enemies, turning the other cheek, and serving others were so radical to Jesus' first-century audience—so far removed from the conventional wisdom of the day—that many people had a hard time understanding them.

Jesus' *power* over sickness and disease, the natural world, and even death itself has no precedence in human history. His miracles, which are thoroughly documented in the Gospels, can be explained only in supernatural terms. We can rule them out as mere illusions or parlor tricks because Jesus often performed them in front of skeptics and people such as the Pharisees who were desperately trying to prove that He was a phony. We can assume that the miracles occurred in a way that left little room for doubts about their authenticity. Many people throughout history have claimed to be God, but only one of them had the credentials to prove it.

Jesus' *life*—the fact that He was sinless—stands as a testament to the truth of His claims about Himself. Who else but God could have spent so much time in the public eye, dealing with the scum of society day in and day out, yet still emerge with an absolutely spotless record? Jesus Himself threw down the gauntlet to His enemies in John 8:46, when He asked, "Can any of you prove me guilty of sin?" The fact that no one uttered a peep in response speaks volumes.

### *Challenge #4: Why is Christianity better than any other religion?*

This final objection is often fueled by political correctness and expressed in earnest questions such as these:

- "Don't you think that whatever religion works for a person is the right one?"
- "Don't all religions basically worship the same God?"
- "Are you saying that all Muslims, Hindus, and Buddhists are going to hell?"

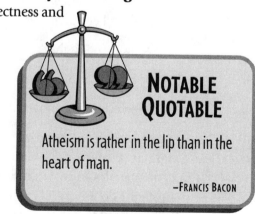

**NOTABLE QUOTABLE**

Atheism is rather in the lip than in the heart of man.

–Francis Bacon

As much as we might like to be thought of as

tolerant and open-minded, the fact is, we can't give the answers that people want to hear to these questions. As *Christians*, we have no choice but to follow *Christ's* lead. And, where salvation is concerned, He's pretty clear about the pecking order of religious beliefs.

In John 14:6, Jesus says, "I am the way and the truth and the life. No one comes to the Father except through me." Jesus was so convinced that He was the only way for us to be reconciled with God that He allowed Himself to be mocked, tortured, and executed in order to pay for our sins.

**NOTABLE QUOTABLE**

The writers against religion, whilst they oppose every system, are wisely careful never to set up any of their own.

—EDMUND BURKE

If there's another way to God—that is, if the practices of Islam, Hinduism, or Buddhism can get us into heaven—it makes Jesus look really, really bad. Specifically, it makes His crucifixion and resurrection completely unnecessary.

In responding to the argument that all religions are basically the same, it's important to point out that Christianity is the only major religion that offers its followers complete assurance of salvation. Buddhism, Hinduism, and Islam all base their requirements for heaven (or nirvana) on human deeds. In other words, followers can receive eternal rewards only if they are . . .

- kind enough,
- moral enough,
- aware enough,
- faithful enough, and
- self-denying enough.

The problem is that there are no clear-cut guidelines as to how much kindness, morality, awareness, faithfulness, and self-denial are required in order to qualify for eternal blessings. As a result, followers of those religions are compelled to constantly do more and more to improve their chances and then simply hope for the best when they die.

Christianity, on the other hand, teaches that we can't earn our way to heaven, no matter how hard we try. Christianity holds that salvation is a gift from God. Accepting that gift—by believing in Jesus' power to save us—is all that's required to receive eternal life. As a result, Christians never have to worry about how our quest for heaven is progressing.

## The Art of Defense

As we suggested earlier in this chapter, it's tough to anticipate the specific questions and challenges you'll face regarding your faith. That doesn't mean you can't prepare yourself for them, though. Certain principles can be applied to any type of opposition you encounter.

Here are six key strategies that will greatly improve your "defensive" skills.

### *1. Educate yourself.*

The "official" term for defending or offering proof of your faith is *apologetics*, and you can find an entire section devoted to it in any well-stocked Christian bookstore. You can find titles dealing with everything from how to feel secure in your own faith to how to defend the "hot points" of Christianity. You can also find books on what Muslims, Hindus, and people of other religions believe—all written from a Christian perspective.

Depending on your budget, choose a couple or more books that offer what you're looking for. But don't just read them; treat them like textbooks. Underline or highlight passages that you think will be especially applicable. Jot down in the margins any thoughts or questions that occur to you. Refer back to the books (and your notes) from time to time to keep the material fresh in your mind.

The more you read about Christian beliefs, the more comfortable you'll be discussing, debating, and defending them.

### *2. Listen.*

If someone challenges your faith, it's natural to assume that they believe they have a better or more logical alternative. Your first order of business should be to find out what that alternative is. Ask the person to explain why they doubt specific Christian beliefs or why they choose to believe other things.

The better listener you are, the more information you'll be able to draw from the person. If you listen closely enough, you may discover underlying causes and unspoken motivations for the person's challenges and questions. For example, a person who questions God's existence may not be struggling with intellectual objections, but emotional ones, such as the loss of a loved one ("If there's a God, my sister would still be alive today").

By listening carefully, you can craft an answer that addresses not only the person's spoken objections, but the unspoken ones as well.

**JUST WONDERING**

**What should I do if I get stumped in the middle of defending my faith—like, say, if someone raises a point or a question that I can't answer?**
Keep in mind that defending your faith isn't an all-or-nothing proposition. You don't necessarily have to have a snappy comeback for every question you get asked. If you don't know the answer to a question, say so. If that means your debate opponent wins a "point," so be it. Remember, your goal is not to defeat the person, but to help him or her ultimately see God's truth.

### 3. *Don't take it personally.*

It's easy to take things personally when it comes to our faith. As Christians, our faith lies at the center of our identity. Having our beliefs questioned, challenged, or opposed can feel like personal rejection.

And while it may be tempting to unload with a blast of "righteous" anger and blow the challenger out of the water with biblical truth after biblical truth, there's a better solution. Proverbs 15:1 lays it out this way: "A gentle answer turns away wrath, but a harsh word stirs up anger."

No matter how angry, facetious, or condescending people are when they question or challenge our beliefs, we must avoid the temptation to respond in kind. The more heated they get, the calmer we have to stay. That may be frustrating at first to the person looking for a knock-down-drag-out confrontation, but, over time, our cooler heads—and softer answers—will succeed in keeping the discussion civilized and productive.

### 4. *Speak the truth in love.*

In listening and offering "gentle" answers to the people who question or challenge our faith, we need to guard against swinging to the opposite extreme and being too accommodating and too accepting of their beliefs. Ephesians 4:15 instructs us to speak "the truth in love." So, while our loving spirit should always be apparent in our interaction with unbelievers, so should our commitment to God's truth. We cannot deny or downplay what the Bible teaches—even if it directly contradicts what other people believe.

Such a commitment to truth may cause difficulties for you occasionally, especially if you're non-confrontational by nature. Your refusal to accept, say, that there's more than one way to get to heaven will likely get you branded as "narrow-minded," "old-fashioned," or "a self-righteous fundamentalist." Some may call you "unfriendly," "hostile to new ideas," or "discriminatory."

So be it. God doesn't call us to be popular. He calls us to boldly and lovingly introduce others to His truth. If we respond to that call, the Holy Spirit will guide our words and help people see us for who we really are.

### On a Personal Note

You will make mistakes in defending your faith. That's a given. You may even make some big mistakes. That's okay. What's important is that you learn from your mistakes. To help you do that, keep a diary of your faith-defending encounters and confrontations. Honestly assess each one, identifying the things you did right and the things you did wrong–the things you're glad you said, the things you wish you'd said, and the things you wish you hadn't said.

### *5. Get a response.*

After you've had an opportunity to defend, explain, or offer evidence for your faith, get a reaction from the person you're talking to. This isn't about asking someone to make an immediate, 180-degree change in their way of thinking. (Although, that's always a welcome response.)

This is about making sure that you're understood. It's about asking questions like . . .

- "Does what I'm saying make sense to you?"
- "Do you have any questions about the things I've been talking about?"
- "Do you understand why I believe the things I do?"

- "Has anyone else ever talked to you about Christianity?"

This is about eliminating misunderstandings and making sure that the person you're talking to has an accurate set of facts to work with, just in case he or she decides to explore your side of the debate a little more closely.

### *6. Keep the door open.*

Short of leading the person to Christ, the best response you can hope for from someone who challenges your faith is a willingness to talk about it again. The best way to keep that possibility open is through affirmation. At the end of your conversation, say something like . . .

- "I respect the way you approach spiritual matters."
- "With your passion, you could make a real difference in the world."
- "It's great to talk about things that really matter, isn't it?"
- "You've asked a lot of intelligent, thoughtful questions."
- "This conversation is too good to end. What do you say we continue it another time?"

The last thing you want to do is "add up scores" at the end of your conversation and try to determine a "winner" ("you stumped me two questions, but I stumped you with three, so nah nah nah-nah nah"). Putting a competitive spin on the discussion will only make the person dig in harder the next time you talk.

To the best of your ability, make the person feel positive about your discussion. Create a conversational relationship that you're both comfortable with.

> **JUST WONDERING**
>
> **What if I'm talking to a person I've never met before and will probably never see again? How should I end the discussion?**
>
> If you're comfortable with the idea, give your name, phone number and/or e-mail address to the person and ask him to contact you if he ever wants to continue the discussion or learn more about the forgiveness and salvation that God offers. At the very least, let the person know that you'll be praying for him.

# Being Prepared

If this all seems like Christian "overkill" to you, consider the apostle Peter's words in 1 Peter 3:15: "Always be prepared to give an answer to everyone who asks you to give the reason for the hope that you have."

That's a pretty tall order—especially when you consider that you never know where the next challenge or opposition to your faith is going to come from.

Being prepared means making yourself an "expert" on the Christian faith, anticipating potential encounters, practicing for all kinds of scenarios, and, most importantly, staying in constant contact with the Holy Spirit, who can and will guide you through any situation.

# Know What You Believe

How much do you know about defending your faith? Here's a quiz to test your knowledge.

1. Which of the following is not true of the Christian faith?
   a. It's impossible to defend rationally or intellectually.
   b. It will be opposed as long as there are unbelievers on the planet.
   c. As many as 425 people lose their lives because of it every day.
   d. Almost all of the apostles and New Testament writers were executed because of it.

2. Which of the following is not one of the common questions Christians get asked regarding their beliefs?
   a. How do you even know God exists?
   b. How do you know the Bible is true?
   c. How do you know Jesus is who He claimed to be?
   d. How do you know the church ushers don't divide the tithe money among themselves when they get out to the lobby?

3. Which of the following is not one of the four options proposed by C. S. Lewis for who or what Jesus must be?
   a. Legend
   b. Lawyer
   c. Lord
   d. Liar

4. Which of the following statements is unique to Christianity among the major religions?
   a. Followers *truly* believe the teachings of the faith.
   b. Followers have a written word to guide them in their faith.
   c. Followers can be assured during their lifetime that they will go to heaven when they die.
   d. Followers use terms and phrases that aren't easily understood by outsiders.

5. Which of the following is not a good strategy for dealing with people who disagree with your faith?
   a. Educating yourself
   b. Speaking the truth in love
   c. Getting a response after you respond to their comments
   d. Screaming "Heretic!" over and over again at the top of your lungs until they back down

*Answers: (1) a, (2) d, (3) b, (4) c, (5) d*

CHAPTER 17

# "To Do" List

## SNAPSHOT

"Check this out," Jeff said as he tossed a CD case across the car seat.

Jake picked up the case and looked at it. "Oh, dc Talk," he said. "This is a great album."

"I bought their entire catalog, including a couple bootlegs of live shows," Jeff explained.

"People sell Christian *bootlegs?*" Jake asked. "Isn't that like selling counterfeit Bibles?"

Jeff shrugged. "I didn't ask a lot of questions," he said. "I was too busy trading in my CDs."

Jake smiled. "It's funny how you start to notice the lyrics of songs a lot more after you become a Christian, isn't it?" he asked. "I remember I ended up getting rid of about a dozen CDs after I accepted Christ. How about you?"

"All of them," Jeff said.

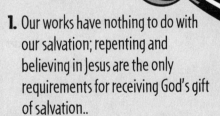

### SNEAK PREVIEW

1. Our works have nothing to do with our salvation; repenting and believing in Jesus are the only requirements for receiving God's gift of salvation..
2. Salvation is just the first step in the Christian life.
3. Growth in the Christian life requires commitment, dedication, and sacrifices of our time and resources.

"Your whole collection?" Jake asked.

"The whole thing," Jeff said with a smile. "I told you I was serious about this Christianity thing."

"I can see that," Jake replied. "So have you thought any more about joining our Bible study on Wednesdays?"

"I don't think I'm comfortable with that idea yet," Jeff admitted.

"That's cool," Jake assured him. "No hurry. I remember I wanted to get comfortable with the Bible myself before I started talking to other people about it. So how's your personal study going, if you don't mind my asking."

"I don't mind, but there's nothing to tell," Jeff said. "So far I haven't had a chance to spend much time in the Bible. But did you notice this?" He held up his left wrist.

Jake nodded. "I've got one of those bracelets at home," he said. "But it's not as nice as yours."

"I had it custom made," Jeff said as he pulled a cross necklace out of his shirt, "as a matching piece to this."

"Looks good," Jake said. "Hey, have you talked to anyone about getting involved in the homeless ministry yet?"

"I changed my mind about that," Jeff admitted. "My schedule is already tight. I just don't know that I can afford to give up another two hours a week. By the way, you didn't happen to notice the back of my car when you got in, did you?"

"No, why?" Jake asked.

"I put on a 'Honk if you love Jesus' bumper sticker."

"Oh, really?" Jake said. "I'll bet you'll find that the slower you drive, the more people love Jesus."

Jeff smiled. "I want to put another one on," he said. "But I couldn't decide between 'Beam me up, Jesus' and 'Ask me about rapture insurance.'"

"Yeah, that's a tough choice," Jake said.

"You were right when you said that accepting Jesus is just the first step," Jeff said. "I've got so many things to think about now."

"That's right," Jake said. "Like the men's fellowship breakfast next Saturday morning."

"Actually, I was thinking more about redesigning my business cards. I can't decide between a dove and a cross. I was going to do a Bible verse, but they charge by the word. What do you think I should do?"

Jake paused for a moment to consider how to word his response. "What do I think you should do?" he finally said. "Well . . ."

* * * * * * * * * * * * * * * *

The Christian life is a race. The author of Hebrews says so: "Therefore, since we are surrounded by such a great cloud of witnesses, let us throw off everything that hinders and the sin that so easily entangles, and let us run with perseverance the race marked out for us" (Hebrews 12:1).

The apostle Paul seconds the notion: "I have fought the good fight, I have finished the race, I have kept the faith" (2 Timothy 4:7).

If you're a Christian, you're entered in the race, too, whether you realize it or not. In fact, if you've repented and made a decision for Christ, you're already at the starting line—and the gun's gone off!

What a scene it is. All of the Christians in eternity who have run the race before you—not to mention God Himself and His host of angels—are standing trackside (spiritually speaking), cheering your efforts, and urging you on.

Before you exhaust yourself trying to make up lost ground, though, we need to point out that this race is not a sprint—it's a marathon. A lifelong marathon. And while there's nothing we can do to make your race easier or shorter, we can lay out the course for you.

In the pages that follow, you'll find a dozen "stations" that you'll want to "check in" at during your race—that is, twelve tips that will start you on your way to

**NOTABLE QUOTABLE**

A thought which does not result in an action is nothing much, and an action which does not proceed from a thought is nothing at all.

—GEORGES BERNANOS

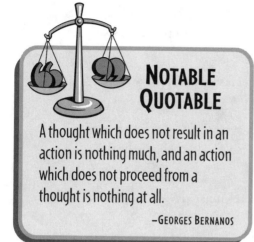

spiritual growth and maturity. This "To Do" list is by no means comprehensive, but it should give you a good place to begin.

## 1. Find a Church.

Babies cannot grow or become healthy without the assistance of caring adults. Likewise, new Christians cannot mature in their faith or develop healthy Christian lives without the assistance of caring brothers and sisters in Christ. If you're a new believer, you need interaction with other Christians, whether you realize it or not. The most obvious place to go for that interaction is church.

Not just any church, mind you, but a church that's right for you. To help you determine what's right for you, we've come up with a list of questions for you to consider while you "shop" for a place to worship:

- What am I looking for in a pastor or spiritual leader?
- What kind of worship style feels most natural to me—formal, informal, or a combination of the two?
- What am I looking for in the people I worship with?
- What kind of church ministries would benefit me?
- What kind of church ministries would allow me to use my spiritual gifts?

Once you've got a pretty good idea of your preferences, you can start to figure out your nonnegotiables. The fact is, no church is perfect. If you look hard enough, you can always find fault with the service, the pastoral staff, the congregation, or the generic grape juice used for communion.

What you have to determine is which imperfections you can overlook and which ones will actually have a negative impact on your ability to worship and fellowship. For example, if the spirit of fellowship in a particular church rates a

"10" in your book, but the song selection rates a "5," you may decide that you can live with an average music ministry for the sake of excellent fellowship. On the other hand, if the pastor's leadership skills rate a "1," you may want to keep looking.

When you find a church that meets your needs, commit yourself to it—not only through regular attendance and tithing (which we'll discuss later in this chapter)—but also through membership. Sign up for membership classes, complete the necessary requirements, and share your commitment to fellowship and worship with the entire congregation.

### Just Wondering

**I don't have a lot of experience with church. How can I tell what's good or bad about the churches I visit?**
Get the Holy Spirit involved in your church search. Ask Him to give you the wisdom to recognize the pros and cons of various congregations. Ask Him also to give you a sense of peace when you find the "right" church for you.

## 2. Talk to Your Pastor.

As soon as you find a church to call "home," schedule an appointment with your pastor, an informal meeting that will allow you to get to know him and him to get to know you. You might start off the meeting by explaining who you are, where you're at in your spiritual life, what you need from the church, and what you have to offer in ministry.

After you've introduced yourself, shift the focus to your pastor. Ask him to talk a little about his background, his leadership philosophies, and his vision for the future of the church. Obviously, you don't want to be nosy or presumptuous in your questioning. However, if you have a legitimate question that you'd like your pastor to answer, fire away. Remember, you need to feel comfortable about him as a spiritual leader.

If you have any time left in your meeting, get your pastor's input on some of the challenges you're facing. Work up a list of questions you have about the Christian life and areas in which you need guidance. Depending on your personal circumstances, your list might include questions such as the following:

- Now that I've accepted Christ, what's my next step as a Christian?
- Where should I start in my Bible study?
- How can I find a group Bible study to get involved in?
- Do you have any tips for maintaining a healthy prayer life?
- What would be a good ministry opportunity for me?
- How can I begin applying my Christian faith to my dating life?
- What should I do about the fact that my spouse isn't a Christian?

> **NOTABLE QUOTABLE**
>
> Determine never to be idle. No person will have occasion to complain of the want of time who never loses any. It is wonderful how much may be done if we are always doing.
>
> —Thomas Jefferson

If possible, e-mail, fax, or deliver a copy of your list of questions before the meeting. Give your pastor a chance to prepare. Do everything you can to maximize your time together. If you don't get all of your questions resolved, schedule another appointment, and then another, until you do.

If you maintain a positive, eager approach to these meetings, you don't have to worry about becoming a bother. Most pastors absolutely love these kinds of encounters. They're besieged every day by people with complaints about the church or people facing difficult times in their lives. Meeting with someone eager to get started in the Christian life is like a breath of fresh air for them.

## 3. Make Yourself Known at Church.

If you're new to the church, make it a priority to get to know your fellow worshipers. After all, if you're going to commit yourself to the church for the long haul, there's a good chance that some of the strangers in the pews around you may end up being instrumental in your spiritual growth—and vice versa.

That's why you might want to consider setting fellowship goals for yourself. For example, you might draw up the following goals:

- ➤ Introduce myself to at least one new person each week before the worship service.
- ➤ Serve as a "greeter" at the door a couple times a month, welcoming people to the church and handing out programs.
- ➤ Invite a single person, a couple, or a family from the church to my house for Sunday lunch at least once a month.
- ➤ Get to know everyone in my Sunday school class.
- ➤ Join the planning committee for the church's semiannual or annual fellowship activities.

The point is not to become the most popular person in the congregation or to have everyone call out your name when you walk into your Sunday school class (a la "Norm!" on old *Cheers* reruns). Your goal is to get to know the people you worship with and to lay the groundwork for meaningful fellowship—that is, relationships that will deepen from week to week.

## 4. Start Tithing.

Everything good and useful in our lives comes from God. As Christians, we'd be hard-pressed to deny that. Tithing is a way of recognizing God's good gifts by giving portions of them back to Him for use in His work. The word *tithe* means "one tenth." So, for Christians, the traditional practice of tithing involves giving one-tenth of our income back to God in the form of weekly "offerings," which are usually collected during Sunday morning worship services.

The tradition of tithing has its origin in the Old Testament story of Abraham and Melchizedek, the king of Salem (or Jerusalem). Genesis 14 tells us that after Abraham (or, as he was originally known,

**ON A PERSONAL NOTE**

Many churches list their congregation's prayer requests in the weekly program or newsletter. If your church does this, refer to the list during your personal prayer time. After worship services, seek out the people you've been praying for, introduce yourself, and check on their situations. You won't find a better icebreaker than demonstrating to people that you care about their needs.

Abram) defeated the kings who kidnapped his nephew Lot, and recovered the possessions of all the people who had been kidnapped with Lot, he encountered Melchizedek. The king-priest of Salem blessed Abraham. In return, Abraham gave Melchizedek one-tenth of everything he had.

Fast-forward to the New Testament book of Hebrews, and you'll find this declaration about Christ: "You are a priest forever, in the order of Melchizedek (7:17)." To make a long theological principle short, everything that was due to Melchizedek is due to Christ. For those who follow Christ, that means one-tenth (or more) of our resources.

**JUST WONDERING**

**What happens to the money that's tithed at church each week?**

Generally tithes are used to pay church expenses, including staff salaries, and to fund ministries. You can find out exactly where your tithes go by checking your church's annual budget.

Let's get one thing straight, though. A tithe isn't a "cover charge" for church or some kind of "dues" that Christians have to pay. You're not going to get called to the pastor's office if you forget to tithe two weeks in a row. You won't be placed on probation by your church at the end of the year if your tithes don't add up to 10 percent of your salary.

You see, tithing has less to do with you and your church than it does with you and God. Tithing is a way of acknowledging that everything we have is God's and demonstrating our willingness to use it for His work.

This isn't a matter of financial means, either. Whether you make $1,000 a year or $1,000,000, the responsibility remains. If it's been given to you by God, it must be given back to Him by you.

If you're not sure how to go about tithing, here's a quick and easy step-by-step guide:

- Add up your total annual income. Include not just your salary (if you have one), but all forms of income, from investment dividends to game show prize money. If you have to estimate, go ahead; but the more precise you can be, the better.

- Divide that total by 52 to get your weekly salary or income. If you make $52,000 a year, your weekly income will be $1,000 (because 52,000 divided by 52 is 1,000).
- Divide that total by 10 (as in one-tenth, or 10 percent) to get your weekly tithe. If your weekly income is $1,000, your weekly tithe will be $100 (because 1,000 divided by 10 is 100).
- Write a check for that amount—or more, if you choose to give above the 10 percent figure—and put it in the offering plate at church each week.

If you're wondering how in the world you can possibly reduce your available income by 10 percent and still get by, financially speaking, you need to consider the *X* variable of the tithing equation: God's generosity.

Luke 6:38 says, "Give, and it will be given to you. A good measure, pressed down, shaken together and running over, will be poured into your lap. For with the measure you use, it will be measured to you." If you are faithful to God in your tithing—regardless of your financial situation—He will be faithful in taking care of you, your family, and your future.

> **JUST WONDERING**
>
> **Do I tithe 10 percent of my net income or my gross income?**
> The Bible doesn't offer specific financial guidelines, so perhaps the better question is, "Does God deserve 10 percent of your net income or 10 percent of your gross income?" As long as we're talking about specifics, let's not forget that 10 percent is simply a starting point. Some people choose to give 15 percent back to God; others choose to give 20 or 25 percent–or more. A few people even choose to reverse the tithe principle and give 90 percent of their income back to God, while keeping only 10 percent for themselves!

If, on the other hand, you wait until you're financially "able" to tithe, you'll never do it. You'll find that there's always another thing to buy, save for, or pay off. And that would be a shame, to say the least—not for your church, not for God, but for you. You see, if you never tithe—that is, if you withhold from God what's rightfully His—you will miss out on the blessings that come from supporting His work.

## 5. Get Involved in a Ministry.

Tithing your financial resources is one thing. But what about your *physical* resources—specifically, your time and talents? Those are God's, too. And the way to acknowledge that is to give those things back to Him in ministry.

In chapter 13, we talked about how to discover your spiritual gifts. If you have a good idea of what your spiritual gifts are, you'll have a head start in finding a ministry. If your spiritual gift is, say, evangelism, make some inquiries at church about getting involved in an outreach program. If your gift is teaching, consider volunteering in a children's Sunday school class. The specifics are up to you. Just make sure that your gifts don't go to waste.

**NOTABLE QUOTABLE**

Action is the proper fruit of knowledge.

–THOMAS FULLER

If you're not sure what your spiritual gifts are, look for a ministry that appeals to you, something that makes you say, "I could bring something good to that." If you love kids, volunteer to help out in children's church. If you're good with babies, try the nursery. If you have a heart for hurting people, volunteer your time in a hospital ministry.

When you start to get involved in church ministries, you'll find that it not only enhances your spiritual growth, it increases your fellowship opportunities. Nothing brings people together like ministry.

## 6. Start Your Personal Bible Study.

Don't put this off. Don't wait until the beginning of the year, the beginning of the month, or even the beginning of the week. Don't wait until your schedule clears. In fact, give yourself no more than two days to prepare. (If you're reading this on a Wednesday, make sure you're studying by Friday.) In that time, you can secure a Bible and notebook, plus any other tools you care to use, and rework your schedule to accommodate your new priority.

As for how often you should study, our sincere recommendation is every day. Remember, your goal is to develop a Bible study *habit*. A habit isn't something you do once or twice a week. Generally speaking, a habit is something that occupies your daily routine. If that reasoning doesn't work for you, there's always this question: What else in your daily schedule is more important to you than God's Word?

The next consideration is the best time of day for your study. Whether you're a morning person or night owl, there are three rules that you need to keep in mind:

1. Don't just wait for a good opportunity during the day.
2. Take drowsiness out of the equation.
3. Find a time that you can protect.

Some people try to keep their Bibles handy, so that when they have an open block of time, they can do their Bible study. Unfortunately, that haphazard approach to Bible study doesn't boast a very high success rate. The problem is obvious: If and when an open block of time does present itself, it's hard to work up the enthusiasm and interest necessary for meaningful study on the spur of the moment.

If you're especially sleep-deprived, drowsiness can be a problem at any time of the day. But it's especially problematic right before you go to bed and right after you get up. It follows, then that the further away from your bedtime you schedule your Bible study, the better chance you have of making it work.

When it comes to choosing a time you can protect, morning is probably your best bet. Generally speaking, if you work or attend school, your schedule is not necessarily your own—at least from eight to five. If you have any kind of social life, your evening hours may be a little iffy, too.

Your morning, on the hand, can be yours—if you plan it right. If you want to talk specifics, how about breakfast in the Word every morning? With a little advance planning—and perhaps a disarming of the "snooze" feature on your alarm clock—you can carve out a block of pre-work (or pre-school) time to accommodate a shower, followed by a leisurely breakfast/Bible study.

And what better way is there to begin your day?

**ON A PERSONAL NOTE**

Here's an extra Bible study tip at no extra charge for you, the consumer. If you choose to do a morning study, get in the habit of reading each passage the night before, just before you go to bed, so that the material's fresh on your mind when you wake up. You'd be surprised at how much a "sneak preview" of the passage can help you concentrate on it later.

As for the amount of time you should spend in study each day, let's not beat around the bush. Anything less than fifteen minutes simply isn't enough. If you want to shoot for something, make it a half hour. After all, you need time to . . .

- pray for the Holy Spirit to guide your study,
- read the passage carefully,
- pray again, if you find your mind wandering during your study,
- ask yourself questions about the passage,
- look up related passages,
- write down your thoughts, and
- pray about applying the passage to your life.

The final area of Bible study you need to consider is where to begin. If you have a topic or passage that you really want to explore and understand, by all means start there. If, however, you're not sure where to start your study, consider one or more of these suggestions:

- *Matthew.* The first Gospel provides a fairly comprehensive look at the life and ministry of Jesus. It's a great starting place for acquainting yourself with Him. If and when you choose to tackle the book, plan to spend at least a couple of days studying Jesus' Sermon on the Mount in chapter 5.
- *Romans.* This letter of Paul offers perhaps the most comprehensive explanation in all of Scripture as to what it means to be a Christian. You'll find a lot of helpful passages on topics such as sin, grace, faith, and holiness.
- *James.* Here's where you'll find some of the most practical advice in the Bible on how to make the most of your walk with Christ.
- *The Faith Hall of Fame.* Hebrews 11 contains summaries of the faithful

lives of over fifteen different Bible "heroes." To help yourself understand the kind of faithfulness God rewards, study the original biblical story of each character.

You don't need book smarts, a church background, or even a natural curiosity about Scripture to develop and maintain a successful personal Bible study. Aside from the guidance of the Holy Spirit, all you really need is a truckload of commitment—a stubborn refusal to allow apathy, frustration, busyness, or anything else to distract you from your work.

## 7. Start a Prayer Habit.

Well, well, well, if it isn't another commitment to add to your already busy schedule. How can you make time for prayer? The good news is that prayer is a lot more flexible than Bible study. If you think about it long enough, you can probably find at least a dozen places in your daily routine in which you can go to the Lord in prayer—even if it's for just a couple minutes at a time.

For example, there's the time you spend. . .

- commuting to and from work or school,
- eating alone at lunch,
- showering,
- working out, or
- cleaning the house.

With a little planning and a lot of concentration, you can turn any of those routine situations into a meaningful prayer time.

We'll remind you, though, that the smaller your window of prayer time is, the more important it is to maintain the order of the ACTS prayer model we introduced in chapter 9:

- Adoration
- Confession

> **NOTABLE QUOTABLE**
>
> The Christian's chief occupational hazards are depression and discouragement.
>
> –JOHN STOTT

- Thanksgiving
- Supplication

Take care of the most important things—giving God His due and restoring your relationship with Him—first. That way, if your prayer time ends early, all that will be lost are your requests. Having said that, we also warn you against rushing through the first three steps of the ACTS prayer in order to get to your requests.

Be sure to keep a journal handy throughout the day so that you can record (1) the date of your prayer; (2) a brief description of your adoration, confession, and thanksgiving; and (3) a fairly comprehensive list of your requests for others and for yourself. Your purpose is to create a written record of God's work in your life. By referring back to old requests, you can gain an appreciation for the way God has answered your prayers.

## 8. Find a Mentor.

Think about when you were a freshman in high school. How cool would it have been to have a senior showing you the ropes, advising you on what to do and what not to do? If you're a new Christian, that's the kind of relationship you need—someone to show you the ropes of the Christian life and advise you on what to do and what not to do.

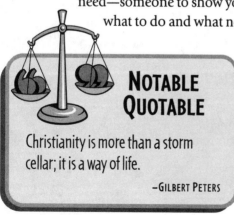

> **NOTABLE QUOTABLE**
>
> Christianity is more than a storm cellar; it is a way of life.
>
> –GILBERT PETERS

If you don't know anyone personally who fits the bill as a mentor, your pastor may be able to introduce you to a candidate or two. Obviously, you'll also want to get the Holy Spirit involved in the search, too. Ask Him to help you recognize potential mentors that you may have overlooked because they didn't meet some preconceived notion of what a mentor should be.

Keep in mind, too, that we're not talking about

developing an authoritarian master-student relationship with someone. Instead, your mentor should be a mature Christian whom you can call up from time to time with questions about the Christian life—someone you can have lunch with once or twice a month to talk about your growth and health as a Christian.

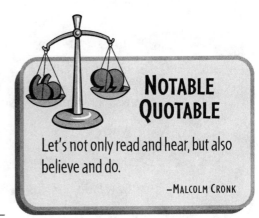

**NOTABLE QUOTABLE**

Let's not only read and hear, but also believe and do.

—Malcolm Cronk

## 9. Join a Bible Study Group.

Accountability can be a powerful motivator. And accountability is exactly what a Bible study group offers. Ideally, each member of a Bible study group has a vested interest in the spiritual growth of every other group member. If you've got four or five other people cheering you on and encouraging you, you stand a good chance of remaining faithful in your Bible study.

What's more, when you study the Bible with other people, you benefit from the different information, interpretations, background, and context other group members bring to the table. Often you'll find that simply talking about a passage with other people can open your eyes to truths in that passage you hadn't seen before.

Finding the right Bible study group for you is another dilemma your pastor may be able to help you with. He may know of current groups in the church looking for new members. If not, he may be able to recommend people to recruit for your own study.

## 10. Prepare Your Testimony.

Preserve for posterity a written record of your personal experience with Jesus, from your first encounter to your present relationship. Include as many details as you can remember, such as . . .

- what you were like before you came to Christ,
- what made you start thinking about God, Jesus, and salvation,

- how salvation was explained to you,
- why that explanation appealed to you,
- who led you to Christ,
- where you were when you finally repented and believed in Christ,
- how you felt after you prayed for forgiveness and salvation, and
- how God has changed your life since then.

The thing is, you never know when your testimony is going to come in handy, so you always have to be prepared to share it. Not only will it benefit others who are curious about Christianity, it may also come in handy for you, should you ever have doubts about whether or not you actually gave your life to Christ.

## 11. Start Sharing Your Faith.

You don't need to be a Bible scholar in order to share your faith. In fact, all that's really required is, well, your faith. If you've had a personal experience with Christ—that is, if you've prayed for forgiveness and asked for His gift of salvation—you have something meaningful to share with an unbeliever. You may not be able to answer all of the questions people ask about your faith, but you can find those answers. Remember, sharing your faith is simply a matter of one beggar telling another beggar where to find food.

> **NOTABLE QUOTABLE**
>
> The Christian is a person who makes it easy for others to believe in God.
>
> –Robert M. McCheyne

What was true of tithing is true of sharing your faith. If you wait for the "right" time to do it—that is, until you feel comfortable in your knowledge of the Bible and in your ability to communicate God's truth to others—you'll never do it.

So here's a challenge to motivate you. Choose three people in your life—one family member, one friend, and one casual acquaintance—to share your faith with in the next week.

We're not talking about making a full presentation of the gospel, although that's certainly an option, if you'd care to do it. We're talking about simply introducing the topic of Christ, eternity, or salvation into a conversation and then openly and honestly answering any questions you're asked. We're talking about making people aware of who you live for and what's ultimately important to you.

## 12. Facilitate Your Personal Worship.

In chapter 10, we mentioned that music is one of the great motivators for worship. If you're serious about developing a personal worship habit, one of your first orders of business should be to assemble a worship "mix tape"—a collection of songs or instrumentals that turn your thoughts to God and make you want to praise Him.

If you don't know anything about Christian music, ask your friends for suggestions or visit your local Christian bookstore and tell the sales rep what you're looking for. If you don't have the cash to build your Christian CD collection just yet, check out the local Christian radio programming in your area (or on the Internet). Chances are, you may be able to find one or two programs that offer just what you're looking for to get your personal worship off the ground.

If you prefer something a little more traditional, buy a hymnal from your local Christian bookstore and read it or sing from it as part of your own personal worship. Many modern hymnals offer a blend of traditional hymns, gospel songs, and contemporary choruses, so it's likely that you'll find tunes and lyrics that appeal to you.

## Opportunities and Growth Await

Let's be clear here. Your salvation is not dependent on completing any of the steps we've outlined in this chapter. Repenting and believing in Jesus are the *only* requirements for receiving God's salvation.

On the other hand, living a stagnant Christian life is simply not an option for a believer. God has a world

**NOTABLE QUOTABLE**

The devil's No. 1 tool is not an active sinner, but an inactive Christian.

—UNKNOWN

of opportunities and growth experiences waiting for you. He has life-changing things to teach you. He has work for you that will actually make a difference in the world—for eternity. He has unimaginable blessings waiting for you.

Claiming those opportunities, experiences, lessons, jobs, and blessings will require your complete sacrifice and dedication. Salvation is God's gift to you. Your life is your gift to God.

Okay, you have your race instructions. The rest is up to you and your running mate, the Holy Spirit.

On your mark . . . get set . . . go.

## Know What You Believe

How much do you know about running the race that is the Christian life? Here's a quiz to test your knowledge.

1. Which of the following is not a helpful question to ask your pastor?
   a. What's my next step as a Christian?
   b. Where should I start in my personal Bible study?
   c. Do you have any tips for maintaining a healthy prayer life?
   d. Why do you suppose I have such a hard time staying awake through your sermons each week?

2. Which of the following is not true of tithing?
   a. By definition, it involves 10 percent of your income.
   b. Ushers receive commission on every dollar they collect.
   c. It's the responsibility of all Christians, and not just the ones who can "afford" it.
   d. God rewards it when it's done cheerfully and sincerely.

3. Which of the following is not a helpful tip for your personal Bible study?
   a. If you study in the morning, read the passage the night before so that you have time to think about it.
   b. Pray before you begin your study, asking the Holy Spirit to guide your thoughts.

c. Don't overdo it; anything more than ten minutes is counterproductive.
d. Make sure that you include time to write down your thoughts, feelings, and questions about each passage you study.

4. Which of the following is a helpful principle to keep in mind when it comes to your personal prayer habits?
   a. Save the supplication for last.
   b. Don't worry about confession unless you've done something really bad.
   c. If you take care of adoration, you don't have to worry about thanksgiving.
   d. Always mention your requests first, in case you run out of time later.

5. Which of the following is not a helpful tip for growing in your Christian life?
   a. Load up on Christian bumper stickers.
   b. Find a mentor.
   c. Join a Bible study group.
   d. Start sharing your faith.

*Answers: (1) d, (2) b, (3) c, (4) a, (5) a*

# Index

## A



## B

## R



## S